David Brown, formerly Professor of Musicology at South-
ampton University, is a leading British authority on Russian
music. He is the author of, among other books, the definitive
biographical and critical studies of both Glinka and Tchaikovsky, the latter in four volumes.

*In the same series*

DEBUSSY REMEMBERED
edited by Roger Nichols

GERSHWIN REMEMBERED
edited by Edward Jablonski

# Tchaikovsky
# Remembered

## DAVID BROWN

Amadeus
Press

AMADEUS PRESS

Keinhard G. Pauly, *General Editor*

PORTLAND, OREGON

First published in Great Britain in 1993
by Faber and Faber Limited
3 Queen Square, London WC1N 3AU

First published in North America in 1994 by
Amadeus Press
(an imprint of Timber Press, Inc.)
9999 S.W. Wilshire, Suite 124
Portland, Oregon 97225, USA

Phototypeset by Intype, London
Printed in England by Clays Ltd, St Ives Plc.

ISBN 0–931340–65–9 (hardback)
ISBN 0–931340–66–7 (paperback)

2 4 6 8 10 9 7 5 3 1

*To Gabrielle and Hilary*

# Contents

# List of Illustrations

# Introduction

> We cannot forget that, without any effort or intention on his
> own part, Pyotr Ilich through his presence alone brought into
> everything light and warmth. And if Europe mourns in him a
> major artistic force, one of the greatest in the second half of the
> nineteenth century, then it is only those persons who had the
> happiness of knowing him closely who know what *a man* has been
> lost through his death.[1]

Such was Tchaikovsky's fame and reputation that he became the first
Russian commoner to be given a funeral at state expense, and his compat-
riots' heartfelt response to his death precipitated 60,000 applications for
admission to his funeral service in the Kazan Cathedral in St Petersburg.
Posthumous tributes to such a man will be suspected of sentimental excess,
even hagiography. Yet I chose the above words from one obituary to end
my biographical and critical study of Tchaikovsky[2] because they seemed to
summarize so well all that I had discovered about him in nearly twenty
years of close research contact. Herman Laroche, who wrote them, was
one of Tchaikovsky's closest friends. But he was no blind acolyte. On
occasions he had upset the composer by his criticisms, and he knew as well
as any the man himself, his foibles and his eccentricities. He was familiar,
too, with the sometimes disconcerting signs of those inner turmoils that so
often determined his outer life. But Laroche also had good cause to know
that abundant humanity which had issued in innumerable acts of kindness,
of generosity, and of practical help, sometimes sustained over very prolonged periods. And he knew his old friend's many other traits, often so
different from what we have imagined. Forty years ago my own ill-
informed image of Tchaikovsky was not untypical. As a composer he was
little more than a naïve creator, the limitations of whose rather simple-
minded technique were effectively masked by an instinctive gift for good
tunes and a flair for orchestral colour; as a man he was little more than a
neurotic homosexual who vented his torments through these emotion-laden
tunes and overheated climaxes, and probably felt better afterwards. And

how wrong I was on both counts! It was not only that Tchaikovsky possessed that rich humanity Laroche points to. Whatever his inability to
regulate certain crucial areas of his own personal life, he could show
admirable commonsense, even wisdom, in observing the problems of
others. He could be intensely practical and energetic, he could combine
bluntness and firmness with compassion, and he had an acute, if sometimes
curious, sense of fun. He was one of the best of troubleshooters . . .

But to develop all this further here would be to spoil the following
pages. My most valuable single source for the present volume has been the
collection of reminiscences of Tchaikovsky which first appeared in Russian
in 1962, and has since passed through three supplemented and corrected
editions.[3] This volume had, however, to be approached with great caution.
Sometimes the recollections written in the Soviet period were manifestly
conditioned by the prevailing political and ideological attitudes and con-
straints, and by far the greater part of these I have rejected totally. Nor had
I any alternative but to exclude a number of the other, untainted contributors who also set their reminiscences down late in life (some over fifty years
after Tchaikovsky's death), simply because their memories had by then
become too self-evidently misted. And throughout this whole Russian
volume there is a tendency to chattiness, even prolixity; total objectivity
and scholarly accuracy are rarely these memoirs' principal concern, and
occasionally they are at variance with the known facts, though normally in
only very minor ways. Yet they have a very positive side to them, for their
vividness of narrative and their intense involvement with Tchaikovsky
the man produce a life and liveliness which present his personality with
sometimes wonderful immediacy. They are not photographs but portraits
– and, as in portraits, it is the intuitive, personal perception which creates
their unique 'truthfulness'. Taken together, they build a very special image
of the human Tchaikovsky – and one that I find totally consonant with that
which I have quite independently conjured for myself from the more
'reliable' evidence of his letters and diaries. Inevitably I have been unable
to avoid repeating some reminiscences already used in my earlier four-
volume study; to have excluded Fanny Dürbach's memories, for instance,
would have denied the present reader uniquely valuable insights into the
personality of the little boy who was to grow into one of the greatest and
most famed composers of the later nineteenth century. But by far the
greater part of what follows has never before appeared in English.

From the list of more than eighty correspondents, journalists and memoirists represented here, Laroche emerges as the most valuable, not only because he was so well placed to observe the composer from the time the two of them were students together at the St Petersburg Conservatoire in the early 1860s, but also because he was the most intelligently perceptive, not only about the man but about his music, as Tchaikovsky himself recognized. Next comes Nikolay Kashkin, Tchaikovsky's colleague and close friend from 1866, when the composer joined the staff of what in a few months was to become the Moscow Conservatoire. Kashkin's main memoirs (Moscow, 1896) are more homely; he lacked Laroche's literary gifts and deeper personal insights, but his descriptions are sometimes very revealing. Above all there is his later narration of the circumstances of Tchaikovsky's marriage, with its vivid retelling of the composer's own account of his marital experience, to which I have allocated a whole chapter.

Laroche and Kashkin, being colleagues and friends of very long standing, were not disposed to the excessive veneration shown by some of those who met the composer perhaps only once when he was already a national icon. I am very aware of the heightened tone of some of these later reminiscences – that at times they romanticize the man – but I have included a number of these where I have judged that beneath the froth of adulation there is an essential substance; I leave the reader to decide the degree of credence to be given to each.

Between these two extremes lie the majority of this present volume's memoirs. The man who was closest to Tchaikovsky was the also homosexual Modest Tchaikovsky. Ten years younger than his composer-brother, Modest likewise was to become a creative artist, though his gifts as a playwright were only mediocre. His three-volume biography of the composer (Moscow, 1900–2) was mostly compiled using direct quotations from his subject's letters, but in dealing with Tchaikovsky's youth he had to rely upon his own memories and, for the fifteen or so years before that, upon the recollections of others; hence his trip to France in the year following his brother's death to draw from Fanny Dürbach her touching reminiscences. Though Modest's own memories are heavily conditioned by conflicting emotions of admiration and jealousy when they deal with the composer's professional years, there is no cause to question his accounts of the composer-to-be during the period of Modest's own childhood.

Nor is there any reason to doubt the essential truthfulness of the recollections which were written by some of the children of Tchaikovsky's close friends. True, Nadezhda Kondratyeva's have a certain literary rosiness, but her description of the composer's lifestyle when staying on her father's estate at Nizy in the 1870s fits fairly with what is known from more summary accounts, while the little-girl thrills within her narrative remind us of the ease with which children seem to have related to the composer, and he to them. Alexandra Jurgenson and Vladimir Nápravník substantiate this in ways more balanced and mature, and between them provide the clearest picture of the eternal-child side to Tchaikovsky's personality. Sofiya Kashkina, too, sounds reliable, and though she is recording her parents' memories rather than her own, they often amplify incidents which are alluded to in her father's memoirs.

Of the remaining more major contributors, Alexandra Panayeva is one of the most precious, even though she wrote down her memories late in life, in 1933. Vladimir Pogozhev's are especially interesting for uncovering a little the less amiable sides of Tchaikovsky's personality. Alina Bryullova, writing on all sorts of aspects of the composer, is also a seemingly trustworthy source, as is Ivan Lipayev who, in his lengthy account of Tchaikovsky's involvement with professional musicians and of his concern for their welfare, vividly highlights just one of the many generally unknown sides of his subject's very human personality (though I suspect that some of the events in Lipayev's narrative have been reordered to make a neater, more effective – and perhaps more comprehensive – piece of writing). Especially to be treasured, too, is the highly detailed account by Yulian Poplavsky of two days with the composer at his Klin home only a fortnight before his death.

There is an abundance of Russian reminiscences such as these, and a useful, if modest, supply from both English and American sources. Tchaikovsky visited England three times in his later years to conduct his own works; on the last occasion the prime object of his visit was to receive an honorary degree of D. Mus. from Cambridge University, and his more than a fortnight in this country enabled a considerable number of people to meet him and later to set down their impressions in autobiographies and memoirs. In 1891 he was invited to the United States to participate in the inauguration of the new Carnegie Hall, and during the three and a half weeks he spent not only in New York, but in Philadelphia, Baltimore and Washington, he was much observed both on and off the rostrum. Americans are especially aware of the image the man presents, and some of their observations are as pointed as they are brief.

My greatest disappointment has been the dearth of recollections from German and especially French musicians. With Hans von Bülow Tchaikovsky enjoyed a long and mutual admiration, and I include one brief comment from him, while Mahler provided an aside after Tchaikovsky had attended a performance of *Eugene Onegin* which Mahler conducted in Hamburg in 1892. In 1888 and 1889 Tchaikovsky himself had conducted in Germany, meeting Brahms and many other German musicians; yet few of them seem to have recorded their impressions of him – though there is the delightful account from the wife of the violinist Adolf Brodsky of a meal in Leipzig with Brahms, Grieg and Tchaikovsky as guests, and I thought this well worth a little chapter to itself. Tchaikovsky's visits to France were far more numerous. Paris was his favourite European city, and there he became personally acquainted with many leading French composers and performers. His brother Modest noted that his visits as a celebrity in the late 1880s coincided with a fashion for all things Russian, and when Tchaikovsky first appeared in Paris as a conductor in 1888 he was subjected to close public scrutiny as an incarnation of this fashion, as the examples I have been able to incorporate show. Yet the vigour and boldness of much of his music clearly had little appeal to the French temperament (as may be detected in the high-toned but woolly critical assessment of Tchaikovsky which had already appeared in the 1881 supplement to Fétis' *Biographie universelle des musiciens*). In any case, by the early 1890s the social climate was changing; as the pianist Alexander Ziloti reported in bitter bewilderment to Modest after including some pieces by Tchaikovsky in a recital at the Trocadéro in 1892: 'They hate Pyotr Ilich; he is too elevated for them.'[4] Certainly the popularity of Tchaikovsky's music had begun waning with the fashion, and this may well be why so few French musicians seem to have mentioned him in their later recollections. That there are few allusions to him as a person in French sources I can say with confidence, for though I have begged the help of many scholars of both German and French music, their accumulated knowledge has been able to turn up very little material. But my gratitude remains to them for what they have been able to provide, for replying so courteously and helpfully to my letters, and in some cases for taking a very great deal of trouble on my behalf. My thanks must go especially to Paul Banks, Antony Beaumont, Edward Blakeman, the late John Clapham, Joël-Marie Fauquet, Christopher Fifield, Marie d'Indy, André Lischke, Hugh Macdonald, Elisabeth Malfroy, Edward Morgan, Marie-Claire Mussat, Jean-

Michel Nectoux, Roger Nichols, Robert Orledge, Robert Pascall, Danièle Pistone, Manuela Schwartz, Andrew Thomson, Damien Top and John Warrack. For providing translations from French, German and Czech sources I am grateful to my wife Elizabeth, Sigrid Chadwick and Lubor Velecky respectively. To my wife I am also heavily indebted for help in checking.

In the Chronology I have provided supplementary information only when it has some direct relevance to Tchaikovsky's own life, or when it may help to fill out a little the perspective in which he lived. Thus historical events are recorded if they are known, or were likely, to have moved him or ultimately to have affected him in some way. Being a voracious reader he was very aware of the literary scene, and so new publications, both Russian and West European, were of great significance to him. So, of course, were new compositions by his Russian contemporaries, and by certain Western composers, especially French. However, to have noted the appearance of all the new works (or new books) which drew his attention would have been merely to produce a confusing catalogue, and I have done no more than note enough pieces composed, or books written, during his lifetime to sketch some sort of picture of the creative environment in which he grew up and subsequently worked.

The chapter structure has been largely determined by the material available, but I have followed a chronological order as far as possible. In the penultimate chapter I have extended my coverage beyond recollections of Tchaikovsky himself as a person. The matter of how Tchaikovsky came to die has always been a subject for debate. The official version was that he died of cholera as a result of drinking a glass of unboiled water, a story that was first widely disseminated through Modest's biography. However, in his account of his brother's last months Modest is so at pains to stress his good spirits that an impression consolidates that he is desperate to counter any suggestion that they could have been otherwise – and, in any case, the inconsistencies and sometimes plain contradictions within the documentary evidence about Tchaikovsky's end must trouble all but the most credulous reader. Clearly many of the people closest to Tchaikovsky concealed crucial facts, yet still failed to silence rumours, and in attempting to stifle these, they sometimes produced even more glaring contradictions. Did Tchaikovsky drink the unboiled water in Leiner's Restaurant on 1 November or in Modest Tchaikovsky's apartment on the 2nd? How could the laboriously detailed accounts of Tchaikovsky's illness by Modest Tchaikovsky and Lev Bertenson, one of the doctors who attended him, be so at variance, especially over the duration of the composer's illness? Indeed, did Tchaikovsky in fact die on 5 November, as the arithmetic of Bertenson's record would indicate, news of his death being withheld for reasons best known to Modest, Bertenson and others? And why were bulletins of his illness's progress only, it seems, posted outside Modest's apartment as from 5 November? Again – had the composer already died, and were these fabricated to provide further visible evidence to support the following day as the date of his death? Whatever the truth about the composer's end, it was not what the outside world was meant to believe.

In fact, it can hardly be doubted that Tchaikovsky committed suicide, and this was accepted privately by many in the old Soviet Union to be self-evident, though it could not be stated openly. But in the West the matter has been a specially live, and sometimes very sensitive, issue ever since 1979, when the Soviet scholar Alexandra Orlova emigrated to the USA and introduced a new element into the controversy. This was the story of a 'court of honour' that is alleged to have condemned Tchaikovsky to take his own life. The story sounds almost bizarre (though it is scarcely more so than some other strongly documented incidents in Tchaikovsky's life), and the mode in which it was transmitted to Mrs Orlova is far from satisfactory.[5] In the fourth volume of my *Tchaikovsky* I have already set out a summary of the main evidence concerning Tchaikovsky's death, and also my own judgement of the matter: that Tchaikovsky committed suicide, and that the court-of-honour story should be taken seriously, though it is certainly not proven.[6] However, there still exist some people, especially in the United States, who are implacably determined to believe the official version, and since Orlova's revelations the issue has become with them, it seems, a very emotional one. Because there have been so many contradictory judgements, suggestions and speculations flying around, readers who have already encountered some of them may now feel totally confused, and would wish to be able to make up their own minds more objectively. And so in 'How did Tchaikovsky die?' I set out, without further loaded comment, the crucial evidence. I do not believe for one moment this will silence the controversy, but I hope it may make it possible to conduct the debate on more secure and rational grounds than has sometimes been the case in the past.

DAVID BROWN
Braishfield, Hampshire
*January 1993*

# NOTES

1 Laroche (H.), 'Pamyati P.I. Chaykovskovo' ['Memories of Tchaikovsky'], in *Yezhegodnik Imperatorskikh Teatrov, 1892–3 [Yearbook of the Imperial Theatres, 1892–3]* (St Petersburg, 1894); Reprinted in Laroche (H.), *Izbrannïye stati [Selected Articles]*, ii: *P.I.Chaykovsky [Tchaikovsky]* (Leningrad, 1975), p. 189.

2 *Tchaikovsky: a Biographical and Critical Study*, 4 vols (London, 1978–91; paperback, 1992).

3 Protopopov (V.) and others, eds, *Vospominaniya o P.I. Chaykovskom [Recollections of Tchaikovsky]* (Moscow, 1962; further edns 1973, 1979, 1980). I have mostly used the fourth edition as being the most recent and the fullest, though I have also referred to the earlier editions for details included in these, but subsequently suppressed.

4 Letter of Alexander Ziloti to Modest Tchaikovsky: 13 July 1892; published in Ralben (A.), ed., *Alexandr Ilich Ziloti, 1863–1945. Vospominaniya i Pisma [Ziloti, Recollections and Letters]* (Leningrad, 1968), p. 177.

5 Alexandra Orlova's detailed examinations of the whole matter are contained in her article 'Tchaikovsky: the last chapter', *Music and Letters*, lxii (1981), pp. 125–45, and in the final chapter of her book, *Tchaikovsky: a Self-Portrait* (Oxford and New York, 1990). A counterblast to Orlova was provided by Alexander Poznansky in his article 'Tchaikovsky's suicide: myth and reality', *19th Century Music*, xi, no. 3 (Spring, 1988), pp. 199–220.

6 The emergence in 1987 of this story through a second, completely different source seems to me to strengthen very considerably its plausibility.

# Chronology

*Tchaikovsky's Life and Works*
*Contemporary Figures and Events*

1840    *7 May* Pyotr Ilich Tchaikovsky born in Votkinsk, some 800 miles east of St Petersburg; second son of Ilya Petrovich Tchaikovsky, a mining engineer, and Alexandra Andreyevna Tchaikovskaya (*née* Assier). His half sister Zinaida is 11 and his brother Nikolay 2.

1840        Berlioz (37), Glinka (36), Dargomïzhsky, Verdi and Wagner (27), Gounod (22), Serov (20), Lalo (17), Anton Rubinstein (10), Borodin and Brahms (7), Saint-Saëns, Cui and Nikolay Rubinstein (5), Delibes (4), Balakirev (3), Bizet (2), Musorgsky (1)
            Victor Hugo (38), Gogol (31), Thackeray (29), Dickens (28), Turgenev (22), Dostoyevsky (19), Tolstoy (12)
            Manet (8), Cézanne (1)
            Zola and Monet born

1841        Dvořák and Renoir born

1842    Tchaikovsky's sister Alexandra (Sasha) born

1842        Glinka's *Ruslan and Lyudmila* and Wagner's *Rienzi* first performed
            Gogol, *Dead Souls* and *The Marriage*
            Massenet born

1843    Tchaikovsky's brother Ippolit born

1843        Grieg born

1844    With sister Sasha makes up a song: 'Our mama in St Petersburg'
        Starts lessons with Fanny Dürbach, governess to his elder brother Nikolay and cousin Lidiya

1844        Rimsky-Korsakov and the painter Ilya Repin born

1845    Starts piano lessons; is soon better than his teacher

1845        Glinka, First Spanish Overture (*Capriccio brillante*)
            Fauré born

1846        Dostoyevsky, *Poor Folk*

1847        Turgenev, *A Sportsman's Sketches*
            Mendelssohn dies

1848    Tchaikovsky family moves to Moscow, then St Petersburg. As a result Fanny Dürbach leaves the family; Pyotr is terribly distressed

1848                    Glinka, *Kamarinskaya* and Second Spanish Overture (later
                       revised as *A Summer Night in Madrid*)

1849     *February–June* Suffers nervous illness, probably psychological in origin.
         Family moves to Alapayevsk in Ural Mountains

1849                   Strindberg born
                       Chopin dies

1850     Tchaikovsky's twin brothers Modest and Anatoly born

         *September* Is enrolled in the preparatory class of the School of Jurispru-
         dence in St Petersburg; traumatic parting from his mother

1850                   Wagner's *Lohengrin* first performed
                       Anton Rubinstein, First Piano Concerto

1851                   Rubinstein's Ocean Symphony (no. 2: first version) completed
                       St Petersburg to Moscow railway opened

1852     Tchaikovsky's family returns to St Petersburg

1852                   Tolstoy, *Childhood*
                       Gogol dies

1853                   Brahms's Piano Sonata in C, op. 1, completed
                       Van Gogh born

1854     *June* Tchaikovsky's mother dies of cholera; Tchaikovsky is devastated

         *August* First known attempt at written-down composition (a waltz for
         piano)

1854                   Britain and France declare war on Russia; Crimean War

1855     Begins serious piano lessons for three years with Rudolf Kündinger

1855                   Reforming Alexander II succeeds reactionary Nikolay I as Tsar
                       Lyadov born

1856     Under influence of singing teacher, Luigi Piccioli, composes a song:
         *Mezza notte* (his first published composition)

1856                   Treaty of Paris ends war with Britain and France
                       Alexander II begins relaxing censorship laws (in 1855 in Russia
                       1,021 books are published, 1,836 in 1864 and 10,691 in 1894)

Restored Bolshoy Theatre opens in Moscow

Dargomïzhsky's opera *Rusalka* first performed

Schumann dies

Taneyev and Bernard Shaw born

1857      Cui's opera *A Prisoner in the Caucasus* begun

Glinka dies; beginning of Balakirev's mission as leader of nationalist cause in Russian music

1858      Is requested by the singing teacher Gavriil Lomakin to make his first attempt (unsuccessful) at conducting the school choir, of which he had been a member since his entry to the school

1858      Balakirev's Overture on three Russian songs composed and incidental music to *King Lear* begun

Brahms's Piano Concerto no. 1 and Berlioz's *Les troyens* completed

1859      *May* Graduates from the School of Jurisprudence

*June* Begins work as a clerk in the Ministry of Justice

1859      Russian Musical Society (RMS) founded by Grand Duchess Elena Pavlovna and Anton Rubinstein to promote concerts and institute classes in which might be laid the foundations for a professional career in music

Goncharov, *Oblomov* and Turgenev, *A Nest of Gentlefolk*

Wagner completes *Tristan und Isolde*

Gounod's *Faust* first performed

Ippolitov-Ivanov born

1860      Tchaikovsky's sister Sasha marries and moves to her husband's family estate at Kamenka in the Ukraine

1860      Turgenev, *On the Eve*

Chekhov born

1861      *July–October* Travels through Germany, Belgium, England and France as interpreter to a friend of his father

*October* Begins studying thorough-bass in the RMS class run by Nikolay Zaremba; his interest in music deepens

1861    Emancipation of the Russian peasantry from serfdom
        Arensky born

1862    *September* Enrols in the new St Petersburg Conservatoire which had grown
        out of the RMS's classes

1862    Railway line from St Petersburg to Warsaw inaugurated
        Anton Rubinstein appointed director of the new St Petersburg
        Conservatoire
        Free Music School founded in St Petersburg by Balakirev and
        Lomakin, promoting concerts and offering classes in opposition
        to the 'westernizing' tendencies of the Conservatoire
        Borodin begins First Symphony
        Turgenev, *Fathers and Sons* and Hugo, *Les misérables*

1863    *May* Finally resigns from the Ministry of Justice; continues Conservatoire
        studies with Zaremba and Rubinstein

1863    Law granting greater academic freedom to Russian universities
        Serov's opera *Judith* first performed
        Tolstoy's *The Cossacks* published
        Thackeray dies
        Edvard Munch born

1864    *Summer* Overture *The Storm* (after Ostrovsky) composed

1864    In Russia, creation of elected *zemstva* (district councils) devolves
        more power to local assemblies; trial by jury introduced
        Population of St Petersburg: 539,400 (by 1893 over 1 million)
        Rubinstein, Fourth Piano Concerto
        Balakirev's First Symphony begun
        Dargomïzhsky's orchestral fantasia *Kazachok* premièred

1865    *Characteristic Dances* composed and performed (*11 September*) under
        Johann Strauss the younger at Pavlovsk

        Is prescribed Schiller's *An die Freude* as the text for his graduation cantata
        (*November–December*)

1865    Publication of Tolstoy's *War and Peace* begun (completed 1869)
        Rimsky-Korsakov's First Symphony, Serov's opera *Rogneda* and
        Wagner's *Tristan und Isolde* first performed
        Glazunov born

1866    *10 January* Absents himself from the performance of his graduation can-
        tata but is still awarded a silver medal. Promptly moves to Moscow to
        become teacher of musical theory in the classes of the Moscow branch of
        the RMS, presided over by Anton Rubinstein's brother Nikolay

        *March* Begins work on his First Symphony; comes close to nervous col-
        lapse over it

        *September* Moscow Conservatoire grows out of RMS classes; Nikolay
        Rubinstein is the director, Tchaikovsky one of the staff

1866            Dostoyevsky, *Crime and Punishment* and *The Gambler*

1867    *March* Begins his first opera *The Voyevoda* and composes *Scherzo à la russe*
        for piano, published as op. 1 no. 1

        *June–August* Holiday in Hapsal (Estonia) with family of Lev Davïdov, his
        brother-in-law; to his distress, Lev's sister, Vera Davïdova is attracted to
        him.
        Three piano pieces, *Souvenir de Hapsal*, op. 2, composed

        *December* Meets Berlioz

1867            Berlioz visits Russia to conduct
                Balakirev's symphonic poem *Tamara* begun
                Borodin's First Symphony and Wagner's *Die Meistersinger* com-
                pleted
                Gounod's *Roméo et Juliette* first performed
                Turgenev, *Smoke* and Zola, *Thérèse Raquin*

1868    *January* Meets Balakirev, as well as Rimsky-Korsakov, Cui and Vladimir
        Stasov, a polymath and art historian

        *15 February* First Symphony performed with considerable success

        *March* First article as a music critic

        *June–August* Visits Berlin and Paris

        *September* Begins close acquaintance with Belgian opera singer Désirée
        Artôt, with whom marriage is discussed; composition of symphonic poem
        *Fatum*

1868            Grieg, Piano Concerto

Cui's opera *William Ratcliff* completed

Musorgsky's *Boris Godunov* begun

Dostoyevsky, *The Idiot*

1869    Collapse of plans for marriage with Artôt

*11 February* Première of *The Voyevoda*

*January–July* Second opera *Undine* composed (later destroyed); Balakirev conducts and criticizes *Fatum* savagely. Meets Borodin

*June–July* Summer holiday with Sasha at Kamenka

*October* At Balakirev's suggestion (and following his ground plan) begins composition of fantasy overture *Romeo and Juliet*

*December* First set of songs (Six Romances, op. 6) composed

1869        Balakirev's *Islamey* for piano

Borodin's Second Symphony and *Prince Igor* begun

Berlioz and Dargomïzhsky die

1870    *February* Begins third opera *The Oprichnik*

*May* Learns of *Undine*'s rejection

*June–September* Visits Paris (where his friend Vladimir Shilovsky is ill), Mannheim (for the Beethoven centenary festival) and Switzerland (to escape the Franco-Prussian War)

*Romeo and Juliet* revised, but few new compositions

1870        Franco-Prussian War

Population of Moscow: 602,000 (by 1893 nearly 1 million)

Delibes, *Coppélia*

Dickens dies

1871    First String Quartet composed (performed *28 March* in first concert solely of Tchaikovsky's compositions)

Meets Turgenev

*June–September* Visits Kamenka (where, in domestic theatricals with his nieces and nephews, the idea of the ballet *Swan Lake* was probably born), Nizy (his friend Nikolay Kondratyev's estate) and Usovo (Shilovsky's estate); writes his textbook on harmony. Continues work on *The Oprichnik*

Turn-of-year holiday with Shilovsky in Nice

1871          Rubinstein's opera *The Demon* completed
              Dostoyevsky's *The Devils* begun
              Serov dies

1872   *February–March* Peter the Great bicentenary cantata composed

       *April The Oprichnik* finished

       *June–August* Holiday at Kamenka, Nizy and Usovo

       *September* Begins regular work as a music critic

       *June–November* Second Symphony ('Little Russian') composed (first version)

1872          First volume of Karl Marx's *Das Kapital* (1867) translated into
              Russian
              Dargomïzhsky's opera *The Stone Guest* (completed by Cui,
              orchestrated by Rimsky-Korsakov) first performed
              Musorgsky begins *Khovanshchina*
              Skryabin born

1873   *March–April* Composes incidental music to *The Snowmaiden*

       *June–August* Stays at Nizy and Kamenka, then travels through Germany,
       Switzerland, Italy and France

       *August* Symphonic fantasia *The Tempest* sketched at Usovo

1873          Rimsky-Korsakov's opera *The Maid of Pskov* performed
              Dostoyevsky, *The Devils*
              Rakhmaninov born

1874   *January* Second String Quartet composed

       *24 April* Première of *The Oprichnik*, against which he turns violently

       Visits Italy

       *June–October* Opera *Vakula the Smith* composed at Nizy and Usovo

       *November* First Piano Concerto begun

1874                Musorgsky, *Pictures at an Exhibition* and Lalo, *Symphonie espag-
                   nole*
                   Musorgsky's *Boris Godunov* performed

1875    *February–April* Composes eighteen songs (opp. 25, 27, 28)

        *June–September* At Usovo, Nizy and Kamenka

        *June–August* Third Symphony composed; ballet *Swan Lake* begun

        *December* Begins his set of twelve piano pieces *The Seasons*; meets Saint-
        Saëns

1875                Bizet's *Carmen* performed; Bizet dies
                   Grieg's incidental music for Ibsen's *Peer Gynt* (1867) completed
                   Publication of Tolstoy's *Anna Karenina* begun (completed 1877)

1876    *January* In Paris is overwhelmed by Bizet's *Carmen*

        *January–March* Third String Quartet composed

        After restless holiday in Nizy, Kamenka and Vichy with brother Modest
        and Modest's pupil Kolya Konradi (a young deaf-mute), attends opening
        of Wagner's opera house at Bayreuth with first ever *Ring* cycle (*August*);
        meets Liszt. Takes decision in principle to marry in order to defeat his
        homosexuality

        *October–November* Composes symphonic fantasia *Francesca da Rimini*

        *December* Composes Rococo Variations for cello and orchestra; meets Tol-
        stoy and has first exchange of letters with the wealthy widow Nadezhda von
        Meck

1876                First telephone transmission of human voice by Bell in USA
                   Delibes, *Sylvia*
                   Brahms's First Symphony and Borodin's Second Symphony
                   completed

1877    Fourth Symphony begun

        *May* Receives written declaration of love from former Conservatoire stu-
        dent Antonina Milyukova, who is unknown to him; opera *Eugene Onegin*
        begun

        *18 July* Marries Antonina; after a disastrous honeymoon and escape to

Kamenka by himself, returns to Moscow and attempts suicide

*October* Flees from Antonina; taken by brother Anatoly to recover in Switzerland, France and Italy

Given leave of absence by the Conservatoire. Nadezhda von Meck settles an allowance upon him which gives him financial independence

1877          Saint-Saëns, *Samson et Delila* and Massenet, *Le roi de Lahore*
              Turgenev, *Virgin Soil*

1878    *March–April* Violin Concerto composed, Piano Sonata begun

*April* Returns to Russia but avoids contact with former associates as far as possible. Spends time at Kamenka and Brailov (Nadezhda von Meck's country estate) while she is away

*August* Begins to compose his First Suite

*October* Resigns from Moscow Conservatoire

*December* Settles in Florence; begins opera *The Maid of Orleans*

1878          Brahms, Second Symphony

1879    *March* Returns to Russia for première of *Eugene Onegin*

Summer mainly passed at Kamenka and Brailov

*October* Begins Second Piano Concerto

*November* Begins four-month trip to France and Italy

1879          Ibsen, *A Doll's House*

1880    *April–November* Stays mainly at Kamenka and Brailov; composes Serenade for Strings (*September–October*) and overture *1812* (*October–November*)

1880          Dostoyevsky, *The Brothers Karamazov*

1881    *March* In France hears of death of Nikolay Rubinstein; is offered vacant directorship of Moscow Conservatoire, but declines

Summer passed at Kamenka; begins opera *Mazepa* (*June*) and edits an edition of Bortnyansky's church music

*December* In Rome begins his Piano Trio in memory of Rubinstein

1881          Alexander II assassinated; Alexander III succeeds him

Borodin, Second String Quartet

Repin paints portrait of Musorgsky

Ibsen, *Ghosts*

Musorgsky and Dostoyevsky die

1882     *April* Returns to Russia

*June–August* At Grankino (the Konradi estate), where he works systematically on *Mazepa*, composition of which is completed at Kamenka (*September*)

1882          Telephone system established in Moscow

Rimsky-Korsakov's opera *The Snowmaiden* and Glazunov's First Symphony performed

Wagner completes *Parsifal*

Stravinsky born

1883     *January–May* In Paris, mainly caring for his niece Tatyana (who is expecting an illegitimate child) and fulfilling three commissions for the coronation of Alexander III (including cantata *Moscow*)

*June* Second Suite begun; completed at Kamenka (*October*)

1883          Arensky, First Symphony

Wagner, Turgenev, Manet and Karl Marx die

1884     After première of *Mazepa* (*15 February*) visits Paris until summoned to an audience with, and investiture by, the Tsar (*March*)

*April* At Kamenka; Third Suite begun

*October* Overwhelming public success of new production of *Eugene Onegin* in St Petersburg confirms Tchaikovsky as Russia's most respected – and popular – composer

1884          Statute deprives Russian universities of autonomy granted in 1864

Massenet's *Manon* first performed

1885     *February* Settles for the first time into a house of his own in the country at Maidanovo near Klin outside Moscow

*February–April* Revises *Vakula the Smith* (renaming it *Cherevichki*)

*April–October* Manfred Symphony composed

*October* Opera *The Enchantress* begun

1885        Brahms's Fourth Symphony completed
            Zola, *Germinal*

1886 Spring holiday in Tiflis where brother Anatoly now works

*May–June* Business trip to Paris

*August* Sketches of *The Enchantress* completed

1886        Musorgsky's *Khovanshchina* (completed and orchestrated by
            Rimsky-Korsakov) first performed
            Liszt dies

1887 *January* Conducts first performances of *Cherevichki*, thus initiating his career as a professional conductor

*June* Second visit to Tiflis

*July–September* In Aachen at bedside of Kondratyev, who is dying

*November* Conducts first performances of *The Enchantress*

*December* Sets out on first international tour as a conductor

1887        Russia has 7000 telephone subscribers
            Rimsky-Korsakov, *Spanish Capriccio*
            Strindberg, *The Father*
            Borodin dies

1888 Conducts in Leipzig (where he meets Brahms and Grieg), Hamburg, Berlin, Prague (where he meets Dvořák), Paris and London

*April* Third visit to Tiflis

Begins Fifth Symphony (*May*) and fantasy overture *Hamlet* (*June*)

*October* Makes first sketches for ballet *The Sleeping Beauty*

*December* Conducts first Prague performance of *Eugene Onegin*

1888        Rimsky-Korsakov, *Sheherezade*
            Massenet's *Le roi d'Ys* first performed

Strindberg's *Miss Julie* published (performed 1889)

Shaw begins writing music criticism

1889 *February* Embarks on second international tour, conducting in Cologne, Frankfurt, Dresden, Berlin, Geneva, Hamburg (where he again meets Brahms) and London

*April* Fourth visit to Tiflis

*September The Sleeping Beauty* finished. Heavy conducting commitments

1889 New *Zemstva* Law restricts these councils' independence and effectiveness

Rimsky-Korsakov's opera-ballet *Mlada* begun

1890 *January* Opera *The Queen of Spades* begun in Florence. Visits Rome

*June–August* String sextet *Souvenir de Florence* composed

*August–November* Visits Grankino, Kamenka and Tiflis

*October* Nadezhda von Meck breaks their relationship, to Tchaikovsky's deep distress

1890 New 'Land Captains' law weakens the independence and effectiveness of the justice system

Zola, *La bête humaine* and Ibsen, *Hedda Gabler*

Rakhmaninov's First Piano Concerto begun

Van Gogh dies

1891 *February* Ballet *The Nutcracker* begun

*March* Arrives in Paris to conduct. By chance learns of death of his sister Sasha, but still proceeds with trip to USA in connection with the opening of the Carnegie Hall (*April*). Conducts in New York, Baltimore and Philadelphia; visits Washington

*June* Back in Russia

*July* Opera *Iolanta* begun

1891 Construction of the trans-Siberian railway begins

Brahms, Clarinet Trio and Clarinet Quintet

Arensky's opera *A Dream on the Volga* performed

Delibes dies

1892    *January* Visits Kamenka, conducts in Warsaw, visits Paris

        *May* Begins a symphony in E flat (later destroyed)

        Visits Paris and Vichy (*June-July*), Vienna and Prague (*September-October*)

        *December* Visits former governess Fanny Dürbach in France

1892        Skryabin, First Piano Sonata and Rakhmaninov, opera *Aleko*
            Shaw's *Widowers' Houses* performed
            Lalo dies

1893    *January* Conducts in Brussels. Triumphant concert appearances in Odessa, Moscow and Kharkov

        *February* Begins Sixth Symphony

        *May* Composition of Six Songs, op. 73, his last completed works

        *May–June* In England to conduct in London and Cambridge and receive an honorary D.Mus. from Cambridge University. Visits Austria and Grankino

        *September* In Hamburg for first performance there of *Iolanta*

        *28 October* Conducts première of Sixth Symphony in St Petersburg

        *6 November* Dies in St Petersburg, officially of cholera, but evidently by his own hand

1893        Gounod dies
            Edvard Munch paints *The Scream*

# Editorial and copyright note

In quotations dates are adjusted to the Western Calendar, which in Tchaikovsky's time was twelve days ahead of that used in Russia. Less precise chronological references have been adjusted to an approximate Western equivalent (for example, 'at the end of June' has been changed to 'at the beginning of July', 'in the middle of October' to 'at the end of October', and so on).

I am grateful for permission to quote from the following copyright material (detailed source references are given at the end of each extract):

Walter Damrosch, *My Musical Life* (Charles Scribner's Sons, 1923: now Curtis Brown Ltd); Bjarne Kortsen, *Grieg the Writer*, i, *Essays and Articles* (Bjarne Kortsen, 1972); Alexandra Orlova, *Tchaikovsky: a Self-Portrait* (Oxford University Press, 1990); Galina von Meck, *Piotr Ilyich Tchaikovsky. Letters to his Family: an Autobiography* (Dennis Dobson, 1981); Igor Stravinsky and Robert Craft, *Expositions and Developments* (Faber & Faber, 1962)

# Abbreviations used in the text

## BOOKS AND ARTICLES

*PVC4*  Protopopov (V.) and others, eds, *Vospominaniya o P.I. Chaykovskom [Recollections of Tchaikovsky]*, 4th edn (Leningrad, 1980)

*CIT*  Shaverdyan (A.), ed., *Chaykovsky i teatr [Tchaikovsky and the Theatre]* (Moscow, 1940)

*CVP*  Glebov (I.), ed., *Chaykovsky: vospominaniya i pisma [Tchaikovsky: Recollections and Letters]* (Leningrad, 1924)

*IRM*  Ippolitov-Ivanov (M.), *50 let russkoy muzïki v moikh vospominaniyakh [My Memories of 50 years of Russian Music]* (Moscow, 1934)

*KVC*  Kashkin (N.), *Vospominaniya o P.I. Chaykovskom. [Recollections of Tchaikovsky]* (Moscow, 1896)

*LIS2*  Laroche (H.), *Izbrannïye stati, vïpusk ii: P.I. Chaykovsky [Selected Articles, ii: Tchaikovsky]* (Leningrad, 1975). Two articles in this volume are themselves identified by abbreviations:

    *MTC*  'Iz moikh vospominany: Chaykovsky v Konservatory' ['From my recollections: Tchaikovsky at the Conservatoire'], first published in *Servernïy Vestnik [Northern Herald]* (1897), nos. 9–10

    *VOC*  'Vospominaniya o P.I.Chaykovskom' ['Recollections of Tchaikovsky'], first published in *Novosti [News]*, no. 323 (1893)

*OTL*  Orlova, (A.), 'Tchaikovsky: the last chapter', in *Music and Letters*, lxii, no. 2 (April, 1981), pp. 125–45

*PRM*  Glebov (I.), ed., *Proshloye russkoy muzïki: materialï i issledovaniya. 1: P.I.Chaykovsky [The Past of Russian Music: Materials and Researches 1: Tchaikovsky]* (Petrograd, 1920)

*PTS*    Poznansky (A.), 'Tchaikovsky's suicide: myth and reality', in *19th Century Music*, xi, no. 3 (Spring, 1988), pp. 199–220

*RKL*    Rimsky-Korsakov (N.), *Letopis moyei muzikalnoy zhizni [Manuscript of my Musical Life]*, 9th edn (Moscow, 1982)

*TZC 1–3*    Tchaikovsky (M.), *Zhizn P.I. Chaykovskovo [Tchaikovsky's Life]*, 3 vols (Moscow, 1900–2)

## PERIODICALS

*IV*    *Istorichesky Vestnik [The Historical Herald]*

*KP*    *Komsomolskaya Pravda [Young Communists' Truth]*

*M&L*    *Music and Letters*

*MV*    *Moskovskiye Vedomosti [Moscow Gazette]*

*NBG*    *Novosti i Birzhevaya Gazeta [News and Stock Exchange Gazette]*

*NV*    *Novoye Vremya [New Time]*

*RMG*    *Russkaya Muzikalnaya Gazeta [Russian Musical Gazette]*

*RS*    *Russkaya Starina [Old Russia]*

*SM*    *Sovyetskaya Muzika [Soviet Music]*

*SV*    *Servernïy Vestnik [Northern Herald]*

*TG*    *Teatralnaya Gazeta [The Theatrical Gazette]*

*YIT*    *Yezhegodnik Imperatorskikh Teatrov [Yearbook of the Imperial Theatres]*

*ZK*    *Znamya Kommunï [Banner of the Commune]*

## MISCELLANEOUS

*RMS*    Russian Musical Society

# I
## Prelude:
*Childhood and student years*

Pyotr Ilich Tchaikovsky was born on 7 May 1840 in Votkinsk, a mining town in the Ural Mountains some 800 miles east of St Petersburg. His father, Ilya Petrovich, was a mining engineer, and his mother, Alexandra Andreyevna (*née* Assier), who was half French by extraction, was eighteen years younger than her husband. Tchaikovsky was the couple's second surviving child.

# Prelude

## FANNY DURBACH
### (1822–95)

By 1844 a governess was needed for the Tchaikovskys' eldest son Nikolay and their niece Lidiya. This brought into the family Fanny Dürbach, a 22-year-old governess. Though she seems to have been trained in St Petersburg, Fanny was of French Protestant extraction. After serving the Tchaikovsky family from 1844 to 1848, she worked for other families in Russia before settling in France at Montbéliard with her sister Frederica. It was here, in January 1893, that Tchaikovsky paid her a visit that proved for both a very moving occasion. In the year following Tchaikovsky's death his brother and first biographer, Modest, visited Fanny and was able to inspect his brother's exercise books and his childhood letters to Fanny, all of which she had kept. Modest also noted down Fanny's recollections of those early years, including her first impression of the family.

Mrs Tchaikovskaya, Nikolay and I took about three weeks from St Petersburg to Votkinsk, and during the journey we became so closely acquainted that when we reached the factory we were on thoroughly intimate terms. The kindness and courtesy of Mrs Tchaikovskaya, the good looks, even handsomeness, of Nikolay disposed me towards my companions, while the meticulous good manners of the latter [Nikolay] were an assurance that the task before me would not be difficult. Yet, all the same, I was very uneasy. All would be well if, on my arrival, I had to deal only with Mrs Tchaikovskaya and her son. But before me lay acquaintance with people and a way of life that were completely unknown. And so the closer we got to the end of our journey, the more my concern and uneasiness grew. But when at length we arrived at the house, one moment sufficed to show that all my fears were groundless. A host of people ran out to meet us, there began rapturous embracing and kissing, and it was difficult to distinguish family from servants in the crowd. All were made one by an undivided, living joy: everyone greeted the return of the mistress of the house with equal warmth and affection. Mr Tchaikovsky came up to me and, without a word, embraced and kissed me like a daughter. This simplicity and the patriarchal character of his action at once set the stamp of approval upon me, and sealed me almost as one of the family. I had not just arrived; rather, like Mrs Tchaikovskaya and her son, I too had 'returned home'. Next morning I set about my work without the slightest agitation or fear for the future.

Fanny Dürbach, Recollections, as reported in Modest Tchaikovsky's articles in *RMG* (1896), nos. 3–5, and repeated in *TZC1*. In the above and following extracts from Fanny Dürbach's recollections, and in the recollection from Modest himself, only the locations in *TZC1* and *PVC4* are given (here p. 21 and pp. 11–12 respectively).

## Childhood and student years

> The most valuable portions of Fanny's recollections are those which relate to Tchaikovsky himself, exposing many facets of his early character and the first signs of his response to music. It is clear that he was Fanny's favourite among her pupils. Modest's record of Fanny's recollections are sometimes in direct, at others in indirect, speech.

From our first meeting – so said Fanny – she felt a special sympathy towards the youngest of her pupils not simply because he outstripped the older ones in his abilities and his diligence in his work, nor because, compared with Nikolay, he was a good boy and had to be reproved less often for getting up to pranks, but because in everything he did there shone through something uncommon, something that inexplicably enchanted everyone who came into contact with [him] . . .

In his outer appearance . . . he could in no way compare with Nikolay, and he was also distinguished by his untidiness. He was always shock-headed, carelessly dressed, grubby as the result of some unthinking act . . .

Fanny Dürbach, Recollections, as reported in *TZC1*, p. 24, and *PVC4*, p. 12.

When I [Modest Tchaikovsky] asked how this exceptional childish charm declared itself, the former governess replied: 'Not in anything in particular, but positively in everything he did. In class no one could have been more diligent or quicker; during play no one thought up more diverting pastimes. When there was general reading [aloud] to a group for enjoyment, no one listened more attentively, and at dusk on the eve of a holiday, when I had collected my fledglings around me and made each in turn tell some story, no one made up tales more delightfully . . .

His sensitivity knew no bounds and so one had to deal with him very carefully. Every little trifle could upset or wound him. He was a child *of glass*. As for reproofs and admonitions (with him there could be no question of punishments), what would have been water off a duck's back to other children affected him deeply, and if the degree of severity was increased only the slightest, would upset him alarmingly. Once in connection with some assignment that both brothers had done badly, I reproached them and said, among other things, that I pitied their father who worked to earn money for his children's education while they were so ungrateful that they set no store by this, and were careless in their work and duties. Nikolay listened to this and ran out as happily as ever . . . But Pierre remained pensive all day and, going to bed that evening (when I myself had forgotten the reproof I had administered that morning), suddenly dissolved in tears, and began talking about his love for his father, and making excuses for the ingratitude towards his father that was unjustly imputed to him . . .'

Fanny Dürbach, Recollections, as reported in *TZC1*, pp. 25–6, and *PVC4*, pp. 13–14.

> On one occasion near the end of Fanny's term as governess there was a wrestling match which got out of control between two of her pupils, Nikolay Romanov, who was fond of such trials of strength, and Venichka Alexeyev, son of one of Ilya Petrovich's employees. Karolina, nurse to the younger children, in some alarm reported the fracas to Fanny.

Hardly had Karolina left than my boys [including Pyotr] returned . . . Not saying a word my pupils sat down on the divan facing our school bench.

'I'm very upset,' I began, 'that I cannot trust you to behave quietly when you're with the younger children. Because of your disobedience you, Venichka, will go and tell the coachman to harness up and take you home.'

Hardly had I uttered these words than I regretted them. The poor child burst into tears. Then Pierre stood up and said:

'M-lle Fanny, you've forgotten that Venichka has no mother and that you, being in her place, have no right to send an orphan away.'

'Does that mean, Pierre, that my pupils may be disobedient and I have no right to punish them?'

'Punish him with the same punishment as us, but don't invent one specially for him. All three of us are to blame, and we must all be punished in the same way.'

Venichka could only say 'forgive me' – Nikolay also. I wanted all the more to forgive them, for though I had only sent Venichka home for one day, I had all the same transgressed against the rules given me by your mother.

Fanny Dürbach, Recollections, as quoted in *TZC1*, p. 27, and *PVC4*, pp. 14–15.

A touching, thoroughly exceptional attachment to everything Russian accompanied him throughout his whole life, right to the grave . . . He sang his love for his native land in verses, but along with this he sometimes revealed it very amusingly. Thus Fanny tells how once, during a break for recreation, he sat down before an atlas and examined it. Coming to a map of Europe he suddenly began to cover Russia with kisses, and then made as if to spit on all the rest of the world. Fanny stopped him and began explaining to him that it was shameful to behave thus to beings who, just like himself, addressed God as 'Our Father', that it was bad to hate fellow men because they were not Russians, and that it meant he was spitting on her also, because she wasn't Russian.

'You don't need to scold me,' replied Pierre. 'Didn't you notice I had covered France with my hand?'

Fanny Dürbach, Recollections, as reported in *TZC1*, p. 28, and *PVC4*, p. 15.

On weekdays, from six in the morning, all the time was strictly allocated, and the day's programme was carried through punctually. Because the free hours during which the children might do what they wanted were very restricted, I insisted they should devote them to physical exercise, and on this matter I always had to wrangle with Pierre, who invariably wanted to go to the piano after a lesson. However, he always obeyed readily enough, and ran around, playing happily with the others . . . Left to himself, he most readily turned to music, reading, or writing verses.

Fanny Dürbach, Recollections, as quoted in *TZC1*, p. 28, and *PVC4*, p. 16.

After work or long periods of letting his imagination loose at the piano he was always nervy and on edge. Once the Tchaikovskys had guests, and the whole evening was spent in musical entertainments. Because it was a holiday the children were allowed to join the grown-ups. Pierre was initially very lively and happy, but towards the end of the evening became so tired that he went upstairs earlier than usual. When Fanny went to the nursery some time later he was not yet asleep but, his eyes glistening, was weeping agitatedly. When asked what was the matter with him, he replied:

'O, it's the music, the music!'

But there was no music to be heard at that moment.

'Get rid of it for me! It's here, here,' said the boy, weeping and pointing to his head. 'It won't give me any peace!'

Fanny Dürbach, Recollections, as reported in *TZC1*, p. 44, and *PVC4*, p. 18.

# MODEST TCHAIKOVSKY
## (1850–1915)

> Modest and Anatoly, the composer's twin brothers, were to play very important roles in his personal life. But whereas Anatoly was heterosexual, Modest was homosexual, and he became, of all people, the one closest to Tchaikovsky; besides being his brother's biographer, he was to be the main custodian of the museum established at the composer's final home at Klin. 'Sister' was the nickname given to Tchaikovsky's cousin, Anastasiya Popova; Zinaida (1829–78) was Tchaikovsky's half-sister.

Among Pyotr Ilich's own memories of this time the first he retained was of a trip with his mother and 'Sister' to the spa, Sergiyevsk, in 1845. He recalled especially clearly how, on the way there, after a long and boring journey into the late evening, they arrived at a well-lit manor and stayed for several days with one of Alexandra Andreyevna's [his mother] relations. The impression of a comfortable, bright house after the terrors and tedium of a journey at night cut so deeply into his imagination that this, according to his own words, was the embryo of that deep love, which never left him, for life in the country. Then staying at the spa itself, where he had no one with whom he had to share the caresses and attention of the mother he idolized, the novelties of the place, the acquaintances – all this remained the brightest and most joyful memory of his childhood. The other memory which he loved to recall from this period of his life was the return of his parents at the end of 1846 after collecting Zinaida Ilinishna who had finished her course at the Ekaterinsky Institute. This event took place one winter evening before Christmas. He would recall that rapturous joy which he experienced along with all the members of the household when the approaching kibitka's bell rang out – how they all with cries rushed to the entrance hall, how the door was opened and a cloud of freezing air burst into the room and there flew in the small, uncommonly pretty being whom he was seeing for the first time in his life (for Zinaida Ilinishna had entered the Institute before he was born). He would recall also the unearthly happiness he experienced as he pressed himself to his mother's breast after three or four months of separation. For a very, very long time, even when he was a completely mature man, he could not speak of his mother without tears; in consequence those around him would avoid talking about her.

Modest Tchaikovsky, *TZC1*, p. 29; reprinted in *PVC4*, p. 16.

> With the departure of Fanny in 1848 Zinaida took over her role as teacher.

# LIDIYA TCHAIKOVSKAYA

## (1830–92)

Lidiya Tchaikovskaya was one of Tchaikovsky's cousins.

In the morning until midday we have lessons with Zina[ida]; then we work, read in the evenings, and sometimes we dance with one another or sing to Petya's accompaniments. He plays very nicely; you might believe he was a grown man. You can't compare his present performance with his playing in Votkinsk.

Lidiya Tchaikovskaya, from a letter of 1849, quoted in *TZC1*, p. 50, and *PVC4*, p. 22.

In 1850 Tchaikovsky was enrolled in the preparatory class of the School of Jurisprudence in St Petersburg, one of Russia's leading schools, whose pupils were shown special favour when seeking appointment within the Civil Service.

# FYODOR MASLOV
## (1840–1915)

Fyodor Maslov was one of Tchaikovsky's schoolfriends and a colleague at the Ministry of Justice, becoming an eminent lawyer. Besides being responsible for vocal music at the School of Jurisprudence, Gavriil Lomakin was to be one of the most prominent figures in the choral life of St Petersburg and the founder, with Balakirev, of the Free Music School in 1862. Alexey Apukhtin, homosexual like Tchaikovsky, became a leading poet, five of whose lyrics the composer was later to set. Apukhtin, though a very difficult person, was one of Tchaikovsky's lifelong friends.

In regard of music Pyotr Ilich of course occupied the first place among his comrades, but none of them noted a serious concern for his [subsequent] calling. We were diverted only by the musical tricks he could do: guessing the key, and playing the piano with a towel covering the keyboard. From the day of his entry he sang in the choir and for his first three years was leader of the second trebles. This was necessary because that was where they put the trebles whose voices and ears were poor. The proximity of these off-pitch comrades caused him suffering . . .

The conductor [during certain of the choir's activities] was always a pupil in the top class because a more than purely musical responsibility rested on him; he had to assemble his comrades for rehearsal and this, in regard of the grown-up boys, required the authority of a person senior in age and position in the School . . . In the autumn of 1858 Tchaikovsky [was appointed]. He was not the conductor for long, not more than two months, because he showed neither an ability nor a will to command . . .

Pyotr Ilich began smoking very early, though his closest friends were not among those who smoked.

In his daily life he was distinguished for his disorderliness and untidiness. He filched nearly all his father's library for his comrades – but when he himself used the books of others, he did not bother to return them. In 1869 in Moscow, at the home of the Conservatoire professor [i.e. Tchaikovsky himself] who [now] had nothing to link him with the judiciary, I found legal works 'overdue' even when he was still at the School . . .

Pyotr Ilich never had his own textbooks and tried to borrow them from his comrades. But his own desk was also, as it were, on open access, and whoever wanted could rummage in it. During the examinations in the top class Pyotr Ilich and I for some reason did our preparing together. We chose the Summer Garden as our workplace, and so that we should not have to lug around our notes and textbooks, we concealed them in a hollow in one of the linden trees, shielded from the rain by boards. At the end of the examinations I removed my papers, but Pyotr Ilich constantly forgot to do this, and his study materials are perhaps still decomposing in one of the trees planted by Peter the Great.

Pyotr Ilich was drawn to literature and took an active part in the journal, *The School Messenger*, which was published in the fifth class under the editorship of Apukhtin and Ertel. A very fluent and sharply written 'A History of Literature in our Class' in it came from his pen.

In his later years at school Tchaikovsky kept a diary entitled *Everything*, where he poured out all the secrets of his soul, but was so naïvely trusting that he did not keep it under lock but in that same desk lying in the general pile of his own and others' books and exercise books.

Fyodor Maslov, Recollections, printed in *PVC4*, pp. 29–30, and partially in *TZC1*, pp. 96–8.

# VLADIMIR GERARD

## (1839–1903)

Vladimir Gerard was one of Tchaikovsky's closest schoolfriends.
Later a prominent barrister, he was also the founder of a society
for the prevention of cruelty to children. He was to deliver the
oration at Tchaikovsky's graveside. According to Modest Tchaikovsky, his brother's unrequited passion for Gerard was later to
be an important factor in the creation of his fantasy overture
*Romeo and Juliet*.

Besides an instinctive sympathy for each other, we shared a love of the
theatre. For some reason Pyotr Ilich took me to a performance of [Rossi-
ni's] *Guillaume Tell* at the Italian Opera. Tamberlik, Debassini and
Bernardi were singing . . . From that day I became a passionate lover of
opera and often went to it with my friend. Besides this we loved the
French Theatre which was generally in fashion with boys at the School of
Jurisprudence . . .

Although Pyotr Ilich's reputation as a musician was overshadowed by
that of Apukhtin as a poet, in whom we all saw a future Pushkin, his
talent still attracted attention, though none of his schoolfellows seriously
anticipated the fame the future composer would acquire. I remember very
well how, on Lomakin's departure after choral rehearsals in the White
Room, Pyotr Ilich would sit down at the harmonium and improvise on
Western themes. You could show him some melody and he would make
endless variations on it. For the most part the themes for these improvisations were from new operas we had recently heard.

As a student Pyotr Ilich was talented, but only moderately diligent and
very absent-minded . . .

We were both fond of society. I remember that, thanks to a meeting
with the pretty sister of one of our schoolfellows, we both tried to get
invited to a ball at the Zalivkina boarding school, that these efforts were
crowned with success, and that we both danced assiduously.

Vladimir Gerard, Recollections, printed in *PVC4*, pp. 27–8, and partially in
*TZC1*, pp. 96–7, 104.

# RUDOLF KÜNDINGER

## (1832–1913)

Rudolf Kündinger was a German pianist and teacher who settled in Russia in 1850; later he was a professor at the St Petersburg Conservatoire. In 1855 Tchaikovsky began piano lessons with him.

From 1855 to 1858 our work was interrupted only in the summer months. During this time my pupil had his successes, though these were not such as to arouse in me any particular hopes on his account. To Ilya Petrovich's [Tchaikovsky] question whether it was worth his son dedicating himself ultimately to a career in music I replied in the negative, in the first place because I did not see in Pyotr Ilich the genius which subsequently manifested itself, and secondly because I had myself experienced how hard was the lot of a professional musician in Russia at that time . . .

It did not occur to me with what sort of musician I was dealing, and so the details of the course of my pupil's musical development are very unclearly preserved in my memory. Certainly his abilities were outstanding: a strikingly fine ear, memory, an outstanding hand, but all this gave no cause to foresee in him even a brilliant performer, let alone a composer . . . The one thing that to a certain extent did arrest my attention was his improvisations; in them could certainly be dimly sensed something not quite ordinary. In addition his harmonic flair sometimes struck me. At that time he scarcely knew anything of musical theory, but when it chanced that I showed him my own compositions, he several times gave me advice on the harmonic aspect – advice which for the most part was sensible.

Rudolf Kündinger, Recollections, printed in *PVC4*, pp. 31–2, and partially in *TZC1*, pp. 122–3.

# ANNA MERKLING

## (1830–1911)

Anna Merkling was Tchaikovsky's favourite cousin. From 1852, when Tchaikovsky's parents settled in St Petersburg, the Tchaikovsky family became a particularly close-knit clan, and the

future composer enjoyed a happy and healthy social life during the
school holidays. After the death of his mother in 1854 (one of the
two most shattering emotional traumas of his whole life), his
father and his brother, Uncle Pyotr (Anna's father), decided to
share their existences for three years, and this consolidated the
future composer's relationship with Anna, even though she was
ten years older than he. Tchaikovsky was to retain lifelong contact
with her, helped when her husband found himself in financial
difficulties, and dedicated to her his piano piece *Menuetto scher-
zoso*, op. 51 no. 3. Anna's following account, recorded by Modest
Tchaikovsky, probably refers to 1852, when Tchaikovsky was 12.

According to her [Anna], when he was not with his mother he was always
with her. They were united in a love of practical jokes, for which the
future composer manifested an unusual flair. As an example I cite the
following. Alongside the Tchaikovsky's [summer] dacha there lived a
certain cantankerous Polish woman of dubious morals, who was a passionate turkey-fancier. And so Pyotr Ilich with his bosom companion set out to
tease this neighbour. Near her poultry-run they launched into the duet:
'Have you seen this boat?' The turkeys began cackling, and then the Polish
woman appeared at the window and hurled abuse at the pranksters. This
sent them into raptures, and they repeated this prank until the occasion
when there appeared at the window a man with a large moustache who
managed to frighten them sufficiently for them not to do it again. Being
Anna Petrovna's companion in escapades, he felt himself obliged to be her
shield and protector on other occasions. One summer evening, when the
three girls [Anna, Lidiya Tchaikovskaya and Tchaikovsky's half sister,
Zinaida] were on the balcony of their upstairs room confiding to one
another the secrets of their hearts before going to bed, an alarmed Petya
dashed off to tell them that Kolya [his brother Nikolay] and Anna's
brother Ilya . . . had set up a ladder and were eavesdropping on the girls'
confidences. The reward of these two inquisitive admirers was cold water
poured onto their heads.

Anna Merkling, Recollections, as reported by Modest Tchaikovsky in *TZC1*,
p. 77.

When Tchaikovsky left the School of Jurisprudence in 1859 he
proceeded straight to a post in the Ministry of Justice.

# FYODOR MASLOV

[During his years of service] the side of his nature that was aristocratic (in the sense of having a refined sensitivity about outward impressions) manifested itself in a striving to draw close to the upper echelons of society in both the figurative and literal meaning of the word, and also in that he nourished a deep aversion to the temper that was prevailing in the army. Meanwhile an attraction to all that was beautiful, that pleased the eye, declared itself in his care for his outward appearance. Being impecunious he could not dress elegantly, and this caused him distress.

Fyodor Maslov, Recollections; published in *PVC4*, p. 30.

# ALINA BRYULLOVA

## (1849–1932)

Alina Bryullova was the mother by her first husband of a deaf mute, Kolya Konradi, to whom Modest Tchaikovsky became personal tutor in 1876 and, after the death of Kolya's father in 1882, guardian. Tchaikovsky had good relations with Bryullova and very close ones with Kolya, and frequently visited their family estate at Grankino. To Bryullova he dedicated the piano piece *Echo rustique*, op. 72 no. 13. Efim Volkov, who recounted to Bryullova the following incident which happened while he and Tchaikovsky were working in the Ministry of Justice, subsequently became an artist.

The latter [Tchaikovsky] was an assistant to the 'head of the table' while Volkov, quite uneducated and not bright, was a sort of clerk and, of course, it was very difficult for such small fry. It happened that Tchaikovsky passed the room where Volkov was working and noticed his downcast expression.

'What's up with you?'

'They've taken away my "goose", and I'd counted on this money to pay my debts.' (In civil servant jargon 'goose' was the name given to the bonus payment made for Christmas.)

'And how much is it?'

The amount was not large, but in the finances not only of Volkov but of Tchaikovsky it represented a handsome sum.

Immediately Tchaikovsky thought of helping the poor man.

'Hold on,' he said. 'This is certainly a mistake. I'll go and sort it out.'

A half-hour later he returned.

'There has indeed been a misunderstanding. Here's your money; they gave it to me.'

Alina Bryullova, Recollections (1929); published in *PVC4*, pp. 114–15.


# MODEST TCHAIKOVSKY

From after their sister Alexandra's [Sasha] marriage in 1860, Pyotr assumed the role of mother to his twin brothers, Modest and Anatoly, and a very close and affectionate relationship built between them. Their age difference seems to have been no impediment.

When he [brother Pyotr] agreed 'to torment' us, he did not do it patronizingly but threw himself into it wholeheartedly, and this made his participation in the frolic so enjoyable for us. He would improvise, invent some [game] and, in consequence, would relish it himself. His games were like nothing else: everything issued from his strange and enchantingly charming nature . . .

In 1861 Tchaikovsky travelled to Western Europe for the first time as interpreter to a friend of his father. Just ahead of this he had begun taking lessons in basic composition techniques with Nikolay Zaremba in the newly established classes of the Russian Musical Society (RMS). Briefly, there is a shift in his relationship with his twin brothers. Herman Laroche was to be one of his closest friends.

[I can see my brother when] he had just returned from Paris . . . That winter he seemed to me, as before, mad about, and very involved in, amateur theatricals. I remember him in the company of Apukhtin . . . Meshchersky, Adamov [former schoolfriends] . . . constantly either talking about performances in houses I didn't know, or rehearsing at home . . . I remember him in the play *The Peasant as Mistress*, where in the second act he played the supporting role of the landowner and amused everyone with his mime of catching mosquitoes, and in *Misfortunes of a Tender Heart*, where he played a young man, a part which he considered his best . . . In ballet he rated smoothness, absence of sharp, mincing movements as the chief virtue, and when he danced he demonstrated what this meant . . .

Later, when Zaremba's courses began, Petina's musical associates began to appear, and he began playing piano duet arrangements of Beethoven symphonies with them . . . I dimly remember a charity concert for a student, a certain Siluyanova, in one of the Technological Institute's halls, where Petya played . . . a polonaise for solo piano by Weber – his virtuoso war horse. I remember he was hurt that the audience had not applauded much, though in his heart of hearts he also did not rate his performance highly. After that, as his [RMS] courses at the Mikhailovsky Palace progress, Petya's choice of pieces to play becomes ever more incomprehensible to me, and finally he begins for hours to play certain ugly pieces; fugues by Bach. In vain did he try to interest me in them . . . During this phase Petya often improvised – particularly, I seem to remember, at twilight: never on request, and for the most part avoiding listeners. And if by chance such were around and praised him, he would retort sharply: 'It is of no importance . . . there's nothing of merit in it . . .'

From the autumn of 1862 there was talk neither of amateur theatricals nor of social acquaintances. Music swallowed up everything. He is teased for growing his hair long . . . people are surprised at his decision [to attend the RMS classes], he is censured for it, they lament it. Laroche appears . . . Petya seems to me a totally new person. There is his tenderness towards Father, his remaining at home, his increasing carelessness about his appearance, the assiduity with which he works, his attention to my and Anatoly's needs, his concern for matters such as formerly had been incompatible with the image of a brilliant man about town. His tender caresses, the complete absence of talk about theatricals and balls – all this taken together both surprised, touched and pleased . . .

Having rejected social pleasures, Petya, except for visiting his closest friends and the theatre, also liked to play dominoes at the 'Noble Assembly'. Besides these amusements, on Mondays Petya would go to an at-home at a certain Khristianovich's, where a very interesting company gathered . . . After this, if mention is made of the 'Five Kopecks' – that is, the little restaurants where for five, ten, fifteen or twenty copecks you could get a tolerable meal, and where Petya 'caroused' with Laroche – then this exhausts all his amusements. At this time an increasing estrangement from his former friends is to be noticed in Petya. He speaks of their emptiness with disdain, and little by little cuts himself off from them completely.

Modest Tchaikovsky, Recollections; published in *PVC4*, pp. 33–6.

In 1862 Tchaikovsky entered the newly founded St Petersburg Conservatoire which had grown out of the success of the RMS classes; he did not, however, resign from his post in the Ministry of Justice until 1863. He graduated from the Conservatoire in December 1865.

## Tchaikovsky as student performer

# HERMAN LAROCHE
## (1845–1904)

Herman Laroche was one of the closest of Tchaikovsky's lifelong friends. They were fellow students in the St Petersburg Conservatoire and for a time Laroche was a colleague at the Moscow Conservatoire. But Laroche, whose upbringing had been very mother-dominated and whose first wife died young, leaving him with responsibility for a young family, declined helplessly into a very disordered lifestyle marked by personal dissipations and long periods of total indolence. Yet he had a brilliant mind, and as a writer on music was in the first rank, as Tchaikovsky recognized; indeed, so anxious was the latter that Laroche's talents should not be wasted that in his later life, even when the pressures of his own fame were at their strongest, he would on occasion still make time to act as Laroche's amanuensis in order to draw an article from him. For his part, Laroche was to become the most supportive – and the most penetrating – critic of Tchaikovsky's music. As noted in the present volume's Introduction, this, combined with his lifelong knowledge of his composer-friend, makes him perhaps the single most valuable source of information about him. Tchaikovsky met the 17-year-old Laroche for the first time at the St Petersburg Conservatoire in 1862, and the two immediately became inseparable in their musical activities and pursuits.

He [Tchaikovsky] played [the piano] . . . in general very well, boldly, with brilliance, [and] could play pieces of the greatest difficulty. To my taste at that time his playing was somewhat rough, lacking in warmth and depth of feeling – exactly the opposite of what the contemporary reader might have imagined it to be above all. The point is that Pyotr Ilich feared sentimentality like the plague and consequently disliked over-expressive piano playing, making fun of the expressive marking 'play *with feeling*' . . . The musical feeling within him was controlled by a certain *chasteness*, and out of fear of vulgarity he could go to the opposite extreme.

Herman Laroche, *VOC*; reprinted in *PVC4*, pp. 37–8, and *LIS2*, pp. 167–8.

From September 1862 to New Year 1863 Tchaikovsky twice a week (on Mondays and Thursdays at eight a.m.) attended Anton Gerke's [piano] class . . . He [Gerke] tended towards the lightly sentimental; when imparting to us the various shades and refinements of phrasing for which he was a great enthusiast, he was not averse to lecturing us on where it was and was not opportune to play in tempo rubato – which did not please Pyotr Ilich at all. At about that time at one of the concerts of the RMS we became acquainted with Konstantin Lyadov's choral fantasia on the theme 'Vozle rechki, vozle mosta'. Under the influence of this Pyotr Ilich composed and dedicated to me a facetious one-page piano piece on that very same theme. To make his point he wrote above the piece, instead of a tempo direction: 'Maestoso, misterioso e senza gherkando'.

Herman Laroche, *MTC*; reprinted in *PVC4*, p. 49, and *LIS2*, pp. 282–3.

Within him there went, along with the amateur pianist, an amateur singer. He had a small baritone voice, to my ears very pleasant, of unusual cleanness and accuracy of intonation . . . That he liked Italian coloratura was remarkable. He himself sang cleanly and rapidly; perhaps because of this he readily, though half in fun, adorned his repertoire with such pieces as arias and duets from [Rossini's] *Semiramide* and *Otello*.

Herman Laroche, *VOC*; reprinted in *PVC4*, p. 38, and *LIS2*, p. 168.

> The St Petersburg Conservatoire's principal, Anton Rubinstein,
> wanted to have a student symphony orchestra, and to ensure that
> the necessary players could be recruited he allotted 1500 roubles
> of his own money each year for free student lessons on orchestral
> instruments.

Students turned up, one of the first being Pyotr Ilich, who expressed a
wish to learn the flute. Before entering the Conservatoire he was well
acquainted with his teacher, the renowned Cesari Ciardi, and had more
than once accompanied him at musical soirées. His lessons with Ciardi
went on for two years. In performing symphonies by Haydn and other
pieces in the normal student repertoire Tchaikovsky played in a thoroughly
satisfactory manner, and once, together with [fellow] students Pugni,
Gorshkov and Pomerantsev, he played in a flute quartet by Kuhlau at a
soirée graced by the presence of Clara Schumann. As was to be expected,
when the need had passed he quickly gave up the flute and forgot how to
play it.

Herman Laroche, *MTC*; reprinted in *PVC4*, p. 53, and *LIS2*, p. 287.

> Rubinstein also paid for students in theory classes to have organ
> lessons, and these included Tchaikovsky.

It fell to his lot to have as his teacher a celebrity: Heinrich Stiehl, at that
time still very young, was close to being one of the foremost European
organists . . . On Pyotr Ilich's impressionable and poetic soul both the
majestic sound of the instrument and the inexhaustible variety of its
resources – and the very location of the lessons in the deserted and mysteri-
ously dark Petropavlovsky Lutheran Church – could not fail to have an
effect. But this effect was transitory; his imagination was drawn to another
world, and the Bach who was king throughout all musical countries was
one of the most alien [of composers] to him. It is notable that later, when
he played Bach for his own pleasure, he chose only his piano and not his
organ pieces, though they were readily available in transcriptions. As a
student conscientious and meticulous in everything, he worked with Stiehl
to his [Stiehl's] complete satisfaction. But once he had left his class he no

longer showed any interest in the instrument and did not compose a single piece for it.

Herman Laroche, *MTC:* reprinted in *PVC4*, pp. 53–4, and *LIS2*, pp. 287–8.

## Tchaikovsky and his teachers

Nikolay Zaremba was Tchaikovsky's first teacher in the RMS classes in which he enrolled in 1861. Zaremba was a pedantic technician in the Germanic tradition, whose drilling by his own teacher, Adolf Marx, in textbook counterpoint had given him a total command of this tramline technique; he was implacably insistent that his pupils should follow Marx's precepts exactly. Though the initial grounding he gave Tchaikovsky in basic compositional procedures was no doubt of enormous value, Zaremba was devoid of any creative imagination and ignorant of contemporary composers (for him music ended with Mendelssohn), and he was unable to offer any help when it came to real composition. Yet Laroche believed it was Zaremba's admonition of Tchaikovsky to apply himself more rigorously to his work that laid the foundations of the systematic diligence which marked Tchaikovsky's composing activities for the rest of his life.

But because he [Nikolay Zaremba] . . . was not a practising contrapuntist and could not, having pointed to a deficiency in a piece of work that had been brought to him, correct it on the spot, many of us distrusted him . . . Pyotr Ilich, who was inclined to look at things empirically, who was a natural foe of all things abstract . . . did not like his superficial structural logic in which he sensed an arbitrariness and a violence against truth. This incompatibility between professor and pupil was exacerbated by the fact that Nikolay Ivanovich [Zaremba] referred more readily and more often to Beethoven, while for Mozart he had a secret and sometimes even open dislike which he had caught from Marx. But Tchaikovsky nourished for Beethoven, with the exception of a very few works, far more esteem than enthusiasm, and in many respects was in no way prepared to follow in his footsteps. In general Tchaikovsky was of a somewhat sceptical cast of mind, with an unusual need for independence; in the whole course of my acquaintance with him I never witnessed a single instance in which he would submit wholeheartedly and blindly to any influence, would bow *in verba magistri*; but he was capable of personal enthusiasms which for a time to a greater or lesser degree coloured his way of thinking.

Herman Laroche, *MTC*; reprinted in *PVC4*, pp. 47–8, and *LIS2*, pp. 280–1.

> Anton Rubinstein was the most important single formative influence upon Tchaikovsky's creative skills. As a composer his reputation was great, though in most of his works he was no more than a competent and fatally fluent craftsman; as a pianist he had a reputation second only to Liszt, and all his life he pursued an international solo career. But Rubinstein was also an idealist who saw the desperate need to develop Russia's musical life, and he was the driving force behind the foundation of the RMS. When the classes this had inaugurated grew into the St Petersburg Conservatoire in 1862, Rubinstein became the new institution's first, and very active, director.

[Regarding Anton Rubinstein] he retained his complete independence of judgement, recalled not without humour the shortcomings of logic and grammar in his lectures, not without distress surveyed the mass of colourless and shallow compositions in which Rubinstein, in effect, swamped the memory of his few masterpieces; but neither the oddities of the professor nor the ever mounting sins of the composer could weaken in Pyotr Ilich's soul the enchantment he experienced from the man. This attachment began almost before personal acquaintance, but was strengthened enormously as a result of the link which [the process of] tuition forged between them, and however far subsequently the paths in life of these two Russian musicians may have diverged, it was retained by Tchaikovsky to his dying day, though he never had with Anton Rubinstein those intimate or unaffectedly friendly relations such as he had with his brother, Nikolay . . . Seeing the uncommon zeal of his pupil, and perhaps judging his work process by that enormous facility with which he himself worked, Rubinstein was less and less sparing in the scope of the tasks [he set Tchaikovsky]. But in proportion to the increasing demands of his professor, so the industry of the pupil became more frenetic; [though] endowed with a healthy youthful capacity for slumber, and loving to have a good sleep, Pyotr Ilich would sit through whole nights without a break, and in the morning would carry off to his insatiable professor his scarcely dry, newly completed score. As far as may be seen from the facts, this inordinate labour had no harmful consequences for Tchaikovsky's health.

Herman Laroche, *MTC*; reprinted in *PVC4*, p. 51 and *LIS2*, p. 285.


## Tchaikovsky's early musical tastes

I began visiting him in the evening about once a week, when I invariably brought along music for piano duet which, thanks to the kindness of Osip Jurgenson, currently the chief salesman at Bernard's shop, I was able to enjoy in unlimited quantities. I can tell you exactly what we played during our first year. There was the Ninth Symphony of Beethoven, the Third of Schumann, 'The Ocean' [no. 2] of Rubinstein, *Genoveva* by Schumann (not the overture but the opera in its entirety) – then, I think, *Das Paradies und die Peri* [by Schumann] and *Lohengrin*. Pyotr Ilich grumbled a little when I made him perform with me long vocal compositions with a mass of recitatives which did not make sense on the piano, though subsequently the beauty of the integral numbers these linked disarmed him. He liked Richard Wagner least of all. He even damned the celebrated prelude to *Lohengrin*, and only many years later became reconciled to the whole opera. To this day I remember how once, trudging with me through the spring-time mud along the Fontanka, he intrepidly declared: 'I know only one thing: that Serov has far more talent as a composer than Wagner.' This conversation must have taken place around Lent 1864 because [Serov's] *Judith* had been given for the first time in late spring of the preceding year . . . From all I have listed, Schumann's Third Symphony and Rubinstein's 'Ocean' made the strongest impression on him. We managed to hear the latter some time afterwards under the composer's own direction at a concert of his own which he gave in the Bolshoy Theatre, and which strengthened yet further our enthusiasm for this work . . .

Many readers will be surprised to learn that Henry Litolff was one of Pyotr Ilich's greatest enthusiasms in these youthful years – or, more precisely, his two overtures, *Robespierre* and *Die Girondisten*, especially the second. It could be said without exaggeration that it was with these very two overtures, and also Meyerbeer's overture to *Struensee*, that there began Tchaikovsky's passion, which haunted him all his life, for programme music. In his early overtures, not excluding *Romeo and Juliet*, the influence of Litolff is still fully to be felt, while at the same time Pyotr Ilich came slowly, indecisively, distrustfully to Liszt, who would have seemed to have had more qualities to attract a young musician. Of the symphonic poems only *Orfeo* roused any real enthusiasm during his time at the Conservatoire; only much later did he take to the Faust Symphony . . .

It is worth observing that during the period of youth I am describing Pyotr Ilich had a great many unhealthy musical antipathies from which in the course of time (sometimes extremely prolonged) he freed himself completely. These antipathies related not to composers but to whole genres of composition – more exactly, to their sound. Thus, for instance, he did not like the sound of piano with orchestra, the sound of a string quartet or quintet, and most of all the sound of the piano in combination with one or several stringed instruments. Though out of curiosity he became acquainted with the broad piano concerto and chamber music repertoires, though it happened time and again that he was enraptured by the musical content of this or that movement, yet afterwards at the first convenient moment he would damn this music for the 'ugliness' of its timbre. Not just once, nor ten times, nor a hundred times did I hear from him what was almost an oath: that he would never compose a single piano concerto, or a single sonata for violin and piano, or a single trio, quartet, and so on . . . It is even stranger that about this very time he gave a pledge never to compose either short piano pieces or romances. To romances as an art form he expressed the deepest aversion. This aversion was purely platonic because at the same time he was prepared to delight with me in [the songs of] Glinka, Schumann and Franz Schubert . . .

It should be noted that while some pieces stood unshakeable in his pantheon – like, for instance, *Don Giovanni*, [Glinka's] *A Life for the Tsar*, the C major Symphony of Schubert – as regards many others he manifested a strong ebb and flow. One season he made much of Beethoven's Eighth Symphony, in another he found it 'simply very nice and nothing more'; for several years he asserted that the music to *Faust* by Pugni (once a celebrated composer for the ballet) was incomparably superior to that in the opera of the same name by Gounod; yet later he pronounced Gounod's *Faust* a masterpiece. The more remarkable is the loyalty he retained for Serov's *Judith*; several years before his death the vocal score of the opera was published, which he soon obtained and began playing with the enthusiasm of his youth, making me also admire it and persuading me to write a big article about it.

Herman Laroche, *MTC*; reprinted in *PVC4*, pp. 54–8, and *LIS2*, pp. 288–90, 292.

## VALENTINA SEROVA
### (1846–1924)

Valentina Serova, herself a minor composer, was a pupil and then the wife of Alexander Serov, the much-admired creator of *Judith*. On this first occasion when Tchaikovsky met Serov, the latter had been holding forth on his views on art. Tchaikovsky had listened but said nothing, though Serov's wife had sensed he did not agree with her husband.

While we were drinking tea Tchaikovsky went to the piano and absent-mindedly ran his fingers over the keys, seemingly transporting himself elsewhere, away from all that surrounded him. I don't know what prompted me to go over to him and draw him out of this state of self-oblivion; I only remember that I approached him boldly and, with the carefree self-assurance characteristic of a still very young, not fully matured being, asked him in a challenging tone:

'And what are your musical ideals, Pyotr Ilich?'

He started, looked around, and without hurrying replied:

'My – my ideals? But is it really absolutely essential to have ideals in music? I'd never thought of this.'

He turned on me that clear glance of his which had the stamp of an almost childlike naïvety, and added firmly and precisely:

'I have no musical ideals!'

Valentina Serova, 'Trois moments musicales', in *RMG* (1895), no. 2; reprinted in *PVC4*, pp. 373–4.

# II
## The Moscow years

In January 1866 Tchaikovsky graduated from the St Petersburg
Conservatoire with a silver medal, and proceeded straight to
Moscow to work under Anton Rubinstein's brother Nikolay as
teacher of musical theory in the Moscow classes of the RMS. In
the autumn of 1866 the Moscow Conservatoire grew out of these
classes, with Nikolay as its director and Tchaikovsky as one of its
professors. Tchaikovsky was to teach here for the next eleven
years.

# At the Conservatoire

*A fellow teacher's view of Tchaikovsky as teacher*

## NIKOLAY KASHKIN

### (1839–1920)

Tchaikovsky first met Nikolay Kashkin on his arrival in Moscow, where this largely self-taught musician was teaching piano and musical theory for the RMS; subsequently he was for thirty years a professor at the Conservatoire. The hospitality Kashkin and his wife extended to Tchaikovsky ensured that friendship quickly followed, and Kashkin became one of Tchaikovsky's intimate circle until his death. His memoirs of Tchaikovsky (Moscow, 1896) are the most substantial single personal record of the composer as a person.

His [Tchaikovsky's] pupils very quickly came to value and like their young teacher, who was able to explain everything well and in a lively manner, and who was, moreover, irreproachably conscientious and thorough in his work. Pyotr Ilich himself always considered he was a bad teacher, but in this regard he was unfair [to himself]. True, he had no inclination to teaching, engaging in it reluctantly as being by far the most convenient work for making a living, but . . . his conscientiousness and his rigorous attitude towards himself excluded any possibility in him of that moral indiscipline which is called laziness – and so in his work with his students he did not permit such indiscipline in himself. But all the same, his duties themselves were antipathetic to him, chiefly because he did not see any special use in them since the majority of his students of both sexes only with great effort made themselves familiar with no more than the external, formal side of their subject, not penetrating into its very essence. If from time to time he encountered students of high aptitudes wanting to acquire a thorough knowledge of compositional technique, then with such (being himself a musician in love with his subject) he was prepared to occupy himself with the greatest zeal; however, such cases were very rarely encountered, and the obligation to be a simple teacher of musical grammar did not have any attraction for him. He would try by all means possible to encourage talented pupils to diligent, persistent work, but he rarely succeeded because for the most part such students also had in view the narrow, practical aim of teaching the piano, while the more ambitious dreamed of careers as virtuosi, and compositional activity itself attracted hardly any of them because its benefits were too remote and hypothetical. Pyotr Ilich attributed such aspirations in the talented students to a baseness of nature originating in inadequate development and education, and he felt a kind of animosity, joined with a pitiful contempt, towards such students.

As regards composition he never placed any hopes in the female students, though he valued very much their conscientiousness and attentiveness, in which they far outstripped the male students.

Nikolay Kashkin, *KVC*, pp. 12, 98–9.

*Some pupils' views of Tchaikovsky as teacher*

## ROSTISLAV GENIKA

### (1859-?1922)

Between 1871 and 1879 Rostislav Genika studied piano at the Moscow Conservatoire with Nikolay Rubinstein, and also composition and orchestration with Tchaikovsky. On internal evidence the following account must relate to 1871; Tchaikovsky's textbook on harmony appeared in 1872.

For Tchaikovsky his hours taking the theory classes were a cheerless part of life; he was openly bored, with difficulty restraining himself from yawning. How vivid are my childhood memories of his first lessons in harmony! . . . Tchaikovsky would enter the lecture room at speed, always a little fussed, a little irritable as though vexed at the unavoidability of the boredom facing him. He was made irritable by the mundane furnishings of the theory class, with its school desks, its red-lined blackboard, and its ordinary, ancient, battered, yellow grand piano with its rattling, yellowing

keys. Standing at this blackboard Tchaikovsky had to write out exercises
and examples for us; I recall the squeamish way in which, casting aside
the chalk and grey blackboard duster, he would wipe his fingers on his
handkerchief. He was irritated by the slowness of the majority of the
[female] students, the dull, superficial relationship to the essence of art of
all these future laureates, who dreamed only of the concert platform and
were convinced that the public who would applaud their playing would
have no interest in their theoretical knowledge. Reluctantly he had to listen
to the melancholy knocking out of sequences and modulations on the
hideous-sounding piano, patiently mark out with his red pencil forbidden
fifths and octaves. When I entered Tchaikovsky's class his textbook on
harmony was still not published; it appeared in Jurgenson's catalogue the
following year. Pacing among the class, slowly and very distinctly he
would dictate to us and we would take it down. For the whole of the first
half-year he familiarized us with the construction and progression of various harmonies, explained suspensions and appoggiaturas, made us work
exercises on a figured bass; he went on to harmonizing a melody only in the
second half-year. Tchaikovsky's exposition, his observations, explanations
and corrections were remarkably clear, succinct and intelligible. Later in
his class I went through instrumentation and the theory of what was called
free composition, transcribed for orchestra various piano pieces, wrote a
string quartet under his guidance and, for the final examination, an orchestral overture. Simplicity, clarity of thought, smoothness of form,
transparency, lightness in the scoring were the ideals towards which Tchaikovsky made his pupils strive. He loved to exemplify various rules with
examples from Glinka and Mozart.

Pyotr Ilich's manner when dealing with students was surprisingly
gentle, delicate and patient; with some of the older ones he was on close,
thoroughly friendly terms. He never expressed his involuntary, sometimes
sarcastic and fully merited observations in any rude or offensive manner.
The insufferable musical absurdities which students sometimes presented
to him drew from him a characteristic, at once kindly yet derisive, smile at
the corner of his mouth.

Rostislav Genika, Recollections; published in *RMG* (1916), nos. 36–7, 49,
reprinted in *PVC4*, pp. 62–3.

# ALEXANDRA AMFITEATROVA-LEVITSKAYA

## (1858–1947)

Alexandra Amfiteatrova-Levitskaya studied singing at the Moscow Conservatoire, and created the part of Olga in Tchaikovsky's *Eugene Onegin* at its première at the Conservatoire in 1879.

When I entered the Moscow Conservatoire Tchaikovksy was the professor of harmony and composition. Among his students there had formed the most contradictory opinions about him, both as man and teacher. Some considered him not only a composer of genius but an ideal teacher. According to their tales Pyotr Ilich always looked over students' work with great interest and attention, patiently correcting mistakes and giving invaluable directions. Others would have us believe that Tchaikovsky behaved towards them offhandedly, unfairly – that to some students he gave a lot of time while giving no attention at all to others. One of his female pupils told me the following as an example of Pyotr Ilich's offhand behaviour to some of his pupils:

'Tchaikovsky was not only unfair, he was a terrible fault-finder. At my last lesson he found fault with a trifle and struck through my work without even looking it through.

"Why have you done that?" I asked.

You see, I had put the tails on the wrong side of separate quavers. He became angry, struck the whole page through from top to bottom with his red pencil. Returning the exercise book to me, he said irritably:

"You need first to learn about tails, and only then work harmony exercises!" ' . . .

Only once, at the final examination in solfeggio, did it fall to my lot to be examined by him. Having heard contradictory tales about him, I became quite violently agitated when Pyotr Ilich summoned me to the table. I remember how he selected from the musical examples lying before him several bars with a difficult rhythm; besides long notes, you met also short pauses and dotted [notes] and syncopations. When I had sung, Pyotr Ilich said to me:

'All right,' and asked: 'From which bars do you get a bar of $\frac{5}{4}$?'

Again I answered correctly. Tchaikovsky asked me to name an example [of $\frac{5}{4}$]; I cited the girls' chorus from the third act of Glinka's opera *Ivan Susanin*.

'Could you sing a few bars from that chorus, and conduct them?' asked Tchaikovsky.

I began singing 'Razgulyalasya, razleleyalas voda veshnyaya po-o lugam', conducting in $\frac{5}{4}$.

'Good. That'll do for you,' said Pyotr Ilich.

'So – that was no worse than I had expected,' I thought as I went off to the summons for dictation with Langer.

In appearance Pyotr Ilich was quite handsome, but he gave an impression of sternness. His facial expression was as though he was constantly displeased with something. His eyes looked out gloomily from beneath his frowning brows. To the greetings of the candidates he responded with a scarcely perceptible nod of the head. He seemed severe and out of temper.

Alexandra Amfiteatrova-Levitskaya, Recollections (1940); published in *CIT*, reprinted in *PVC4*, pp. 66–7.

# ALEXANDER LITVINOV
## (1861–1933)

At the Moscow Conservatoire Alexander Litvinov first studied
the violin under Ferdinand Laub. He was also a pupil of Tchaikovsky, who later supported him through part of his course.

I first saw Tchaikovsky in 1873 at a lesson on harmony which he taught us at the Moscow Conservatoire. He was a nervous, agile man, not tall. He entered the class at speed with his hands behind his back, his head bent slightly forward and looking straight ahead with a fixed and – so it seemed to us – severe look in his grey eyes. Pyotr Ilich would sit at the piano, take a pencil, slip it between his fingers so that the second and fourth fingers appeared above the pencil while the third was below it (and sometimes the other way round) and without letting it go, would play through our exercises. Stopping for a second, with a quick and sharp movement he would put a bracket round parallel fifths and octaves, and then play on. It was evident that our mistakes irritated him. When explaining the rules of

harmony Pyotr Ilich would continue walking around the class, character-
istically placing his hands behind his back and leaning forward slightly.
We were all very afraid of him (at that time I was 13) . . .

I especially remember the following incident. It happened that my
parents (I was born into a poor Jewish family), being convinced that I 'had
learned how to play the violin adequately' and not having the means to pay
for me at the Conservatoire, decided to withdraw me from it and prepare
me for another career . . .

One morning, however, while sitting in hopeless despair at home and
holding my adored violin (I would never be parted from it, even taking it
with me to bed at night), I suddenly heard the rumble of an approaching
carriage which drew up at the porch of our apartment. An impatient noise
was soon audible, the tread of quick steps up the staircase, a door was
opened, and I saw Tchaikovsky entering. I rushed to him, and in a few
minutes we were bowling along in the carriage to the Conservatoire. On
the way he told me that, having learned of my poverty (I had stopped
coming to my lessons) and of the cause, he had decided to make me his
stipendiary [student] – that is, to bear my Conservatoire costs . . . In
1879 I finished at the Moscow Conservatoire with the great silver medal.

Alexander Litvinov, Recollections; published in *PVC4*, pp. 69–70.

## At home and at play

## SOFIYA KASHKINA

### (1872–1964)

Sofiya Kashkina was the daughter of Tchaikovsky's close friend
Nikolay Kashkin, and she is the main source of information about
the happy and sometimes boisterous social life enjoyed by Tchaikovsky, her father and their circle during the late 1860s and early
1870s.

Tchaikovsky's taste for practical jokes was nothing new. Niko-
lay Bugayev, who was a professor of mathematics at Moscow
University, had a habit of fastening upon one or another of the
Moscow Conservatoire staff, raising a problem, then often

plunging into a complex argument about it and refusing to let the
matter rest until his victim accepted his point.

On one occasion Tchaikovsky, noticing that he [Bugayev] had chosen the
most amiable Ivan [Jan] Voitsekhovich Hřímalý [a professor of violin] as
his victim, lay in wait for the latter and said:

'Look, Ivan Voitsekhovich, Bugayev is a dangerous man. You've only
got to agree with him on some matter, and he'll make something out of
your words that will make your hair stand on end. See you don't give in.'

Hřímalý promised to hold firm. Bugayev set about his arguments – I do
not remember any longer about what – and turned to Hřímalý:

'Do you concede that point?'

Because he had been prompted by Tchaikovsky, Hřímalý replied resol-
utely to everything:

'No, I don't concede it.'

Finally Bugayev moved on to some simpler thesis.

'Do you concede this?'

'No, I don't concede it,' was the immutable reply.

'Then don't you even concede the passing of time?'

'No, I don't concede it . . .'

Tchaikovsky used to recount this incident with delight.

There was also in their company some young and naïve woman, only
just out of boarding school, who was not quick on the uptake and was
therefore a target for jokes. They all amused themselves by telling her
cock-and-bull stories and then waited for her finally to see that they were all
inventions. Once Tchaikovsky recounted a reception at one of Moscow's
wealthy gastronomes, describing a dinner with the most recherché dishes.

'And at the end we were served coffee with pigeon's milk.'

Seeing that the lady was beginning to look sceptical, Nikolay Grigoryevich [Kashkin] quickly picked up the thread:

'But there's nothing special in what you say about pigeon's milk – but if
there's cheese from that milk, that is something truly remarkable.'

And still the bemused woman did not doubt what was being told to her
by these two respected professors of the Moscow Conservatoire – and these
pranks so delighted them that they would laugh about them to me many
years later. Tchaikovsky had an unusually infectious laugh and often
recounted various trifles with such (as it were) childish animation and joy
that even decades later I enjoy recalling it. What is important here is not

what was said, but how it was said. Thus for instance, Pyotr Ilich enters
and says that he has moved to a new apartment and is very pleased with it.

'Is it a good apartment?'

'Yes,' says Pyotr Ilich joyfully, becoming all animated, 'it's splendid,
comfortable, so small, modest, dark, nothing can be seen. It's such a
delight!'

Note: this is said without any irony . . .

Sometimes the tables could be turned on Tchaikovsky.

The friends were not above playing tricks on one another . . . One of
them (Ivan Klimenko [an architect], if I am not mistaken), who was
famed for his ability for telling stories very rivetingly and at the same
time very touchingly, decided to make use of Pyotr Ilich's exceptional
impressionability and amuse the friends at his expense. Everyone knew
how strongly he [Tchaikovsky] was ruled by his emotions: if something
touched his feelings deeply he surrendered to it totally and his reason
then became completely subordinate to it. And so the story teller, having
forewarned the other listeners, so they would not interfere in any way,
began an unusually pathetic tale of the sufferings of a little orphan girl,
how she had been left without her parents, had fallen in with evil people
who had done her injury and exploited her; very touchingly he described
her meekness, her attractiveness, and her undeserved sufferings. As Pyotr
Ilich listened to the story he was completely carried away by it; his lively
imagination presented to him the suffering of this poor child so vividly
that he himself suffered, groaned, winced, bent over just as though he was
in physical pain. Having brought him to a highly emotional state where
the feeling of pity possessed him completely, the story teller pressed yet
harder, and concluded his sad tale by describing how the girl was sent off
to sell (I believe) matches and was ordered not to return until they were
sold. It becomes frosty, a wind arises – a snowstorm – passers-by speed
homewards, no one is buying anything, the girl is in despair, sits there,
presses herself into a corner – for she is frightened to go home – becomes
all numb, and falls asleep. The snowstorm passes, the sun appears, warms
everything, everything in the street is white, bright, merry – 'and . . . she
opens her eyes – and she is dead'.

'How terrible, she opens her eyes – and she is dead,' repeats Tchaikovsky, covering his face with his hands. The loud laughter of the other

listeners recalls him to himself, and in indignation he jumps up and begins
upbraiding the pranksters . . .

> Kashkina describes how her father and Tchaikovsky decided to go
> to a masquerade, and made a bet each would not recognize the
> other. To disguise himself, her father had gone to the barber's,
> had his beard shaved off, and this had been judged sufficient to
> mask his identity. At the ball a friend, who had been let in on the
> secret, introduced him to other guests as a visiting musician. But
> then a new arrival drew the attention of the guests . . .

The appearance of a very elegant, tall lady produced something of a
sensation. She was dressed in an unusually luxurious domino [a kind of
loose cloak with a small mask covering the upper part of the face] made of
black lace, and was wearing diamonds and carrying a fan made, I believe,
from ostrich feathers. She began walking about grandly on the arm of one
of the male partners. Many recognized this domino; it was the only one of
its kind, made to the order of one of the wealthy Moscow ladies. Her
husband, who was attending the masquerade, was very embarrassed. His
friends had forewarned him that his wife was entering, [but earlier] she
had told him she felt unwell and would not be going to the masquerade,
and he had begun paying court to a certain actress to whom he was
attracted, and of whom his wife was jealous. He hastened to make himself
scarce, someone else took over his lady-friend, and the author of this
rumpus continued calmly strolling past the dancers and the guests who
were chatting together. Several times she passed the table near where
Kashkin was chatting with some others – when suddenly, having turned so
that Kashkin became visible to her from behind, she stopped, with a
pronounced gesture struck herself on the forehead, and exclaimed:

'Idiot! Of course he would have shaved!'

The lady had recognized Papa – and by the characteristic gesture and
voice the others had recognized Tchaikovsky, and their anonymity was
broken, to the amusement of all.

Sofiya Kashkina, Recollections (1959); published in *PVC4*, pp. 79–82.

## As musician

*On Tchaikovsky's performing abilities*

# NIKOLAY KASHKIN

When Tchaikovsky had first moved to Moscow he had shared
quarters with Nikolay Rubinstein.

When he arrived in Moscow in 1866 Tchaikovsky read music well, but
subsequently he made constant strides in this, and in his last years he
became a true *Notenfresser* [devourer of notes] as far as one could without
having a really first-class piano technique. It was the same with reading
scores; as far as I remember, at first he read them at the piano competently,
but no more. But later in this also he made enormous progress, because
here experience played a big part. Sometimes we had vocal evenings. Pyotr
Ilich had collected together a large pile of romances by people unknown or
little known to us; on such occasions he would sing and Laroche or I would
accompany . . . In his youth Pyotr Ilich had a very modest but pleasant
voice of a rather baritoneish quality. Among the voices of composers, as
far as I have heard them, his was one of the best, but none of them sang
with such mastery of nuance and musical declamation . . . Because of that
diffidence which he never conquered to the end of his days, Pyotr Ilich
would allow himself his vocal exercises only in my and Laroche's presence,
and also perhaps when our mutual friend, Klimenko, was present . . .
Even the presence of Rubinstein embarrassed him . . . Pyotr Ilich confined himself to singing romances he was unfamiliar with; his own compositions he would never sing, except if it happened he was playing some
extract from a new opera, when he would sing the vocal part as best he
could in an undertone. Regarding his own compositions Pyotr Ilich was
very finicky and would never himself direct the conversation towards
them, though in reality he was always longing to hear any opinion about
them – though he attached no significance to unqualified praise unless he
was convinced of its complete sincerity. But if he noticed that some new
work of his had produced a really deep impression on the circle of those

close to him then, as far as I could see, he must have experienced a feeling of bliss, though he was careful to try and conceal this.

Nikolay Kashkin, *KVC*, pp. 48–9.

## On his relationship with the group of Russian nationalist composers

## NIKOLAY RIMSKY-KORSAKOV
## (1844–1908)

Nikolay Rimsky-Korsakov was one of the group of St Petersburg-based composers around Balakirev whose musical ideals were at first aggressively nationalist. Tchaikovsky had met Balakirev in Moscow in 1868, and relations with Balakirev's circle had begun to develop after he had composed the first version of his fantasy overture *Romeo and Juliet* under Balakirev's guidance in 1869. This relationship was at its height during the early 1870s. Rimsky-Korsakov recalls first his initial impression of Tchaikovsky, then a meeting which probably occurred in 1874.

He proved to be a pleasant conversationalist and a sympathetic person, knowing how to behave simply and to talk always, as it were, with sincerity and candour . . . When on a flying visit to St Petersburg, he readily dropped in on us. His visits often coincided with our musical gatherings. On one visit – I do not remember in which year – to our usual question about what he had composed, he replied that he had just finished his Second Quartet in F major. We begged him to acquaint us with it and, after excusing himself briefly, he played it. Everyone liked the quartet very much. Several years later Tchaikovsky ceased playing his own compositions anywhere.

Nikolay Rimsky-Korsakov, *RKL*, pp. 65, 148.

*On his composing habits*

## NADEZHDA KONDRATYEVA
### (1865–19??)

Nadezhda Kondratyeva was the daughter of Tchaikovsky's close friend Nikolay Kondratyev. Tchaikovsky had first met the latter in 1864, and from 1871 to 1879 frequently visited him on his estate at Nizy, near Kharkov. Tchaikovsky was to dedicate a piano piece to each member of the family: to Nikolay, *Rêverie du soir*, op. 19 no. 1; to his wife, *Valse de salon*, op. 51 no. 1; and to their daughter, *Valse Bluette*, op. 72 no. 11. Although he composed during the Conservatoire session when necessary, most of his work was done away from Moscow during the months of the summer vacation.

His day was spent like this. He always got up at seven o'clock and bathed (the river flowed right past the house, and the bathing was excellent). Often about that time my father would also go off to the river, and the friends would meet while bathing. Two or three of my father's brothers who were staying with us would join them. Laughter, happy cries, jokes would fill the air, and I would listen with delight from my room, whose windows faced on to the river. Pyotr Ilich would bathe for a long while, then return to his own quarters and drink tea or milk with home-made buns and pretzels which were prepared specially for him. At our home each drank his morning tea when he wanted to in his own quarters. Pyotr Ilich always drank two glasses, sometimes substituting milk for tea. Then he would go to my father and they would set out together on their invariable walk along the bank, across the entire garden, the vegetable garden, and back home by other paths. The garden was very large and this walk took up a lot of time. Then Pyotr Ilich would come to greet us, chat a little, then go off to his own room. He would work, look through the morning post, read. At noon he would come to eat on the terrace where everyone congregated at that hour. Pyotr Ilich was a great gourmet; he loved tasty food, and each evening with us would order the menu for the following day. In summer he preferred above everything fresh fish soup, or sturgeon (fresh and cured) which was fetched from the town.

After lunch we all dispersed to our rooms, and Pyotr Ilich would come with me to the nursery, look through my exercise books, make me read aloud. Sometimes he would give me a subject for a [literary] composition, and he interested himself in my successes. Then we would go off to the drawing room where there was a large grand piano, and he would examine me closely, making me play from memory what I knew, would select some piece and make me guess what he was playing, say in what key it was; and sometimes he would play some easy piano duet with me. The examination over, he was always satisfied with his check on my knowledge, for I was a very able girl, I loved learning, and I worshipped music. Having kissed me tenderly on the forehead and praised me for being a good pupil, Pyotr Ilich would go off to his own room.

At five o'clock we again collected for a meal, then took a stroll all together, sometimes went for a drive in the wagonette, sat on the balcony, chatted merrily, drank evening tea, ate fruits, fermented boiled milk, and yoghurt, which Pyotr Ilich liked very much. And after tea I would go off to bed and they would sit down to cards; Pyotr Ilich liked this activity very much and they would play . . . until midnight, when they went off to bed.

Such was the mode of living that Pyotr Ilich followed in normal times; however, when he had – as he put it – a wave of inspiration, he became unsociable, gloomy, and talked with nobody. From morning, having drunk two glasses of milk, thrust paper and pencil into his pocket and taken our house dog, Dog, with him, he would go off for the whole day into the country and wander there until evening, jotting down notes, musical phrases, bits of arias, and suchlike. Sometimes he would come back for our [five o'clock] meal, sometimes even later. Having taken a bath and had a quick drink, he would sit down at the piano and begin playing through [to himself] what he'd written during the day. But being unusually self-critical, Pyotr Ilich almost always ended dissatisfied with his work; then he would tear to pieces the sheets he had written on, and angrily throw them away. The next day he would compose others.

Sometimes Pyotr Ilich would return tired but happy. I learned how to read from his face whether he was satisfied with his work. On such days, after our meal together he would turn to everybody with the words:

'Now, my friends, come into the drawing room and I'll play you my sketches, and you'll tell me what you think of them.' . . .

When the wave of inspiration had passed, Pyotr Ilich would again become affable, and joke with everyone. He would walk for hours on end, and always a long way; but my parents were not walkers and did not go beyond the boundaries of the garden. I, on the contrary, from my childhood loved walking very much. What a joy it was to me when Pyotr Ilich, knowing my taste, would say to my mother after the meal:

'Mariya Sergeyevna, let Dinochka come for a walk with me. Don't worry, we'll be back by tea.'

And so we would set off: me, Pyotr Ilich, my governess, one of my father's pupils, or even all of them (my father took in five peasant children, gave them an education in the town high school, and then set them all up), and the irreplaceable Dog.

Nadezhda Kondratyeva, Recollections (1940); published in *PVC4*, pp. 90–1.

## On the performance of his own works

### NIKOLAY KASHKIN

Tchaikovsky composed his Piano Sonata in G in 1878. Nikolay Rubinstein first played the piece to Tchaikovsky in November 1879. The identity of the eminent foreign pianist is unknown.

Our host [Rubinstein] quickly sat down at the piano and played the sonata magnificently. The composer was thoroughly delighted, and said so in the most enthusiastic terms. By the way, it was during this that one of Pyotr Ilich's peculiarities revealed itself, for he was very rarely completely sure how exactly one should play his compositions, and in this regard relied much more on Nikolay Rubinstein [who had conducted the premières of many of Tchaikovsky's compositions] than on himself. The former drew his attention to the departures from his [Tchaikovsky's] indications which he had permitted himself in several places regarding tempo and nuance. At this the composer exclaimed in the most positive tone:

'Do it your own way, my dear friend; of course that is much better than in my way – for what do I understand in this matter?'

However, Pyotr Ilich felt trust such as this in very few people – perhaps also in Hans von Bülow, whom he placed very highly, especially as a conductor. For the majority of performers he tried in the most careful way to indicate everything: both expression and metronome marks – and he disliked it very much when they departed from these indications without his permission. When the sonata was over, the pianist who had turned up in his turn sat at the piano, though I do not remember anyone asking him to, and played several of his own rather trivial new pieces. After this Tchaikovsky and I left, and we had hardly got on to the street before he suddenly in extreme agitation turned to me with the question: how could I account for the impertinence of sitting down at the piano after such a performance as Rubinstein's? I cannot recall my explanation, but I remember that it was a long time before Pyotr Ilich could recover from his indignation.

Nikolay Kashkin, *KVC*, pp. 127–8.

# ALEXANDRA PANAYEVA

## (1853–1942)

Alexandra Panayeva was a singer who had been a pupil of Pauline Viardot. She is recalling an evening passed in 1879.

At one of the evenings there arose a lively debate concerning the performances of some of his [Tchaikovsky's] romances ('It's both bitter and sweet', 'The fearful minute', 'It was in the early spring'), in which I had not held absolutely exactly to all his directions on the page. I quoted the view of Mme Viardot, who considered that sometimes the performer should be given freedom in interpretation, the more so since often the composers themselves do not give comprehensive pointers to the meaning concealed within their compositions, and not infrequently it is the performers who uncover this. From this it follows that one and the same piece can, depending on the performance, produce a tremendous impression or make no effect. I proposed to test Madame Viardot's thesis by a vote after I had twice performed the above-mentioned romances, leaving it to the listeners to judge which interpretation more truly and faithfully expressed the thoughts of the poet and composer. I had not finished all the romances before Pyotr Ilich capitulated and allowed me to perform his pieces

'freely', and there and then made on the copy pencil markings that corresponded [to my performance].

Alexandra Panayeva, Recollections (1933); published in *PVC4*, p. 127.

# III
## Crisis

By 1876, when Tchaikovsky was 36, a combination of outer and inner pressures brought him to a moment of critical decision. His homosexuality was becoming the subject of increasing public comment, while for himself it was a matter of ever more intolerable inner torment. And so his fate had to be confronted and vanquished; 'I have decided to marry,' he suddenly declared to his brother Modest on 31 August. At that moment he had absolutely no idea who his future wife might be; yet within months, in May 1877, the bridal victim offered herself. There followed a succession of bizarre, chilling events which brought Tchaikovsky to the verge of total mental breakdown – even to a suicide attempt. Though after some years the wounds inflicted by this traumatic episode had healed, the scars remained, and neither the man nor his music could ever be quite the same again.

# NIKOLAY KASHKIN

Tchaikovsky's own letters of the period between June and September 1877 chart the stages of his marital venture with appalling clarity. But some years later Nikolay Kashkin wrote down his own version of the incident, partly from his memories as an outside observer, partly from the composer's own later oral account. Kashkin felt that what he recorded was so personal that it could not be published while any of the principals in the affair were still alive, and so it was excluded from his Memoirs published in 1896; instead he delivered this portion of his manuscript into the care of the Moscow Conservatoire. However, in 1917 Tchaikovsky's widow died in a mental asylum, and in 1920, the year of Kashkin's own death, his account was released.*

Youth passed, the years of maturity approached, and Tchaikovsky began to dream of the ideal of family comfort, for which he needed the presence of a woman – not, however, a servant, but an educated companion capable of understanding his fervent aspirations and of being his trustworthy companion in life, freeing him from, among other things, all domestic cares. The thought of marriage to a middle-aged woman or widow began to enter his head – someone with whom he might have a mutual understanding without pretence to ardent passion. This thought occurred to Pyotr Ilich rather vaguely; all the same, he spoke with me about it more than once. In principle I approved his intention, but counselled the greatest caution and circumspection in the choice of his life's helpmate; I even advised him not to trust in his own choice, but to seek the opinion of Nikolay Rubinstein, in whose ability to weigh up people quickly I had deep faith. I personally considered the fulfilment of Pyotr Ilich's intention, although very difficult, yet possible, the more so since in general he had elicited in a large number of serious middle-aged women a genuine sympathy regarding himself; moreover, he himself was at that time well able to adapt himself to people and circumstances. I am not speaking of the fact that young women had also fallen in love with Pyotr Ilich, for that relates to questions of another

---

*For a fuller account of the circumstances preceding Tchaikovsky's marriage and of the marriage itself, see David Brown, *Tchaikovsky: a Biographical and Critical Study*, ii, pp. 137–58.

kind . . . [But] Pyotr Ilich not only consulted with no one, but, as will be seen, it was precisely from his Conservatoire friends that he tried to conceal his intention as far as possible.

In the spring of 1877 Tchaikovsky was utterly engrossed by the thought of composing the music for [the opera] *Eugene Onegin* . . . I usually moved to a dacha somewhere on the outskirts of Moscow even before the end of the Conservatoire session . . . and would drop in on Moscow only briefly and very rarely, usually for a few hours. On one such visit to Moscow I heard from some stranger (I cannot remember exactly whom) that Tchaikovsky had recently married a former Conservatoire student, and that the wedding had taken place in Moscow . . . The news was so unexpected and strange that at first I simply did not believe it, for not infrequently the most wild rumours would circulate round Moscow . . . However, in this instance I soon had to accept that it was true, and this news induced a kind of chill when Albrecht [a Conservatoire colleague] confirmed it . . . From Albrecht's account I discovered that Tchaikovsky had very carefully concealed his intention, and even Albrecht, who was a close friend, had only been informed after the wedding had taken place; until then he [Tchaikovsky] had kept secret his arrival in Moscow . . . having spent all the time up to the wedding in the country at Konstantin Shilovsky's . . . where he and Shilovsky [a friend] had been devising the libretto of *Eugene Onegin*.

I sensed something sinister in the secrecy with which Pyotr Ilich had surrounded his wedding . . . Meanwhile, however, everything was bound to remain obscure and incomprehensible, since the newly-weds, so Albrecht told me, had left Moscow.

Usually I remained at my dacha as long as possible, and travelled daily to Moscow for the entrance examinations and even for the beginning of the teaching term. When I met with Nikolay Rubinstein and Nikolay Hubert [another colleague at the Conservatoire] we hardly mentioned Tchaikovsky and his wedding at all because everyone was bewildered, felt there was something not good in this event, and feared to talk about it . . . acknowledging, however, that everything depended on who and what Pyotr Ilich's choice, unknown to us, would turn out to be.

It seemed, however, there were some persons who knew this chosen being, for several years earlier she had spent a year as a student at the Moscow Conservatoire. At that time there were fewer than two hundred students, and we knew almost all of them at least by sight and as regards their musical capabilities. But Miss Milyukova, who had now become Mrs Tchaikovskaya, was an exception in this regard, and none of the above-named members of our circle knew or remembered her except Albrecht, who had preserved a faint recollection of someone from whom he, as the Conservatoire's inspector, had taken her papers when she had entered the Conservatoire and given them back when she had left. There remained only the teacher of the piano class in which Miss Milyukova had been enrolled . . . When one of us asked about Miss Milyukova, Langer [the teacher] informed us that in May Tchaikovsky himself had asked about her, and had received in reply an extremely laconic and bluntly negative account of her character, which he [Langer] now repeated because he had nothing to add. We knew that Langer's judgements on his students were conditioned for the most part by the degree of the latters' attentiveness to their studies in general and to his classroom demands in particular, and so from his judgement we could only conclude that Miss Milyukova's work in his piano class had been unsatisfactory.

From Albrecht we learned that Tchaikovsky had taken a new apartment . . . At first Antonina Ivanovna [Tchaikovskaya] appeared in the apartment alone, and busied herself with arranging it, in which, at Tchaikovsky's request, Albrecht helped her; he was the only one of us to have seen her. At that time Tchaikovsky himself was in the Kiev province at his sister's, whither he had gone alone on returning with his wife from St Petersburg, where he had introduced her to his father and brothers.

Tchaikovsky arrived in Moscow markedly late for the beginning of the academic term, and immediately appeared at the Conservatoire. He had an exaggeratedly free-and-easy and cheerful appearance, but this smacked of affectation; Pyotr Ilich was quite incapable of dissembling, and the more he tried, the more apparent became his pretence. Observing his nervous agitation, we all treated him very carefully, asking no questions and waiting for him to introduce us to his wife. But when Tchaikovsky came to the Conservatoire for his classes or for business matters, he always hurried off, pleading the fuss and bustle of arranging his apartment.

We finally met the young couple at the home of Pyotr Jurgenson [Tchaikovsky's chief publisher and another of his closest friends], who had arranged for this purpose a supper evening to which were invited Tchaikovsky's closest friends from the Conservatoire . . . Here for the first time I saw Antonina Ivanovna, who in general made a good impression as much for her appearance as for her modest bearing. I engaged in conversation with her and could not help noticing that all the while Tchai-kovsky himself scarcely left us. Antonina Ivanovna seemed either to be shy or to be having difficulty in finding words, and from time to time, when there were involuntary pauses, Pyotr Ilich chimed in after her or completed what she had been saying. However, our conversation was so trivial that I would not have paid attention to Pyotr Ilich's interventions, had the latter not been over-persistent every time his wife engaged in conversation with anyone. Such solicitude was not quite natural, and, as it were, bore witness to a fear that it would perhaps be difficult for Antonina Ivanovna to carry on a conversation in the proper tone. In general our new acquaintance produced an impression which, though favourable, was rather colourless. On one of the following days, when some of us had gathered in the director's office at the Conservatoire during a break in our commitments, Nikolay Rubinstein, recalling the evening at Jurgenson's and speaking of Antonina Ivanovna, observed: 'You know, she's pretty, and she behaves nicely, but yet she's not particularly winning; it's as though she's not a real person, but some sort of confection.' For all its vagueness such a characterization was nevertheless appropriate, for Antonina Ivanovna really did give the impression of being someone 'not real'.

For the majority of those who were at Jurgenson's that evening this first meeting with Antonina Ivanovna was also the last . . . Day followed day, and Tchaikovsky appeared for his Conservatoire duties with his characteristic undeviating punctiliousness, but left immediately he had finished his classes, visibly avoiding all conversation. The affected jauntiness and cheerfulness of those first days following his arrival had completely gone; his appearance became more agitated and gloomy so that it was difficult to begin a conversation with him – for, knowing him, you could expect a nervous outburst at any moment.

At the end of September he arrived at the Conservatoire at the beginning of a morning session with such a painfully distorted face that even now I can still recall it with total clarity. Without somehow looking at me, he showed me a telegram, and said that he had to go away. In the telegram, over the signature of Nápravník [chief conductor at the Maryinsky Theatre], he was summoned immediately to St Petersburg. He told Nikolay Rubinstein that he was going by the mail train and did not know when he would be able to return.

Two or three days passed and we learned – I do not remember how – that immediately on his arrival in St Petersburg Pyotr Ilich had suffered a very violent nervous attack which had raised the most serious fears for his mental state. A further short time afterwards Anatoly Ilich Tchaikovsky arrived in Moscow, stopping with Nikolay Rubinstein and bearing the most unreassuring news. He told us that Pyotr Ilich's derangement was of a very serious kind, and that the sick man was, on the advice of the then well-known psychiatrist, Balinsky, going abroad with his brother, Modest Ilich . . . He [Balinsky] had immediately recognized that not only was living with his wife impossible, but had declared in the most decisive fashion that a complete and permanent separation between the pair was essential, and even forbade any future meetings between them . . .

The main object of Anatoly Ilich's visit was to inform Antonina Ivanovna of the psychiatrist's instruction, and to arrange matters relating to property and everything else that stemmed from the impending permanent separation of the pair . . . Tchaikovsky was borne off to Italy; we at the Conservatoire received news of his condition which began to give hope of recovery. Nikolay Rubinstein expressed total confidence in a full recovery on the part of the sick man, and the restoration of his powers and faculties. But when he talked to me about it, he added sadly that he considered Tchaikovsky was lost for ever as far as the Conservatoire was concerned.

This difficult period in Tchaikovsky's life passed, and he recovered comparatively quickly . . . Quite a few years passed, probably at least seven or eight (perhaps even ten), and all was forgotten. And Tchaikovsky's own position changed radically. Nikolay Rubinstein was long dead, other figures had come onto the scene. Already Tchaikovsky was enjoying very great popularity, and after several years' absence from Moscow he again returned to it, though not to live in Moscow itself, but near Klin, where he occupied accommodation now in one, now in another rented house, and lived in rural solitude, from time to time inviting over one of his Moscow friends. He rarely left Klin unless for trips abroad, where he already had world-wide celebrity and appeared as conductor of his own works. As for Moscow, he visited it only rarely, staying two or three days, not more.

I rarely visited Tchaikovsky in the country, for my Moscow affairs did not allow frequent absences; but in consequence I sometimes stayed with him for a lengthy period during the summer vacation, or came to spend Holy Week with him – for, like Tchaikovsky, I greatly loved the very beginning of spring . . . On one of my lengthy visits to Tchaikovsky we were for some reason sitting together after a walk. The light was already fading, and though it still was not late, the rooms were beginning to grow dark. The letters and the newspapers had been brought from the post; I had taken the latter while Tchaikovsky looked through the letters. We were both sitting on opposite sides of a round table, each occupied with his own reading. Having hastily looked through the newspapers, I put them down and saw that Tchaikovsky was sitting with his gaze directed to some point alongside him and was deep in serious thought. For quite a while we sat silently. Then Tchaikovsky, as though coming to himself, turned to me and said:

'Read this letter, please,' – and at the same time he handed to me the folded sheets of notepaper which he had been holding in his hand. Having taken the letter, I noticed first of all Antonina Ivanovna's signature, which surprised me greatly, for I had heard from Jurgenson, who had been entrusted with giving Antonina Ivanovna her allotted allowance, that no direct contacts existed between the spouses; in my conversations with Tchaikovsky himself there had been no hint of anything having a connection with his marriage.

The letter turned out to be quite long . . . It was well written and apparently contained some burning questions, for it was peppered with exclamation and question marks. When I had read the letter through and looked at Tchaikovsky, in reply to my silent question he turned to me also with a question:

'Now, tell me, what does this letter say?'

Only then did I grasp that there was absolutely no definite, real content in the letter, even though it was written not only completely grammatically, but even in a good literary style. I had to say that I could not make out the content of what I had read, in reply to which I heard:

'She always writes me such letters.'

We sat for some time in silence. The gloom in the room deepened until I could not see my interlocutor's face properly. Without any preamble Tchaikovsky, in a kind of level, as it were, lowered voice, completely unexpectedly began a tale, and continued it, never changing his tone, as though he was fulfilling something obligatory. In this tale he set out for me in some detail the circumstances of his first meeting with Antonina Ivanovna, and all the subsequent events right up to his separation from her.

I have thought so much of this tale, and checked it against the notes which I made at the time, that I cannot set it out except as though from the person of Tchaikovsky himself, who conjures himself vividly in my imagination at this moment so that I can even, as it were, hear the sound of his voice. My retelling will probably be rather shorter than the tale itself, but in much, even in its greater part, it will be a literal retelling of what I heard. Perhaps I shall leave something out – but in no circumstances shall I add anything.

To begin Tchaikovsky told me how in the spring of 1877 Elizaveta Lavrovskaya [a singer and friend] had given him the idea of writing an opera on *Eugene Onegin* . . .

'Between the middle of April and the middle of May 1877,' said Tchaikovsky, 'I received a longish letter containing a declaration of love. The letter was signed A. Milyukova, who said she had begun to love me several years back when she was a student at the Conservatoire. Although, because I was in the Conservatoire almost every day, I knew most of the students, I had no memory of Miss Milyukova. In the letter she had recalled that she had been in Eduard Langer's piano class – and when I met him at the Conservatoire, I asked him about this former student Milyukova whom, it seems, he remembered and characterized . . . in a single, harshly abusive word, without any amplification. I asked no one else about Miss Milyukova.

At this same time I was totally absorbed with the thought of *Eugene Onegin* – that is, of Tatyana, whose letter [scene] had above all drawn me to this work. Still not having a libretto, nor even any general plan of the opera, I began to write the music for the letter, succumbing to an invincible spiritual need to do this, in the heat of which I not only forgot about Miss Milyukova but even lost her letter – or concealed it so well that I could not find it, and only remembered it when, some time later, I received a second letter.

Being completely immersed in composition, I so thoroughly identified myself with the image of Tatyana that she became for me like a living person, together with everything that surrounded her. I loved Tatyana, and was furiously indignant with Onegin, who seemed to me a cold, heartless fop. Having received a second letter from Miss Milyukova, I was ashamed, and even became indignant with myself for my attitude towards her. In her second letter she complained bitterly that she had received no reply, adding that if her second letter suffered the same fate as her first, then the only thing that would remain to her was to put an end to herself.

In my mind all this tied up with the idea of Tatyana, and it seemed to me that I myself had acted incomparably more basely than Onegin, and I became truly angry with myself for my heartless attitude towards this girl who was in love with me. Because the second letter also contained Miss Milyukova's address, I forthwith set out thither, and thus began our acquaintance.

I found my new acquaintance to be a modest, good-looking girl who in general produced a pleasant impression. At our very first meeting I told her that I could not respond to her feeling of love, but that she inspired in me a true sympathy. She replied that any sympathy on my part was dear to her and she could be satisfied with this – or something like that. I promised that we should see each other often, and I kept my word.

You probably recall that I spoke with you more than once of my intention of marrying a person who was not young but who possessed known characteristics which would enable her to be a good friend and companion in life. Antonina Ivanovna did not correspond in that she was comparatively young, but she expressed such devotion to me, such a readiness to do everything that would be pleasing to me, that somehow there lay upon me the obligation to respond with something similar, for all my lack of feeling towards her. In addition, there was constantly in my heart a genuine indignation at the offhand, thoughtless attitude of Onegin towards Tatyana. It seemed to me that to act like Onegin would be heartless and simply intolerable on my part.

It was as though I was delirious. Focusing all the time on the thought of the opera, I related to everything else unconsciously or half-consciously. However, I remember well my firm conviction that I must tell none of you, my Conservatoire colleagues, anything about my relations with Antonina Ivanovna and of the intentions that had grown from these relations. I was convinced that if you got to know of this, then everything must end, and I should not be able to act as I wished. I emphatically did not know what this conviction was based on, but all the same it was there.

All these vague vacillations were not such as to greatly alarm or agitate me, but they hindered composition, and I decided it would be better to settle this question in order to be rid of it. Having made this resolve, I set out one evening after my day's work to Antonina Ivanovna, and told her again that I felt no love for her and most likely never would feel any – but if, despite this, she still wanted to marry me, then I was prepared to marry. On her part she expressed complete agreement with this – and the wedding was decided upon; all she said was that she needed to make some preparations, to set her papers in order and generally arrange her affairs, to do which she would even have to leave Moscow for a while; on her return the wedding should follow swiftly. I did not forget to tell Antonina Ivanovna that our decision had to remain a very close secret – otherwise the wedding could not happen; by this I meant most of all keeping the secret from my Conservatoire friends who by some means or other – though I did not know how – could obstruct me from carrying out my intention of marrying Antonina Ivanovna.

Having taken such a decision, I simply did not recognize its importance, and was even unaware of its meaning and significance; it was essential for me, even if only for the near future, to remove everything that hindered me from concentrating on the idea that had taken possession of my whole being – the opera – and it seemed to me most natural and simple to do just this. And so, having entrusted to Antonina Ivanovna all the worries about, and preparations for, the wedding, I felt as though I had cast off some burden and immediately went off to the country to Shilovsky, who was already working on the libretto of *Eugene Onegin*, and I spent nearly a whole month there, working all the time and feeling completely content and happy, for there was no one to hinder me, and Shilovsky worked on the libretto with such enthusiasm that his good spirits even infected me.

Glebovo, Shilovsky's estate near Novïy Ierusalem, is a wonderful place, with amazingly beautiful surroundings, and walks which afforded great pleasure. The house and the whole way of life at Glebovo was furnished with every comfort you could fancy, but the most precious thing was that I had been granted as much solitude as I desired, and I had the company of my hosts only when I wanted it. I hardly remembered the new way of life that faced me, and only somewhere deep and distant inside me there stirred an uneasy expectation of something I did not wish to contemplate, considering it quite unnecessary – above all, disturbing and distracting.

The Fast of St Peter (28 June) passed, and I heard from Antonina Ivanovna that she had completed the preparations, and that we could get married.

Although it was extremely unpleasant for me to leave Glebovo, where I had lived and worked so well, the possibility of postponing the wedding for a longer or shorter time did not enter my head; I still lingered some time, wishing somehow to finish work. Of course I did not tell Shilovsky what faced me, and I think I justified my departure by the necessity of visiting my father in St Petersburg.

Arriving in Moscow, I made haste to have done with the matter that was weighing upon me and, among other things, wrote to my father about my intention of marrying, being fully confident that he would be very pleased with my intention. The wedding was only a few days off, and I invited only my brother Anatoly, who quickly appeared in Moscow.

I seemed all the while in a daze. I visited Dmitri Vasilyevich Razumovsky [a priest who was also professor of the history of church music at the Conservatoire] and asked him to marry me in his church. With his characteristic, infinite kindness, he somehow had a good effect on me, cheered me, freed me from certain formalities, and administered the sacrament of marriage with that tasteful refinement characteristic of him, which I could not fail to notice, despite the solemnity of the moment. But all the same I remained a sort of bystander until the moment when Dmitri Vasilyevich, at the conclusion of the ceremony, made Antonina and me kiss. Then a kind of pain gripped my heart, and I was suddenly seized with such emotion that, it seems, I wept. But I tried quickly to gain control of myself and to assume an appearance of calm. However, Anatoly noticed my condition, for he began saying something reassuring to me.

That evening we set off for St Petersburg, where I think we spent a whole week visiting relatives and several friends. Already during these days the terrible import of my action and the hopelessness of the situation in which I found myself became clear to me.

I sincerely wished and I tried to be a good husband, but this proved beyond my powers. From the very first days of our life together I realized with horror that we had no interests in common, and that everything through which and for which I lived was absolutely foreign to Antonina Ivanovna, although she, it seems, tried to understand me and to be nice to me. The way she had developed in general was something peculiar, and I had never even presupposed the possibility of anything like it. She had heard and knew much, but was totally devoid of the ability to find within herself any response to anything except the most commonplace demands of life. And it was not only that she had no wish to understand all this: most horrifying of all was that she could master absolutely nothing except the most basic conditions for existence. I cannot describe to you my state when I recognized that I must pass all the rest of my life with this being who was completely alien to me. My budding sympathy towards her turned into aversion, and, sensing my situation was unendurable, I shamefully fled under the pretext of having to go to the Caucasus to take the waters. I said that on the way I would visit my sister in the Kiev province, and departed alone, leaving Antonina Ivanovna to arrange our apartment.

I did not go to the Caucasus but spent about a month at my sister's, where I again felt myself capable even of work. At Kamenka at my sister's I again breathed freely and tried to muster strength for the battle with myself. But unfortunately the respite was over too quickly, and I had to go to Moscow for my duties at the Conservatoire.

Arriving in Moscow I found my new apartment almost ready. Antonina Ivanovna had added somewhat to the furnishings out of her own money; in all this it emerged she had been helped by Albrecht, who had already managed to meet my wife. Everything in the flat was comfortable and even nice, but the very comfort only made more sharply obvious the impossibility, which was becoming evident to me, of an existence in the given conditions. Antonina Ivanovna, with her even, calm attitude to everything around her, seemed to me even more limited than before, and her very presence weighed terribly upon me. I fully recognized that I alone was the guilty one in all this, that nothing in the world could help me, and therefore it only remained to endure while I had the strength, and conceal my unhappiness from everyone. I do not know what precisely prompted this latter requirement of concealment; was it just my pride, or fear of distressing my relatives and casting over them the shadow of, as it seemed to me, my crime?

In such a state it was completely natural to arrive at the conviction that death alone, which was becoming for me a longed-for dream, could free me, but I could not bring myself to explicit, open suicide for fear of inflicting a too cruel blow upon my aged father, and also upon my brothers. I began thinking of means of disappearing less obtrusively and, as it were, from a natural cause; one such means I even attempted.

Although not more than a week had passed since my return from my sister's, I had already lost all ability to cope with the burden of my situation, and from time to time, so it seemed to me myself, my consciousness became clouded. During the day I still tried to work at home, but in the evenings it became intolerable. Not daring to go off to a friend or even to the theatre, I set off each evening for a walk, and for several hours would wander aimlessly through the distant, out-of-the-way streets of Moscow.

The weather had become gloomy, cold, and at night there was a slight frost. On one such night I came to the deserted bank of the River Moscow, and there entered my head the thought that it would be possible to kill myself by contracting a chill. To this end, unseen in the darkness, I entered the water almost up to my waist and stayed there until I could endure no longer the bodily ache produced by the cold. I came out of the water with a firm conviction that either from pneumonia or from some respiratory illness I should die. At home I told how I had taken part in a nocturnal fishing expedition, and had fallen into the water by accident. However, my health showed itself to be so sound that the icy bath had no consequences for me.

I did not [have time to] hazard any other attempt with this same end in mind, for I felt that I could not exist [a moment longer] in the given circumstances, and I wrote to my brother Anatoly so that he would telegraph me, over Nápravník's name, that I had to come to St Petersburg – which Anatoly did without delay.

As regards my arrival in St Petersburg I remember very little, and that only by chance; I remember the painful nervous attacks, I remember Balinsky, my father, brothers – and that is all.

Modest and I first travelled to Italy, as you know, probably on the doctor's instruction, but this was a very bad choice, for the light and the brilliance of the Italian sun and the luxurance of nature in an Italian spring were too incompatible with my mood at that time, and increased my depression. Remembering stories about this, I even once tried to drive away my melancholy with wine, but because Modest would not let me drink much wine openly, like a thief I secretly carried two bottles of cognac to my room, and hid them. When that evening we went off to our separate beds, I locked my room and began to drink the cognac in great mouthfuls from a glass. You know that in normal circumstances I probably won't drink more than a glass without falling down drunk and insensible – but on this occasion I drank both bottles and did not feel drunk because the melancholy that was weighing upon me grew to such a degree that I don't believe I have ever, either before or since, endured such a frightful feeling as that in which I passed the rest of that night until morning; of course I never again thought to escape from melancholy through drunkenness.

Finally I began insistently asking my brother to transfer to some other place further north, and we set off for Vienna, where I felt much calmer and better. I think it was in Vienna I received your letter, and you cannot imagine how beneficially it acted upon me: so there are people who do not despise me but sympathize with me! Let us assume that at that time I had already become somewhat better and calmer – yet a lively, cheering word was dear to me.

My material circumstances at that time, as you know, had already changed, thanks to Nadezhda von Meck [a wealthy widow who settled an annual allowance upon him], but I felt morally bound to the Moscow Conservatoire, and I proposed that the next year I should return to Moscow and my Conservatoire duties, and thus live out the rest of my days. You know that it worked out differently, for when I tried to resume my duties at the Conservatoire in reality, memories that I could not bear surged up in me, and I then left the Conservatoire and Moscow, as I thought, for ever. However, as regards Moscow that feeling quickly disappeared. It disappeared also in regard of the Conservatoire, and some time afterwards I could easily have taken up duties in it – but, firstly, this would have interfered with my composing and, secondly, [Sergey] Taneyev, who had replaced me, was an incomparably better teacher than I, which I very well recognized. My attachment to Moscow even proved so firm that living close to it was more pleasant for me than anywhere else. In addition I so loved the surroundings of Moscow that among the countries that I had seen there are no places more attractive.'

Just as Tchaikovsky had begun his tale, so he took it to its end in the same even voice, hardly changing its intonation – but at the same time you could hear that he was very strongly agitated, and that this evenness of tone was the result of a great effort to control himself and not give way to his nerves. And I myself, in the role of listener, was so moved that I simply could not remember even approximately how long the tale had lasted. Probably quite a while, for it had grown completely dark, and by the end we could hardly see each other. After the tale was ended we began supper, and passed the evening as usual in reading or playing piano duets – but there was no exchange of thoughts upon the tale either that evening or at any time afterwards. I simply could not have talked about it, for I saw that such memories cost Tchaikovsky dear, and he also never again even hinted at this subject. Perhaps Tchaikovsky had felt the need to tell it to someone close to him, and receiving the letter in my presence provided the jolt for this – and I am probably the only person to whom Tchaikovsky spoke of this sad episode in his life.

Nikolay Kashkin, 'Iz vospominany o P.I. Chaykovskom' ['From recollections of Tchaikovsky']; published in *PRM*, pp. 105–28.

# IV

## First impressions – and more

### I

#### 1879–90

# ALEXANDRA PANAYEVA

Although by 1879 Alexandra Panayeva had long been performing Tchaikovsky's music in concerts, all her endeavours to meet the composer had been thwarted by, it seems, Tchaikovsky himself. In 1879 she travelled from St Petersburg to Moscow for the première of *Eugene Onegin* on 29 March, and saw the composer for the first time when he appeared on stage after the second scene to acknowledge the applause. She had been sitting with Anton Rubinstein in his box in the Maly Theatre. The acquaintance initiated here began while Tchaikovsky was still suffering severe after-effects from the trauma of his marriage, and his difficulties in mixing with people were at their most extreme.

I grappled with my opera glasses and saw a man who was not tall, with greying beard and rather dishevelled hair, confused, red in the face, not elegant, not at all like the person I had imagined.

'So that's him,' I said under my breath, somewhat disenchanted.

'What, you've never seen him before?' Rubinstein said in surprise.

'No, never.'

'And you're not acquainted with him? But you're such an admirer and propagandist for him!' said Rubinstein teasingly.

I then told Anton Grigoryevich about my vain efforts to meet my favourite composer, and his evident unwillingness to yield to my attempts.

'Wait; I'll see to it,' declared Anton Grigoryevich, smiling slyly, and leaving the box.

My father had left earlier and I remained alone. Suddenly the door of the box opened, and I saw Tchaikovsky and, behind him, Rubinstein laughing. On seeing me Tchaikovsky would have retreated, but Rubinstein pushed him from behind and he, stumbling over the threshold, fell into the box. Rubinstein burst out laughing and kept repeating:

'That's where you should be, at her feet, begging forgiveness!'

Pyotr Ilich got up, redder than ever, and sat on the edge of a chair. In the face of all my attempts to begin a conversation with him he remained obstinately silent, his suffering face glancing back at the exit until finally, bidding farewell to Rubinstein, he flew headlong out of the box. It turned out that Rubinstein had lured him to the box by deceit, assuring him that no one was in it, and like a child he was [now] rejoicing in his joke . . .

I think a week had not passed since our trip to Moscow when Anatoly Ilich [Tchaikovsky] arrived with the great news that Pyotr Ilich wanted to drop in on us. If we agreed he asked to be allowed to come to dinner the following day with his two brothers (at that time we were still not acquainted with Modest Ilich) . . . There was a further request: that at dinner Tchaikovsky should be seated between his brothers so that as far as possible I should not converse with him, and should pay as little attention to him as possible. This was quite a difficult assignment – but 'I agree to everything, everything – as long as you'll bring him to us' was, of course, my response.

The whole company arrived, and strained conversation was kept up in the drawing room until dinner. Pyotr Ilich sat, totally confused and with eyes lowered, between his brothers, who did not take their eyes off him. At dinner it was exactly the same . . . After dinner everyone went into the reception room and, having conversed in a whisper about something with Pyotr Ilich, Anatoly Ilich asked me to sing. Pyotr Ilich sat at the piano, I went to the instrument, but the brothers asked me to stand a little further off, while they themselves sat like guards on either side of the composer.

The latter quietly turned to his brother:

'Anatoly, ask her to sing some Mozart.'

In his turn Anatoly Ilich turned to me:

'Pyotr Ilich is asking for some Mozart.'

I sang an aria from *The Marriage of Figaro* and Pamina's aria from *The Magic Flute*. Pyotr Ilich was silent for a moment, sighed, somehow helplessly dropped his hands onto his knees, and barely audibly said:

'How nice!'

– then:

'Modest, ask her for something else.'

Both twins turned to me with beaming faces:

'He liked it, and he asks you to sing something more.'

I then sang an aria from *Don Giovanni* and, at his request, an aria from *Sonnambula*, which he said he had loved in his early youth, and also several of his romances.

By degrees he became livelier, but he communicated his impressions only to his brothers, and then they bore him away . . .

I was satisfied that at last I had managed to see my beloved Pyotr Ilich, but I was also sad because I had decided that probably with this our acquaintance would also cease.

The next day it was reported to me that 'Mr Tchaikovsky wishes to see the young lady'. Fully convinced that this was Anatoly or Modest Ilich, I entered the drawing room with indifference. What then was my surprise when I saw before me Pyotr Ilich himself 'solo soletto'. He approached to take my hand in a free-and-easy manner, and we had a lively conversation. He began by thanking me for having spent such a pleasant evening the previous day. I saw before me a totally different person — cheerful, lively, a thorough man of fashion, even elegant. Having conquered his shyness, he proved to be charming, corresponding completely to that image I had created for myself in my youthful imagination.

> After this Paneyeva came still closer to Tchaikovsky, especially after her marriage to his second cousin, Georgy Kartsov. Tchaikovsky's sensitivity revealed itself increasingly to her.

For instance, once he for some reason invited me to dine with him and, on my agreeing, suddenly became alarmed, and began reproaching himself for inviting me: perhaps it was not convenient for me, perhaps I had no wish to come to him . . . He became so wound up that I said:

'All right, I won't come!'

This upset him even more, and it ended in my having to take the decision upon myself, and I declared firmly:

'I'm definitely coming, and that's an end of the matter!'

> On 6 April 1880 Panayeva sang in an all-Tchaikovsky concert in St Petersburg. Rumours circulated that the composer, who had only that day returned to the capital, was present. In the audience was the wife of the future Alexander III, who, when she was told, pointedly directed her gaze towards where Tchaikovsky was sitting, forcing him to reveal himself and acknowledge the ovations.

Finally he appeared on the platform in the same dishevelled condition in which I had first seen him. He grabbed me by the hand and urgently exchanged bows with me, blushed to the roots of his hair, visibly suffering from all this noise. I turned him to face the audience, the [future] empress smiled graciously, pointedly extending her applauding hands towards the composer. In the artists' room he almost wept that he had had to appear before the public in a shabby travelling suit, and inveighed against the indiscreet individual who had betrayed his presence.

After each item there was no end to the summonses and ovations, and when, after the concert, he was surrounded in the hall by a crowd of friends and unknown admirers, he had already quite lost his head. Mariya Nikolayevna Vasilchikova (the sister of the concert promoter), who had not met the composer before, invited him to supper; he declined, addressing her in reply as 'tï', evidently taking her for someone else.

'I'll come to you another time. Today I have to go to someone called Vasilchikova. It's so unpleasant.'

Then, discovering his blunder, he was so embarrassed that, to our general distress, he did not come to supper. However, Mariya Nikolay-evna did not lose hope of seeing him at her home, and asked me to arrange an occasion for her and to bring Pyotr Ilich to an intimate dinner. When I made the appointment with him he asked me to be there earlier, before his arrival, and to sit alongside him at the meal:

'I don't know any of them and quite certainly will lose my head.'

I did as he had asked, and arrived in good time. Dinner was scheduled for seven o'clock, but neither at seven nor at half-past had Tchaikovsky appeared. They waited until a quarter to eight and, distressed by his absence, decided to begin the meal, with slight grumbles at me as though I were responsible for everyone's disappointment. We had only just left the side table when Pyotr Ilich entered the room hurriedly, confused, red, sweating, with his tie awry, his shoes dusty . . . He muttered some excuses, and then guiltily glanced at me.

'Why were you late?' I asked when we had all sat down in our places.

'I decided not to enter. I was first here at half-past six; when I asked whether you were here they told me you weren't yet. I went off to walk along the embankment. When I came back you were already here, and such terror descended upon me that I again went off for a walk. I walked along the embankment twice more and finally took myself in hand and came . . . Forgive me; don't be angry,' he concluded with such a sweet, guilty look and tone that not only was it impossible to be angry with him but, on the contrary, you wanted to hug and comfort him.

At dinner he said little – that is, he only replied to questions, and I was forced all the time to bolster him up under my breath. After dinner everyone went into the drawing room for coffee, and our hostess whispered to me that she had to go off for half an hour to feed her three-month-old baby, entrusting me in the meantime with occupying our precious guest. Such was not to be! Our hostess had only just disappeared through the door when Pyotr Ilich began begging me to agree that he might use her absence to go home, saying that he could not bear to remain any longer with people he didn't know. However hard I tried to persuade him to suffer a little longer, there was nothing for it, and seeing his genuine distress, I had willy-nilly to let him go. You can imagine our hosts' distress. However, the next day Pyotr Ilich came to us bright and cheerful, with a request to arrange for him an evening at the Vasilchikovs' — 'at those nice people's whom I greatly liked'. Of course they received him with open arms, and after Pyotr Ilich's short visit, we all contrived to pass two very pleasant evenings with him [at the Vasilchikovs'].

Alexandra Panayeva, Recollections (1933); published in *PVC4*, pp. 123–7.

# ALEXANDER GLAZUNOV
## (1865–1936)

Alexander Glazunov's friendship with Tchaikovsky began in the autumn of 1884, at one of Balakirev's soirées. Tchaikovsky first met Balakirev in 1868, and the following year had composed the first version of his fantasy overture *Romeo and Juliet* on a ground plan supplied by him. But by 1872 a personal crisis had caused Balakirev to withdraw completely from Russia's musical life for a number of years, and it was only in 1884 that Tchaikovsky, whose position as Russia's best loved and most respected composer was now firmly established, renewed his face-to-face contact with the old autocrat. Since Tchaikovsky was not considered musically 'of Balakirev's party', his arrival at Balakirev's soirée was awaited with some unease.

Tchaikovsky's appearance immediately put an end to the somewhat strained mood of those present, especially the younger ones. With his combination of simplicity and dignity, and the refined, purely European restraint in his manner of address, Tchaikovsky produced on the majority of those present the most favourable impression. We somehow breathed freely. In his conversation Pyotr Ilich brought a breath of freshness into

our somewhat dusty atmosphere, and talked without constraint about subjects on which we kept quiet, partly out of a feeling of admiration
(combined with a certain fear) for the authority of Balakirev and other
members of the circle. Balakirev, for all the hospitality that was characteristic of him, liked, as they say, to provoke those who were present, sometimes rather caustically and mockingly. On this memorable evening
Balakirev, turning to Tchaikovsky, permitted himself to describe rather
harshly one of the Moscow musicians and his wife who had friendly
relations with Tchaikovsky. The latter straightway extricated himself from
an awkward situation, and in a joking, even somewhat unceremonious
way, repulsed Balakirev, asking him whether he knew these friends.
When Balakirev replied evasively that everyone was talking about them,
Tchaikovsky added that you should not believe rumours. Balakirev was
confused, his eyes shifted nervously, he recognized his tactlessness, and
did not repeat his attacks. The evening passed in a very lively way . . .
Tchaikovsky left before the others, and with his departure we again felt
ourselves in our former, somewhat humdrum situation. Many of the
younger musicians, among them Anatol Lyadov and I, left Balakirev's
enchanted by Tchaikovsky's personality, and went off to sit in an inn to
share our new impressions.

Alexander Glazunov, Recollections; published in *CVP*, reprinted in *PVC4*,
pp. 208–9.

# VLADIMIR POGOZHEV

## (1851–1935)

Vladimir Pogozhev, a former army officer, was in charge of the
secretariat of the Imperial Theatres in St Petersburg from 1882.
His earliest clear memories of Tchaikovsky were of meeting him
in 1884 in the office of Ivan Vsevolozhsky, director of the
Imperial Theatres.

Pyotr Ilich's grey hair and the appearance of his pleasant face, with its
extremely kind, gentle eyes, seemed to me quite unlike the familiar portrait of him in his youth. The first thing on which my attention rested was
Pyotr Ilich's extreme elegance and courtesy, his gentleness of manner and

of speech, the simplicity and, at the same time, refinement of his appearance and apparel . . . From this same meeting with Pyotr Ilich at Vsevolozhsky's I recall another of Tchaikovsky's peculiarities: his frequent
employment, when praising something, of the words 'enchantingly', 'ravishingly', 'charmingly' . . .

   Pyotr Ilich was rarely as talkative as during evenings at the home of
[Emiliya] Pavlovskaya [a singer especially admired by Tchaikovsky, and
a close friend]. His speech was extremely gentle, quite fluent and well-
rounded; from time to time he enunciated passionately pronounced, laconic
terms: 'ravishingly', 'abominably', 'charmingly'. Many of his stories were
not without humour, and some not without venom. When telling a story or
talking about something he found unpleasant, his speech became jaundiced
and dry, and even his face changed — it became malicious. The subjects
that chiefly got Tchaikovsky worked up were the unfairness and bias of
music critics, and also his assessments of musical works he did not
like . . . In his judgements of artists [singers?], of the theatre adminis-
tration, of conductors and musical performers, and also of composers,
Tchaikovsky was very circumspect and even, I would say, evasive and less
sincere than he might have been, and in giving praise he not infrequently
exaggerated.

> Pogozhev speaks of Tchaikovsky's especial hatred of César Cui as
> a critic, and of what he suspected as Tchaikovsky's glee at a
> savagely satirical cartoon of Cui.

Somehow this rancorous trait in Tchaikovsky did not fit with the established image of him as unusually good-natured and soft-hearted. But in
this regard one should observe that Tchaikovsky's ill-will did not carry the
slightest trace of envy in it. As far as I observed it, it always applied to
persons who were significantly lower than Pyotr Ilich on the ladder of
artistic reputation.

   On the other hand there were, during conversations with Tchaikovsky,
subjects where a certain special warmth and even, one might say, his
sentimentality manifested itself. Such subjects were children, whom Pyotr
Ilich regarded with special tenderness, and human (and especially female)
selflessness. An account of some disastrous material predicament would
make a swift, strong, and painful impression upon him; his eyes would
moisten, on his lips would appear a piteous, even mournful smile, his face

would express suffering, and his hand would involuntarily go to his pocket to release from its confinement a banknote which he had (or frequently, perhaps, did not have) . . . This circumstance made many people careful in what they disclosed to such a person, who suffered from atrophy in his powers of self-restraint when it came to his instinct to philanthropy.

> To Pogozhev's surprise, Tchaikovsky readily accepted an invitation to his home.

My friendly relations with Pyotr Ilich lasted more than five years, but it was remarkable that, though Tchaikovsky visited me many times of an evening, I was never once at, nor ever invited to, his home. My first visit to his [in fact, Modest's] apartment on the Malaya Morskaya was not until 7 November 1893, when the unforgettable master of that apartment lay beneath icons on a table surrounded with flowers.

> Three or four times a season Pogozhev would arrange gatherings attended especially by people from the theatre, and by military and medical men – and two good raconteurs. Leonid Yakovlev was a baritone from the Imperial Theatres, Ivan Gorbunov and Pavel Weinberg actors at the Alexandrinsky Theatre.

Among my guests there were always significantly more men than women. We did not usually assemble before ten o'clock; many came from the theatre after the performance. The ingredients of these occasions were most ordinary: conversations mostly in groups, a couple of tables for those playing vint [a card game], a little music, the singing of Leonid Yakovlev – after supper (especially after dessert and coffee) general conversation, sometimes amusing tales and an improvisation of 'General Dityatin' by Ivan Gorbunov, or little scenes by Pavel Weinberg.

Tchaikovsky loved to play a little vint. He played without special skill, but very intensely, animatedly; he avoided disputes, and was genuinely distressed by his mistakes. He was not shy in female company, and he very willingly conversed with ladies.

Vladimir Pogozhev, Recollections; published in *CVP*, reprinted in *PVC4*, pp. 151–2, 163–6.

# HANS VON BÜLOW
## (1830–94)

The German pianist-conductor, Hans von Bülow, was one of
Tchaikovsky's earliest foreign admirers, and in 1875 gave the
première of the First Piano Concerto in Boston, USA. In the
composer's opinion, von Bülow was one of the finest interpreters
of his works, especially as a conductor.

Tchaikovsky was here for a day . . . [The composer] is in my opinion one
of the most truly likeable men I have ever met, and moreover so tolerant
and so full of praise for his colleagues: in short, a gem. Born in 1840, his
hair is already almost white, but he is full of youthful spirit. When he
composes he buries himself in absolute isolation, but when his work is
finished he delights with his cordiality all those companions he finds sympathetic.

Hans von Bülow, letter to Richard Strauss: 30 March 1886; printed in Marie von
Bülow, ed., *Hans von Bülow, Briefe*, vii: *Höhepunkt und Ende, 1886–94* (Leipzig,
1908), p. 33.

# VASILY YASTREBTSEV
## (1866–1934)

Vasily Yastrebtsev was a writer on music, a close friend of
Rimsky-Korsakov, and the author of important reminiscences of
him. Yastrebtsev first saw Tchaikovsky conducting at a concert in
March 1887 (after the concert he slipped onto the platform and
stole Tchaikovsky's baton as a memento of the event). In the
interval of the Borodin memorial concert in St Petersburg on 15
November he asked Tchaikovsky for his autograph, and was told
to call the following morning.

While awaiting Tchaikovsky I went into his study. It was a large, high,
luxuriously furnished room, fully carpeted; at its centre stood a large old
writing desk adorned with portraits and a bronze, and laden with every
kind of writing accessory. The walls were lined with furniture upholstered

with dark green material, and with several bookshelves, some with scores, others empty. To the left of the entrance was situated an elegant upright piano on which lay the orchestral score of [Tchaikovsky's opera] *The Enchantress*. The walls were decorated with pictures in gilded frames; in addition, above one of the bookshelves hung a plaster mask crowned with a laurel wreath.

Pyotr Ilich entered. I greeted him and was about to introduce myself for a second time, but he had remembered flawlessly not only my surname but even my first name and patronymic.

'You see,' I began, a little embarrassed, 'I wanted to ask you to sign your portrait, but unfortunately . . . I simply could not obtain one, because it was too late yesterday after the concert, and this morning when I was coming to you the shops were still closed.'

'That being the case,' said Tchaikovsky, 'perhaps you would like to have my musical autograph?'

I thanked him. Pyotr Ilich took a sheet of letter paper and began writing. While he wrote I talked about yesterday's concert . . .

During this conversation Tchaikovsky suddenly turned to me and said:

'As it happens, I had forgotten I have some pictures to hand. If you like I can give you one of these as a memento.'

Of course I was extremely touched by his kindness. While he went for the photograph I went to the table (on which lay among other things a wonderful boudoir portrait of the French actress, Angel) and began looking over his autograph. It seems Pyotr Ilich had written several bars from his new opera, specifically from the aria of the Enchantress herself. However, Tchaikovsky quickly returned, bearing my photograph already signed. Going on to talk of all sorts of current musical matters and also of Berlioz, of his memoirs, and of his incomparable instrumentation, Pyotr Ilich proffered, among other things, the following interesting thought:

'Both he and I,' he said, 'have extremely complex textures, but with this difference — that Berlioz's works, which present as a whole enormous difficulties in learning, are quite easily and gratefully written for each instrument; but my music is complex and not all that grateful to perform, not only for the whole orchestra but for each separate player, demanding of him veritable virtuosity . . . Writing technically difficult parts for the instrumentalists is my fundamental weakness from which, for all my efforts, I cannot free myself. It is,' Tchaikovsky ended, 'unquestionably the major shortcoming of my style.'

It was time to go. I got up, warmly thanked Pyotr Ilich for his cour-
teous reception, and went out into the entrance hall, with him following.
These were his parting words:

'If in two or three years time you write something larger' (I had brought
with me for him to look over and assess several of my romances) ' – a
quartet or an overture – bring it to show me when I am here again; I'll
always with pleasure help and advise you. And so I hope we'll meet again
on a musical matter.'

You can imagine how happy I was that morning!

Vasily Yastrebtsev, Recollections; published in *RMG* (1899), no. 10, reprinted in
*PVC4*, pp. 212–13.


# EDVARD GRIEG
## (1843–1907)

Grieg met Tchaikovsky in Leipzig in January 1888. Tchaikovsky
was much taken by the Norwegian composer and his wife, and
immediately resolved that the former should be the dedicatee of
his next symphony, though in the end he was to receive the
inscription of the fantasy overture *Hamlet* instead.

In the evenings I am going through an English work, *Tchaikovsky's Life
and Letters*.* It reaches into my innermost soul; it is often as if I were
looking into my own, there is so much of myself that I recognise. He is
melancholic almost to the point of madness. He is a beautiful and good
person, but an unhappy person. I did not think the latter when I met him
in his time, but so it is: either one has others or oneself to fight.

Edvard Grieg, letter to Frants Beyer: 6 January 1906; quoted in Bjarne Kortsen,
*Grieg the Writer*, i: *Essays and Articles* (Bergen, 1972), p. 122.


*Tchaikovsky (M.), *The Life and Letters of Peter Ilich Tchaikovsky*, ed. from the
Russian . . . by Rosa Newmarch (London, 1906).

# FRANTIŠEK ŠUBERT

## (1849–1915)

František Šubert was a Czech dramatist, and from 1883 to 1900 chief administrator of the National Theatre in Prague. He was one of those responsible for Tchaikovsky's first visit to Prague in 1888.

Right from the first meeting – I would even say, from the first glance – Tchaikovsky enchanted us all. His sincerity, transmuted at times into warmth, opened to him the heart of everyone who was able to exchange with him but a few words. At the same time one recognized not only a wholehearted musician, but also an educated and refined man. It has long been known that those who live the intensive life of a musician have a nervous system that is much more sensitive and excitable; this was soon apparent in our guest. The smallest trifle, whether pleasant or less welcome, made a deeper impression on his soul than it would have on another's.

František Subert, *Moje vzpominky* (Prague, 1902), pp. 107–8.

# HUGES IMBERT

## (1842–1905)

Huges Imbert was a French writer and music critic who worked in Paris from 1886. Almost certainly he is remembering Tchaikovsky from the latter's visit early in 1888 to conduct in the French capital.

A head full of intelligence and charm, a well developed forehead which his close-cut, silvery hair leaves very clearly revealed, his eyebrows finely outlining the rather deep arches from where his wide-open blue eyes, full of frankness and kindness, stand out, a well-formed nose, a mouth with sensual lips which his moustache, with its pointed ends, leaves visible, a chin and lower part of a face completely covered by a white, fan-shaped beard: such is the sketch conjured by my memory of Pierre Tchaikovsky.

H. Imbert, *Profils de musiciens* (Paris, 1888).

# ANONYMOUS

Modest Tchaikovsky remarked that the observation on his size greatly irritated his brother, who was in fact of rather above average height. M. de Freycinet was presumably Charles de Saulces de Freycinet, the distinguished engineer.

He is a small man, with a distinguished and diffident bearing which vaguely recalls that of M. de Freycinet. Along with this [there is] in his eyes a flame of melancholy which is reflected in all his compositions.

Newspaper: *Le Gaulois*, Paris, 1 March 1888; quoted in *TZC3*, pp. 231–2.

# 'TOUT PARIS'

The identity of 'Tout Paris' is unknown.

The composer is a charming conversationalist who grows animated as soon as the word Paris passes his lips . . .

The Russian maestro is excessively modest; he avoids speaking about the enthusiastic eulogies emulously bestowed on him by Austrian and German critics, and prefers to express his admiration for Lalo and Saint-Saëns, for Debussy and Bizet.

You should hear him tell how, at a festival (in Weimar, I believe), a symphonic poem by a famous German composer almost made him go to sleep, and how he was saved from doing so by the performance of a delicious morsel by Saint-Saëns! . . .

This Slav, who so readily appreciates our musicians and writers, talks about everything with as much erudition as charm.

His motto should be: *Art and Homeland*. In Prague the demonstrations [of feeling] by the Czechs touched him to his very heart because they were directed equally at the great artist and the Slav.

Anonymous, from 'Bloc-notes parisien' in newspaper: *Le Gaulois*, Paris, 28 February 1888.

# EMIL SAUER
## (1862–1942)

Emil Sauer was a German pianist who had studied with Nikolay
Rubinstein at the Moscow Conservatoire from 1879 to 1881.

[Tchaikovsky] came to Dresden in February 1889 in order to conduct his
F minor Symphony [no. 4] and his [First] Piano Concerto, which I
played . . . Of course I assumed that our Russian colony would take
complete possession of the maestro, and so was very surprised when, at our
greeting in Weber's Hotel, I found him completely alone. The extraordinary circumstance that, inexplicably, nobody seemed to notice his
presence except during the evening of the concert, where he was celebrated
beyond all belief, afforded my wife and me the pleasure of three unforgettable days during which he was most satisfied with that which our house
had to offer. After the concert I had arranged in his honour a small
banquet which passed in animated fashion, and which he was kind enough
to recall later. We had met as good, old acquaintances; now we parted as
dear friends. Tchaikovsky was a man of great charm: a gentleman in the
best sense of the word, a human being full of tact and perfect manners –
moreover, unpretentious and modest: severe towards himself, but lenient
towards others. When his music was discussed he steered the conversation
towards other great names, preferably towards Mozart, whom he adored.
In doing this he tried to indicate how unimportant his merits were compared with those of the godlike figure of Mozart. Often he explained to me
in all seriousness that his First Piano Concerto, and in particular the last
movement, was full of shortcomings, and that he had thoughts of revising
it; moreover, that his Piano Sonata, [and] especially the Concert Fantasia
[for piano and orchestra], was an imposition upon the pianist.

Emil Sauer, *Meine Welt* (Stuttgart, 1901), pp. 206–7.

# MARIYA ANDERSON

## (1870–1944)

Mariya Anderson was a ballerina in the Imperial Theatres; an accident was to cut short her career. In 1888 she had danced a fairly major role in one of the Imperial Theatres' ballets. In fact, the meeting described below, which must have taken place on 2 February 1889, was probably in the St Petersburg Bolshoy Theatre.

Pyotr Ilich Tchaikovsky had taken note of my performance, and at one of the rehearsals of some ballet in the winter of 1889 had asked our ballet master, Marius Petipa:

'What's the name of that young dancer who performed Amourat in the ballet *Vestalka*?'

'Mariya Anderson,' replied Petipa.

I vividly recall that conversation. It took place on the proscenium of the Maryinsky Theatre, close to the orchestra, five or six steps away from the first slips on the right-hand side. Pyotr Ilich was in a blue jacket; as always, his pince-nez hung on a black cord. During conversation Tchaikovsky had the habit of playing with his pince-nez with his right hand.

Petipa's eyes were searching for somebody. Noticing me, with a wave of his hand and the words 'ma belle', he summoned me to him. I approached timidly and stood a little way off. They had not interrupted their conversation in French, and seemed not to be paying the slightest attention to my approach. From the separate phrases that reached me I understood that they were talking about the staging of a new ballet, *The Sleeping Beauty*, and in particular about me, although my name was not spoken.

Imperceptibly, furtively, Pyotr Ilich stole a glance in my direction, evidently assessing me as a dancer. Judging by the expression on his slightly smiling face I satisfied him. Several of his exclamations, clearly and intelligibly repeated in French, confirmed my assumption. Finishing the conversation, Pyotr Ilich took several steps in my direction in his characteristic way – with a slight inclination of his body. Approaching more closely, he began asking me various questions, by habit mixing Russian and French, and playing with his pince-nez.

When Pyotr Ilich had completed his questions, to which I had replied timidly and with reserve, Petipa, thinking I did not understand French, began explaining to me in his broken Russian-French dialect what they had been talking about. 'Translated', this signified that in the ballet *The Sleeping Beauty* I was to dance 'the little cat – so Tchaikovsky wishes'.

Mariya Anderson, Recollections (1943); published in *PVC4*, pp. 202–3.

## LEON BAKST

### (1866–1924)

Leon Bakst was a painter, illustrator and theatre designer; in the last capacity he was to be especially associated with Dyaghilev (in 1921 he was to design Tchaikovsky's *The Sleeping Beauty* for Dyaghilev's company). Through the agency of his older friend Gennady Kondratyev, chief producer at the Imperial Theatres, Bakst had a ticket for the dress rehearsal of *The Sleeping Beauty* on 14 January 1890. Before entering the theatre itself he paid a courtesy call on Kondratyev. There, in the depths of the producer's spacious office, he saw two silhouettes.

One of them was large and stooping with an aquiline nose, with a gentle and roguish smile, with the Star of Vladimir on the left breast of the blue uniform of the director of the Imperial Theatres [Ivan Vsevolozhsky] . . .

The second gentleman was shorter, his hair and beard were white, his face very pink, friendly and modest. He was clearly in a nervous state, and was making visible efforts to control himself.

Who is this? I tried to catch the eye of my older friend who finally noticed me . . .

'Levushka, do come, I'll introduce you to our pride and joy, Pyotr Ilich Tchaikovsky!'

Red with agitation, very short, in my Art School uniform, but wearing white gloves which seemed to me so chic, my red hair cut short – I probably looked ridiculous . . . Without turning a hair, it was I who held out my hand to the famous composer.

'So,' continued the old producer, amid general smiles, 'this little lad worships the theatre, and is already making sketches. The other day,

while telling his friends about your *Sleeping Beauty* over a cup of tea, he improvised designs for it after his own taste . . . Where are they?'
– and he rummaged vainly in the drawer of his desk.

'I find the music of *The Sleeping Beauty* good!' I cried in a voice choking with emotion, amid general surprise which quickly changed to loud laughter.

'Ah! You already know my ballet?' said Tchaikovsky in surprise, continuing to laugh – and his questioning gaze settled on the patriarchal beard of the producer . . .

A never-to-be-forgotten day! For three hours I lived in an enchanted dream, intoxicated by fairies and princesses, luxurious golden palaces, by the enchantment of a fairy tale . . . My whole being, as it were, echoed to these rhythms, to this resplendent and fresh flow of beautiful, already familiar melodies . . . On that evening, it seems to me, my calling was determined.

Léon Bakst, Recollections; published (in French) in the journal *Comoedia* (Paris), 9 October 1921, reprinted (in Russian) in *PVC4*, pp. 200–1.

## IGOR GRABAR

### (1871–1960)

> After graduating in law from St Petersburg University in 1893, Igor Grabar became an artist and art historian and was associated with Dyaghilev's *Mir isskustva*. He recalls his walk home, as an 18-year-old, with Tchaikovsky after meeting him by chance at a mutual friend's.

We walked along the Neva's bank. It was a wonderful moonlit night. At first we walked silently, but soon Pyotr Ilich said:

'But you want to be an artist. Why did you go to the university?'

I explained as best I could, adding that I could ask him a similar question: why had he studied at the School of Jurisprudence before going to the Conservatoire?

He only smiled, but remained silent.

After a long silence I suddenly dared to speak, said something inept, and became confused. I do not remember on what grounds and how it connected with his reply, but I voiced the thought that geniuses create only 'by inspiration'; I had in mind, of course, his music.

He stopped, made an impatient gesture with his hand, and said with annoyance:

'Ah, young man, don't be trite! You can't await inspiration, nor is it alone sufficient; what is needed above all is work, work and work. Remember that even a man gifted with the mark of genius will produce nothing great, nor even anything mediocre, if he does not work like the devil. And the more a man has been given, the more he must work. I consider myself the most ordinary, average of persons.'

I made a gesture of protest, but he cut me short:

'No, no, don't argue; I know what I'm talking about. I advise you, young man, to remember this all your life: "inspiration" is born only of work, and during work. Every morning I sit down to work, and I compose. If from this nothing comes today, I'll sit down again tomorrow at the very same work. Thus I write for one day, for two, for ten days, not despairing if still nothing comes, for on the eleventh day, you'll see, something worthwhile will come. Through dogged work, through superhuman effort of the will, you will always achieve your aim, and you'll always succeed more and better than idlers of genius . . .'

'Does that mean there are absolutely no ungifted people?'

'Whatever the case, far fewer than is usually thought. But also there are many people who do not wish to work, or who cannot work.'

When we stopped at his entrance on the Malaya Morskaya and he rang the door-keeper, I could not restrain myself from voicing a thought which worried me:

'It is good, Pyotr Ilich, if you work for yourself and of your own free will. But what about the man who works to order?' (I had in mind his commissioned works.)

'It is not at all a bad thing: it is even better than of your own will. I am always working to commission, and Mozart worked to commission, and so did your gods, Michelangelo and Raphael . . .'

The door-keeper opened the door, and its dark jaws swallowed up Pyotr Ilich's figure.

I stood a long while thinking over these new thoughts that had so deeply struck me.

Pyotr Ilich's words became the guiding thread to my whole life.

Igor Grabar, Recollections; published in *Ogonyok [Light]* (1940), no. 12, reprinted in *PVC4*, pp. 288–9.

# V

The eternal child – and the 'misanthrope'

The range of Tchaikovsky's responses in personal relationships was as wide as the range of those relationships themselves. He showed both constancy and inconsistency. On the one hand there was his 'misanthropy', as he called it, which was doubtless just one manifestation of the terrible tensions and problems of his inner world. This aversion to human society could lead him to be desperately evasive and sometimes surprisingly rough when contact was demanded (or threatened) by someone other than a close member of his family or one of his small circle of trusted friends. This hypersensitivity was especially evident in the eight or so years following the trauma of his marriage in 1877, and in his later years he learned to cope better; indeed, he openly admitted that he had become so well practised in fulfilling the unpalatable social duties of the international celebrity that not only could he cope with meetings, receptions, and so on: he could almost delude himself that he was enjoying them. But on the other hand, throughout all his life there were deep, close and stable relationships, and he had a flair with children; he himself could be both childlike and childish, sometimes in quite extraordinary ways. So, too, he responded very naturally to the peasantry out of a deep respect for their resilience and fundamental, if sometimes devious, humanity.

# SOFIYA KASHKINA

Nikolay and Alexandra Hubert, mentioned in the following narrative, were close friends of Tchaikovsky. Nikolay and he had
been fellow students in St Petersburg and then colleagues in the
Moscow Conservatoire; Alexandra was to become a member of
the administrative staff there after her husband's death in 1888.
Nikolay was the dedicatee of Tchaikovsky's song 'O sing that
song', op. 16 no. 4.

There was always in Tchaikovsky something childlike and spontaneous
when he was among people with whom he felt no constraint; he could play
with children like a child, and he loved children's amusements, joining in
with genuine delight. I remember once (probably this was in 1887 or
1888), when Tchaikovsky was no longer a permanent inhabitant of
Moscow but was there as a guest, Hubert told his friends at the Conservatoire that Tchaikovsky had promised to spend that evening with them . . .
It was Christmas, and Alexandra Ivanovna [Hubert] said that after dinner
the Christmas tree would be lit and presents distributed. Dinner passed off
very merrily. At its end the guests were not let into the hall where the
Christmas tree was, but sat in the darkened room; then, when the tree had
been lit, the hostess played a march, the doors were opened wide and 'the
children' (all near to 50 years old), under Tchaikovsky's leadership, flew
into the hall holding hands and began to dance a *khorovod* [a processional
dance] around the Christmas tree, describing various figures under their
leader's guidance – and then, leaping up, began dragging down from the
Christmas tree (some of them even using their teeth) the presents that had
been allotted to them. These were all various comic figurines, pictures and
knick-knacks, wittily selected by the Huberts according to the character of
each 'child'. You should have seen the animation with which our old folks
told us, the younger generation, about that evening the next day . . .
According to their accounts, the prime mover in all these pranks and jokes
was Tchaikovsky himself; he had also taken part in thinking up the light-
hearted presents.

Sofiya Kashkina, Recollections; published in *PVC4*, pp. 83–4.

# ALEXANDRA JURGENSON

## (1870–1946)

Alexandra Jurgenson was a daughter of Tchaikovsky's publisher and close friend Pyotr Jurgenson, and the dedicatee of the piano piece *L'espiègle*, op. 72 no. 12.

Pyotr Ilich loved to drop in on us [the Jurgenson children] when we had returned from school and had gathered round the tea table. He loved to observe or join in our childish preparations for festivals, for [decorating] the Christmas tree, for Easter; he loved the festive family bustle. 'I adore it': he often uttered these words, drawing them out in a special way, and applying them to the most varied occasions. He would peep in on our nursery when we were preparing candles, cardboard [knick-knacks] and sweets for the Christmas tree. He once asked that during Holy Week we should not paint the eggs without him. The day was fixed and he came, even though he lived outside the city, and he showed us how to adorn the marble eggs with silken threads drawn out of pieces of silk. He himself painted several, and rubbed them over with olive oil.

There was within him, as it were, a demand to breathe the family life of children and its pleasures. Moreover he liked to tease, to joke. Of the three of us he especially liked to tease me. Probably he was amused by my inability to hide the effect and the agitation this produced in me. It was as though he provoked me in order to draw a protest, because his teasing only consisted of looking at me and repeating endlessly: 'Sasha Jurgenson, Sasha Jurgenson,' and so on, and I became confused and sometimes ran off or hid from his glances.

Once he came for three o'clock tea after we had returned from school. I came with a girl whom my mother had taken under her wing, and for whose schooling she was paying. In the twelve-point system this girl had contrived to get the lowest mark: 'one'. I secretly confided this to Pyotr Ilich, asking him not to tell my mother. But whenever I glanced at him, he indicated 'one' with his finger, and I trembled lest my mother should see, and the girl should see and realize that I had revealed her secret to an outsider.

At such a time when we were in session he brought photographs of himself and inscribed one to his godson: 'To a mastodon, from an old monkey'; to the youngest, a 12-year-old boy, he wrote: 'To the most mordant of mortals'. The lad indeed had a certain enigmatic ironic smile, which said, as it were: 'I know you – you don't deceive me' . . .

He was always interested in our successes at school, and it seems my mother had told him I was preoccupied with an essay on the set subject: 'Everyone is the shaper of his own happiness'. True, what can a 13-year-old girl, as yet unfamiliar either with happiness or unhappiness, pronounce on this subject: And so he disguised his handwriting and sent me a letter through the post as though from the journal *Russkaya Mïsl* [*Russian Thought*], with an offer to publish my composition in that journal – though on the envelope the address was written in his customary hand.

For New Year, Christmas, or our birthdays we sometimes received presents from him. Twice I received from him inscribed books, and once a box of writing paper with very pretty bunches of dried flowers. I liked it very much, but despite my mother's demand that I should say thank you, I was too shy to do so. And so I received a letter in which was inscribed in capital letters: 'INGRATITUDE IS THE MOTHER OF ALL EVILS'. On the envelope his monogram had been pretty well struck through in ink, but you could still make it out . . .

Alexandra Jurgenson, Recollections (1938); published in *PVC4*, pp. 102–3.


## ALINA BRYULLOVA

This recollection refers to the late 1880s or early 1890s.

My youngest daughter (she was not 8 years old when Pyotr Ilich died), a rather cheeky girl, always ran to him when he arrived, climbed onto his knees, and then asked in a whisper: 'My composer, play: I want to dance!' And obediently he would go to the piano, saying in confusion: 'But I don't know what to play' – then would string together some polkas, and she would spin round the room. When I protested and wanted to take the child away, he would say: 'No, let her hop around. It's a pleasure to strum trifles for her.'

Alina Bryullova, Recollections (1929); published in *PVC4*, p. 115.

## ALEXANDRA AMFITEATROVA-LEVITSKAYA

> The following incidents would have taken place in Tiflis in 1889
> or 1890.

Meeting Tchaikovsky each day at Mikhail Mikhailovich's [Ippolitov-Ivanov] I often saw him happy. He joked, laughed, and loved to romp with Tanya, the 2-year-old [adopted] daughter of the Ippolitov-Ivanovs, and when playing with her he himself was drawn into the game like a child. He loved this little girl very much, and called her his 'Little Lump'. It was comical to see how Tanya clambered, trying to pull herself up on Pyotr Ilich's arms, and how he, while continuing to talk seriously with someone, would carefully seat her on his knees.

> Amfiteatrova-Levitskaya recalled what happened at an intimate
> gathering at the Ippolitov-Ivanovs' after their host had gone to
> sleep and most of the others were dozing.

Only Pyotr Ilich played with Tanya, rocking her from side to side. Tanya loved this; she squealed and laughed, and asked 'Uncle Pyotr' to 'turn her upside down' again – which 'uncle' did with pleasure, sometimes even himself rocking from side to side, to Tanya's great delight.

Alexandra Amfiteatrova-Levitskaya, Recollections (1940); published in *CIT*, reprinted in *PVC4*, pp. 241–2.

## VLADIMIR NÁPRAVNÍK
### (1869–1948)

> Vladimir was a son of Eduard Nápravník, chief conductor at the
> Imperial Opera in St Petersburg, who conducted the premières of
> most of Tchaikovsky's operas. These memories must relate to the
> 1880s or early 1890s.

He took part in our charades and games, and himself rejoiced like a child when he succeeded in stumping or nonplussing someone, doing card tricks, or guessing someone else's thoughts. The last was known to us under the title of 'Black Magic' and consisted of one of the guests (one, naturally, who had not been let into the secret of the trick) whispering into the ear of one of us – usually Pyotr Ilich – the word he had chosen. And then Pyotr Ilich would begin saying all sorts of words which for the outsider had no meaning, and from the initial letters of these words we would work out the chosen word. The game's secret is very simple, but no one could ever guess it. And Pyotr Ilich would go into raptures seeing someone struggling to find out how it was done. I remember we once brought Sergey Taneyev to white heat when he could not hit upon the answer.

Once arriving at Pyotr Ilich's, I found him and his nephew, Bob Davïdov, writing a mass of letters addressed to Anna Petrovna Merkling [Tchaikovsky's cousin], whom Pyotr Ilich loved dearly, but on whom he wanted to play a trick. The letters contained the most varied content, starting with funny and ending with tragic things; in one, for instance, he himself wrote that Pyotr Ilich Tchaikovsky had shot himself. I also sat down to write. We wrote fifteen to twenty letters, and Pyotr Ilich himself posted them. He anticipated a tremendous effect, and relished the pleasure of having a good laugh. The next day Pyotr Ilich dined with us along with Anna Merkling, and thought that as soon as she saw him, then immediately she would begin talking in horror about the letters which she had received that morning. But instead our victim maintained a dogged silence and only looked at us knowingly. Pyotr Ilich waited a long time, winking at me, finally could bear it no longer, asked something about the letters, and thus gave himself away. It turned out that Anna Petrovna had immediately guessed who had begun this, and had purposely remained silent to tease Pyotr Ilich.

Vladimir Nápravník, Recollections; published in *SM* (1949), issue 7, reprinted in *PVC4*, pp. 217–18.

# TATYANA SHCHEPKINA-KUPERNIK

## (1874–1952)

From 1870 to 1873 Tatyana Shchepkina-Kupernik's mother had studied the piano with Nikolay Rubinstein and harmony with Tchaikovsky at the Moscow Conservatoire. Tatyana herself

1 The Tchaikovsky family, 1848; left to right: Pyotr, Alexandra
Andreyevna, Alexandra (Sasha), Zinaida (standing), Nikolay, Ippolit,
Ilya Petrovich

3  Herman Laroche

2  Tchaikovsky, 1860

5 Nikolay Rubinstein

6 Nikolay Kashkin

7 Tchaikovsky, 1877

8 Tchaikovsky and his wife,
  Antonina

9 Modest Tchaikovsky

10 Tchaikovsky, 1888

11 The Tchaikovsky brothers, 1890; left to right: Anatoly, Nikolay,
Ippolit, the composer, Modest

12 Tchaikovsky, 1890

13 Herman Laroche and
Alexander Glazunov, 1892

14 Tchaikovsky's home at Klin

15 Tchaikovsky in his doctoral
robes, Cambridge, 1983

became a writer and translator, the authoress of opera libretti, and of verses that were set by, among others, Arensky and Cherepnin. Her father had been responsible for Tchaikovsky's visit to Kiev in September 1889, when he attended a performance of *Eugene Onegin*, and it was here that she first saw him as he acknowledged the ovations. Daniil Rathaus was a student at Kiev University on whose verses Tchaikovsky was to compose his last completed work, the Six Romances, op. 73.

I remember distinctly his well-proportioned, not very tall figure, his silver-grey hair and beard, and his very slightly black eyebrows and moustache . . .

During the interval her father took her to meet the composer.

My heart was beating as I approached him. My father told Tchaikovsky that I wrote verses. He put his hand gently on my shoulder and said to me in his soft, baritone voice:

'Ah, write, write – that's good . . . Maybe you'll write me verses for romances.'

He had a very nice way of talking. Of course, it was of not the slightest interest to him that some little girl wrote verses. But his kind words and the squeeze of his hand made a great impression on me. I was so overcome I could not find anything to say to him.

The following year Tchaikovsky returned to Kiev.

Because of illness I did not go to the theatre, but my father again met him, and here you can judge·all the thoughtfulness Pyotr Ilich showed towards people. He asked my father:

'How are your daughter's verses coming along?' – and added: 'Bring them to me to look over – perhaps they'll be suitable. I'm always looking for words for romances.'

I was dumbfounded when my father told me this; to remember for a whole year the verses of some girl! But I decided not to send my verses; they seemed to me bad. Later I was terribly envious of that student I knew – the languid, fair-haired youth, Daniil Rathaus – on whose verses Tchaikovsky wrote many romances.

Tatyana Shchepkina-Kupernik, Recollections; published in *KP*, 6 May 1940, reprinted in *PVC4*, pp. 265–6.

# IVAN IVANOV

## (1881–1942)

Ivan Ivanov was a dancer in St Petersburg until 1918, when he became chief producer of the Kirov Ballet. He was one of the children in the première of *The Nutcracker*. The children had been given toy instruments to learn, but the results were not as hoped, and so the instruments were practised before each ballet rehearsal. Marius Petipa was the choreographer of *The Nutcracker*, and Riccardo Drigo the principal conductor of the Imperial Ballet in St Petersburg; he conducted the ballet's première.

On one of the following days, after dogged labours with us in the presence of the ballet-master, Marius Petipa – and, sitting alongside him, an imposing gentleman beautifully dressed in a light-coloured suit who from time to time made observations to Drigo and conversed with Petipa in a very lively manner – we several times demonstrated what we had achieved . . . Unfortunately our achievements were deemed unsatisfactory, and after quite long discussions in French between Petipa, the gentleman in the light-coloured suit, and Drigo, the last explained to us that it had been decided each should play as best he could . . . At that rehearsal we learned that the man sitting with Petipa was the composer of the ballet . . . Tchaikovsky . . . After the première of the ballet . . . Tchaikovsky had asked that all the pupils should be told that he was very satisfied with the performance and its performers, that he thanked everyone who had taken part very much, and was sending them sweets. Two of the school porters brought in big baskets, and all the pupils, boys and girls, and the teachers each received a box of wonderful sweets.

Ivan Ivanov, Recollections (1940); published in *PVC4*, p. 394.

## KONSTANTIN DUMCHEV
### (1879–1948)

Konstantin Dumchev was a violinist who later taught at the Novo-cherkassk School of Music. In January 1893, when this incident took place, Dumchev was only 13. Rudolf Felday was a pianist resident in Odessa.

After dinner at Felday's . . . a young pianist, the daughter of a friend of the composer's brother Ippolit Ilich, performed. The girl played one of Liszt's fantasias (*La muette di Portici*) very conscientiously but with little musicality. After she had played, Pyotr Ilich went to the piano and played several notes to test her ear, but she could not name any of them. Because she had played from music Pyotr Ilich suggested she should play some-thing from memory – but she could not do this either. Then Pyotr Ilich said to her father very politely, though with evident irritation:

'The great service your daughter's piano teacher has done her is to get results such as these from her.'

The pianist's father, confused, immediately left for home.

Konstantin Dumchev, *Vstrechi [Meetings]*; published in *ZK*, Novocherkassk, 6 May 1940, reprinted in *PVC4*, p. 417.

## HELEN HENSCHEL
### (1882–1973)

Helen Henschel was the daughter of Sir George Henschel, the singer and conductor. She became a singer and pianist in her own right. The incident took place in June 1893; her father had dated his earlier meeting with Tchaikovsky as 1876.

Another frequent visitor to our house about this time was Tschaikovsky, who had come to England to receive an honorary degree at Cambridge. My father had met him years earlier in Moscow, and described him then (1875) as 'a most amiable, kind, gentle, modest man, with just that touch of melancholy in his composition which seems to be characteristic of the Russian'.

The melancholy was naturally enough not evident to me as a small child, but the gentleness and kindness were. Nobody could have been more charming than he was. One of my life's minor tragedies is that he wrote me a long letter when he left London, that the wind blew it off the table into the waste-paper basket, and that the housemaid lit my fire with it . . . But I do possess a personal remembrance of Tschaikovsky – the photograph he gave to my mother, inscribed: 'À Madame L. B. Henschel, de la part de son fervent admirateur. P. Tschaikovsky'.

Helen Henschel, *When Soft Voices Die* (London, 1944), p. 89.

## NIKOLAY KASHKIN

Tchaikovsky lived in Maidanovo, near Klin, between 1885 and 1888.

Once, I don't remember in which year, I spent Holy Week at Maidanovo. It was still winter rather than spring, though the snow was beginning to thaw a little from below, and when walking you often had to plough through water, though we walked in topboots so that it was not too terrible . . . We went to Easter morning service at the Maidanovo church; in the morning the parish priest visited us, and I think it was towards lunchtime that there arrived from the village of Demyanov (on the other side of Klin) Sergey Taneyev, who then set off for a walk with us. Pyotr Ilich liked the peasant children very much, and indulged them a lot, even spoiled them with tips of all sorts, usually of small change. Taneyev and I reproved him for this, saying that he would corrupt the children; the culprit confessed sadly that this was, frankly, true, but gave us little hope that he would behave better. However, having set out on our walk, he decided to make an heroic effort to avoid such extortion on the part of the children. In the park we went along the bank of the river, directing ourselves to the bridge across the Sestra on the road to Klin. The villagers knew very well the time of Tchaikovsky's walks, and he himself knew they would certainly be watching for his exit from the park; and so he decided to outwit his persecutors and, leaving us to go along the road in the park, he himself descended to the river and, bending down, plunged into the dense willow-bushes, trying to steal up to the bridge unnoticed – during which, from above, the companion he had left with me exclaimed with pain, as he looked at the stooping figure of the fugitive:

'There you have the just reward for corruption!'

However this innocent deception failed; the children had probably studied the character of their victim and had set up observation posts everywhere. Soon we heard in the distance joyful summoning cries, the boys who streamed before us alongside the park threw themselves headlong in that direction, and when we finally got close, the triumphant foe was already retreating in a noisy crowd with their spoils, and our poor friend, quite red with agitation and confusion, was awaiting us, and justified himself by saying there was nothing he could do, but that he had given the children very little, only trifles; he considered the latter an extenuating circumstance in his misdeed. How far he was truthful regarding the insignificant contribution which had been extracted from him I do not know. But once on a walk with me he distributed seven roubles which he had taken along in small silver coins, and in addition took from me all the small change I had in my pocket.

Nikolay Kashkin, *KVC*, pp. 138–40.

From 1888 to 1892 Tchaikovsky lived in Frolovskoye.

The village of Frolovskoye, near Klin, was very dear to its inhabitant for its quiet, its solitariness, and finally because he managed to accustom himself to the house and the surroundings. The men of the village looked after their master very well, generously giving him fare for big festivals and for his nameday . . . and probably also helping him in occasions of need. Knowing there was no bathing to be had in Frolovskoye except in a very unsavoury pond near the house, the peasants used a small spring in the wood, built a dam, and there appeared a small reservoir with water as clear as crystal. But it was so cold that bathing in it was impossible. All the same, Pyotr Ilich was very touched . . .

Nikolay Kashkin, *KVC*, p. 155.

# ALEXANDER GLAZUNOV

During Tchaikovsky's later years Glazunov became a fairly intimate member of his social circle. The incident at the railway
station must have taken place in the late 1880s.

In order to characterize the work of the great Russian composers, I would
compare Borodin with a pre-muscovite warrior-prince, Musorgsky with a
thoughtful peasant, Rimsky-Korsakov with a magician from an old Russian *bílina* [a medieval Russian epic], and Tchaikovsky with a Russian
gentleman from the mental and spiritual world of Turgenev. Tchaikovsky
worshipped the country and, from his own viewpoint, loved and knew the
people. He knew how to treat them, and they all and everywhere loved
him. In 1895 I arrived in Klin to visit the house where Tchaikovsky had
lived. I remember how the coachmen almost came to blows when I
explained the purpose of my trip. I stayed with one of them, whose
nickname was Killer. He proved talkative and observant, and told me
about Tchaikovsky's walks along the avenues with 'a little book in his
hands', into which from time to time he would write something. He
praised his kindness. When bidding me goodbye Killer suddenly asked me
a question: had I known [Tchaikovsky], and was it true that the deceased
was 'a composer of all-Russian music'? All this was thoroughly plausible,
and I replied in the positive.

My late aunt told of another incident. She had arrived at the station of
Podsolnechnaya [near Klin], and was sitting waiting for her train. She
noticed (as she put it) a grey-haired, handsome old man sheltering in a
corner, and beckoned the railway guard, whom she had long known, to ask
who her neighbour was. The guard replied that it was the well-known
Tchaikovsky, who wanted to buy an estate in Podsolnechnaya. My aunt
instructed the guard to tell Tchaikovsky that she would very much like to
make his acquaintance. To this the guard replied:

'Don't think of it, madam; *he* prefers to talk with our brother [i.e. a
peasant].'

And so the introduction did not take place.

Alexander Glazunov, Recollections; published in *CVP*, reprinted in *PVC4*,
p. 210.

## ALINA BRYULLOVA

In all serious artistic and aesthetic matters he [Tchaikovsky] always acted firmly, not giving an inch on something he considered his duty, or which his sensitive heart prompted him to do. But he was certainly a person suffering from a nervous disorder. In the 1870s and 1880s neuroses had still been little studied, had not been separated from temperament and character, and there had been no attempt to cure them. But in the light of present-day scientific investigation, he had a definite neurosis which at times intensified into inexpressible sufferings; a burning, groundless melancholy, from which in no way could he extricate himself, an inability to control his jangled nerves, a dread of people, and a consciousness that this state was unworthy of him, that he *had* to struggle with it; this tormented him unspeakably, and poisoned his life which, it seemed, had every outward chance of being bright.

Alina Bryullova, Recollections (1929); published in *PVC4*, p. 111.

## SOFIYA KASHKINA

For some reason he was going along a street (in Geneva, I believe) immersed in his own thoughts. Suddenly a certain lady stopped him with a joyful greeting in Russian:

'Pyotr Ilich, what an unexpected pleasure!'

'Forgive me, madam, I am not Tchaikovsky,' he said, not noticing that by using his own surname, he had given himself away.

Sofiya Kashkina, Recollections (1959); published in *PVC4*, p. 86.

## ALINA BRYULLOVA

Tchaikovsky often showed unwillingness to meet with former schoolfellows from the School of Jurisprudence. But not with all: for instance, Apukhtin and Meshchersky, both prominent homosexuals, were exceptions to this rule.

I had two friends, his comrades, the nicest of people — and completely antimusical, which also should have constituted an attraction in Tchaikovsky's

eyes: that there would be no conversations about music with ignoramuses.
They often dined with me. Pyotr Ilich always looked at me appealingly:

'Don't invite D. and Sh. when I'm with you.'

Of course this request was fulfilled without question. Tchaikovsky made
an exception only of Apukhtin and Meshchersky. Why he had good
relations with the latter is a mystery . . .

On another occasion Tchaikovsky met Verzhbilovich [a cellist] in a
railway carriage.

'Ah, Pyotr Ilich, how timely. Turgenev is travelling with me in one of
the compartments. He very much wants to meet you. I'll go and fetch
him.'

Verzhbilovich went off, but Pyotr Ilich, like a thief in the night,
secretly stole away into the third class, and hid himself there until the train
arrived in Moscow and the last passenger had departed.

'Why did you do this?' I asked, when he, like a naughty schoolboy, told
me this. 'Surely you like Turgenev?'

'I love him terribly, I bow before him, but what should I say to him? I
should have been very awkward – and I ran away.'

Alina Bryullova, Recollections (1929); published in *PVC4*, pp. 108–9.


# MIKHAIL IPPOLITOV-IVANOV

## (1859–1935)

> Mikhail Ippolitov-Ivanov was a composer and conductor who
> founded the Tiflis branch of the RMS in 1882 and became a
> friend of Tchaikovsky from 1886, when the composer began
> visiting his brother Anatoly, who was living in that city. Nikolay
> Peresleny was a nephew of Tchaikovsky's brother-in-law, Lev
> Davïdov.

When he [Nikolay Peresleny] arrived unexpectedly with his suitcases
while he [Tchaikovsky] was right in the middle of some urgent work, and
was counting on spending some considerable time with him, Pyotr Ilich,
not giving him time to collect himself, engaged the cab for the return
journey, sat [Lev's] nephew in it with his suitcases, and sent him off to the
station without any explanation. Subsequently he had a good laugh as he

recalled the surprised expression of Nikolay Peresleny to whom he had given such an unexpected welcome.

Mikhail Ippolitov-Ivanov, *IRM*; reprinted in *PVC4*, p. 238.

# VI

## Life in the country

The countryside had a lifelong attraction for Tchaikovsky, and from 1885 he made his home at or near Klin, some fifty miles to the north-west of Moscow and conveniently situated on the railway line to St Petersburg. But long before this he had enjoyed periods on the country estates of one or another of his friends.

# ALINA BRYULLOVA

From the early 1870s Tchaikovsky frequently stayed at Grankino
on the estate of Herman Konradi, Alina Bryullova's first husband.

When Pyotr Ilich was our guest in the country . . . his day was strictly
organized. In the morning he always composed; each day he would sit
down to work, whether inspiration came or not. 'Sometimes I'll write two
or three lines, and often I'll cross these out the next day – and always I
discipline my thoughts, set them in order. Sometimes a good melody will
come, a successful musical phrase. Sometimes it comes easily, of its own
accord, sometimes with difficulty – but I do not despair, I do not give up
working, and finally my labour is crowned with success.'

When with us he lived in a separate wing. In the morning coffee was
taken over to him and he did not appear until early country lunch, and no
one, not even his brother, disturbed his solitude. After dinner, whatever
the weather, he would go for a walk across the steppes (which were open to
the full blaze of the sun), then bathed and turned up, fresh and contented,
for five o'clock tea. And he would pass the whole evening with us; we
would make music, read aloud, chat, sometimes play vint. Pyotr Ilich very
much liked to relax by playing cards, and would be as happy as a child
when he got a grand slam. Of books he liked memoirs most of all,
especially about Russian life. When travelling he invariably took an issue
of *Russkaya Starina [Russia's Past]*. Just how much he took to heart what
he read is shown by one little incident. I saw on his table a copy of Zola's
only recently published *Pot-Bouille*, which had been torn to pieces.

'I was reading it,' he confessed, 'and was so indignant at the author's
cynicism that I flung the book a great distance' (he was reading in the
wood). 'Yet all the same he has talent; I shall not be able to resist picking it
up again and finishing it off.'

Alina Bryullova, Recollections (1929); published in *PVC4*, p. 117.

# NIKOLAY KASHKIN

After 1885, when Tchaikovsky took a lease on his first country home in the village of Maidanovo just outside Klin, he was freed from many of the unavoidable interruptions and distractions of life in Moscow. Now he could establish his own routine and invite only those people whose company he enjoyed. Maidanovo had 'a magnificent park' where he could walk, though this did not make the location ideal.

For Pyotr Ilich a major shortcoming of Maidanovo was the lack of a large wood nearby, because each day he liked to have a long walk, taking no account of the weather, and in this matter no park could take the place of a wood. Pyotr Ilich lived in the country almost without a break; he would not show himself in Moscow for several months, and no one would go to him for several months. We, his closest friends, knew very well that the hermit of Maidanovo was constantly engrossed in his work and did not like any hindrance to this, and so we always waited for our invitations, which indicated the completion of some composition, or some general break in work. In the country Tchaikovsky always dined exactly at one o'clock, and had supper at eight-thirty. Usually three or four of us would go on the mail train at four, would dine, stay the evening and the following day, and leave for Moscow by the last train. Usually on such visits with a large group the time passed noisily and gaily; there was, of course, no shortage of wine which our host allowed himself on such occasions, though in the normal course of things he was very restrained in this regard.

Besides participation in such noisy assemblies, from time to time I stayed at Pyotr Ilich's for a more or less extended period either alone or in a very small company. Pyotr Ilich, as I have already said, feared visits of outsiders, sometimes simply would not receive those who came to him without prior agreement – and if this situation arose it only remained to await the train and go back to Moscow . . .

In the country Pyotr Ilich retained a cook, but was very undemanding with food, and since he possessed a good appetite, ate almost everything with pleasure, though he was perfectly capable of judging the worth of good cooking. I am very undemanding in my cuisine, and this was well known to the hermit of Klin; all the same, he began to get alarmed at the uniform simplicity of his dinners and suppers, and tried to think up something new. In exactly the same way, despite the exemplary conduct of his servant in looking after his guests, he was often worried that something was lacking – in a word, the presence of the most undemanding guest still caused him some anxiety . . .

We met for morning tea at a little after eight, sitting over it for about a half-hour, in very good weather strolled a bit, and then at nine we dispersed to our rooms until lunch, always served exactly at one. We both ate very – perhaps too – fast, and the meal usually consisted of two dishes, so that we spent little time on it, and set off to walk at two. We were both accustomed to solitary walks, and so sometimes we went along together without saying a word, scarcely noticing each other; it would happen that I, walking a little faster, would without noticing get ahead and then, suddenly remembering, would look round and note my companion two hundred or more yards behind; having waited for him, then again we would proceed in the same way. Sometimes, however, we would continue talking about something which had been started over lunch but remained unfinished, and in such instances the conversation for the most part would not be broken off until the end of the walk. It would also happen that Tchaikovsky would say at lunch that he would go for his walk alone. That meant that he was occupied with composition, and a solitary walk was his favourite time for thinking out the general plan [of a composition], and sometimes for the invention of themes, because of which he constantly had with him a notebook where he noted down what had come into his head. After the walk at three-thirty there was tea, and then we again dispersed to our rooms until six – in winter even later because we did not go for a walk, whereas in summer we again had a walk before supper, which was served exactly at eight-thirty. After supper Pyotr Ilich did not work except on very rare occasions . . .

Supper being over, his servant would clear the table, leaving a bottle of wine, and at nine or a little after would go off to his own quarters and was free until morning. The pair of us being left alone, we would usually set about playing piano duets; Pyotr Ilich always had a large supply of such arrangements. On such occasions we many times played works by Brahms. Tchaikovsky greatly revered this composer for his sincere seriousness and for not hunting after success, but at the same time he had little sympathy for his works, finding them too dry and cold. He was inclined to attribute his lack of sympathy to his insufficient acquaintance with Brahms, his insufficient understanding of his compositions, but repeated experiences of playing them through did not change his initial attitude. We also quite often played Glazunov, in whom he found much talent. Sometimes music gave way to, or was replaced by, reading aloud, in which I was almost always the reader because our tastes in this matter were complete opposites. Being accustomed to reading quickly with my eyes, I have to force my attention in order not to lose the thread when listening to comparatively slow reading aloud; but I can myself read [aloud] with some pleasure. On the other hand Pyotr Ilich very much liked to listen to the reading not only of new works but also of old favourites from Russian literature; in addition, he found that I read quite well. A new talented work would send him into raptures . . . .

> The increasing pressures of Tchaikovsky's professional commit-
> ments finally decided him that he would also have to have a base in
> Moscow.

Tchaikovsky took an apartment . . . and settled himself into it very comfortably. At first he himself was very contented, but when visits from strangers began and became more and more frequent, and ringing at the bell during the morning hindered him from working, Pyotr Ilich thought to place at the entrance a brass plate with the notice: 'Not at home. Please do not ring.' Every passing schoolboy who read this notice of course considered it his unfailing duty to ring as loudly as possible and then hide, and summons no less frequent than before annoyed the unfortunate composer. Finally, when beginning to think of setting about *The Queen of Spades*, the composer decided that it would be impossible to work on this in Moscow, and therefore speedily departed abroad for Italy . . . With this, life in Moscow ended for Pyotr Ilich, and he made no further attempt to set up an apartment in the city.

> In 1888 Tchaikovsky had moved to a new home at nearby Frolov-
> skoye. The following narrative probably refers to 1890.

During the first half of the summer Modest Tchaikovsky and Herman Laroche were my fellow guests at Frolovskoye. When all four of us collected together in the evening, we sometimes played vint in addition to our usual occupations of music, reading and conversation. Pyotr Ilich would readily play three rubbers, but later would become tired, and we

would abandon cards. In the summer there was a great quantity of mushrooms in the wood and park. Pyotr Ilich busied himself with collecting
these instead of his usual walk, and even became passionately triumphant
because almost always he collected more mushrooms than I, for all that I
was quite experienced in this business. Mushrooms were served at table in
various forms each day and, to our surprise, we did not get tired of them.
One morning, before tea, we went out onto the terrace of the house
with Pyotr Ilich and admired the beautiful weather. Suddenly Pyotr Ilich
dropped to the ground with a loud cry. I did not know what had happened
to him, and was alarmed. It turned out that he had simply seen some white
mushrooms near the terrace, and had cried out for fear I should pick them
before him – and had fallen to the ground with the sole intention of
obstructing my way with his body and of reaching, on all fours, the bushes
more quickly and getting the mushrooms. Afterwards we laughed not a
little at his hunter's ardour. Being very familiar with the wood, Pyotr Ilich
knew where the mushrooms were, but he never showed these places to
anyone. He even feared that people would follow him, and so he would
deliberately take various detours.

Nikolay Kashkin, *KVC*, pp. 135–8, 154, 143–4.

## VLADIMIR NÁPRAVNÍK

Because the woods at Frolovskoye had been cut down, in 1891
Tchaikovsky returned to Maidanovo. In 1892 Vladimir Nápravník stayed four weeks with Tchaikovsky while preparing for
an examination. He was not, of course, in the category of Tchaikovsky's more intimate associates.

Life at Maidanovo followed a strict plan. Exactly at eight o'clock Alexey,
Pyotr Ilich's servant, woke me, and when I arrived for tea at eight-thirty
my host was already sitting at the table, a book in his hand, and was
listening to the morning report of the yardman, Andrey, who was inform-
ing him about the weather – what the temperature was, whether it was
windy, whether the weather was good, and so on. Regarding this, it always
in fact proved completely the opposite to the tone in which it was reported.
After talking with Andrey he would order lunch and supper. Pyotr Ilich
loved Russian cooking very much, and with special pleasure ate cabbage

soup with kasha, bortsch, sauerkraut, and all fish. After dismissing the cook Pyotr Ilich sank into 'stubborn' silence and, while finishing his tea, read his book or the letters he had received.

At nine we got dressed, put on felt boots, and went out together from the house. Pyotr Ilich would go over to greet the yard dog, which sat there on its chain, bestowing upon it the most affectionate epithets. During our walk I saw how affectionately all who met Pyotr Ilich greeted him, and he found an affectionate word for each one.

At ten we returned home. Pyotr Ilich immediately sat down to work and, without stopping, composed at the piano or at the writing table.

At one o'clock we gathered in the dining room for lunch, and told each other what we had achieved that morning . . .

From two to three there was a second walk which Pyotr Ilich always took alone, and during this he thought over his compositions, and on the spot noted down the ideas that came into his head.

The time from three to four was devoted to reading. Tea was at four, during which the host continued reading and silence reigned. After tea until half-past eight – musical work and writing letters. At eight-thirty – supper.

The time after supper we devoted to playing piano duets. Pyotr Ilich had quite a large library of piano duets. We played the classics, or the most recent contemporary composers: Grieg, Bruckner, Brahms. The music of the last said little to Tchaikovsky's soul. Of Russian composers [we played] Borodin, Rimsky-Korsakov, Glazunov, Rubinstein, Arensky, Konyus (*Children's Suite*, to which Tchaikovsky was very attracted), and [the Third Symphony] *The Demon* by my father. Never would Pyotr Ilich permit his own compositions to be played either as piano solos or duets, and he himself never played them.

Vladimir Nápravník, Recollections; published in *SM* (1949), no. 7, reprinted in *PVC4*, pp. 219–20.

# VII

Conductor and celebrity

Though his first appearance on the rostrum was a personal disaster, in his later years Tchaikovsky made an important subsidiary career for himself as a conductor, first of his own works, then increasingly of music by others. His concert tours were to take him not only to Western Europe, but also to the USA. Because it was his most exposed activity, its documentation is very ample – and very revealing. It is also sometimes highly contradictory.

# NIKOLAY KASHKIN

While still a student Tchaikovsky had already done a little conducting within the St Petersburg Conservatoire, but in 1868 he appeared for the first time at a public charity concert conducting one of his own pieces. The work had begun life in 1865 as a set of *Characteristic Dances*, but had subsequently been incorporated into his first opera, *The Voyevoda*.

I went behind the scenes where the debutant-conductor was, and approached him. He told me that, to his own surprise, he was not feeling in the least scared. We talked a little, after which, before his piece, I went off to my seat in the stalls. Soon after this Pyotr Ilich appeared, and my first glance told me that he had gone completely to pieces. The orchestral players were already arranged on stage, and he walked between their desks bending forward just as though he wanted to hide himself. When he finally reached the rostrum he had the appearance of a man who found himself in a desperate situation. He completely forgot his own piece, saw nothing that was in the score, and failed to give the players their cues in those places where it was really necessary. Fortunately the orchestra knew the piece so well that the players paid no attention to his wrong directions, and played the *Dances* quite satisfactorily, simply grinning when they looked towards the composer.

Nikolay Kashkin, *KVC*, p. 42.

In 1877 Tchaikovsky made a second modest attempt at conducting, and coped better. But it was 1885 before he decided that he might make a serious effort to master his nerves.

# PAVEL PCHELNIKOV
## (1851–1913)

From 1882 Pavel Pchelnikov was head of the office of the Imperial Theatres in Moscow. The initial quotation is from a letter from Tchaikovsky of December 1885, in which he offers his services to conduct the first performance of his opera

*Cherevichki* (the revision of his earlier *Vakula the Smith*).

'. . . I am very ungifted as a conductor, but I can attempt it, providing that if I do not succeed, then in the event of a similar proposal from me on some other occasion, you will refuse me without further ceremony.'

Whoever attended operatic performances under Pyotr Ilich's direction will understand how the phrase I have cited speaks of that merciless rigour with which he viewed his work. Because of such an attitude towards himself he was as inordinately agitated when conducting as at the first public performances of his works.

Pavel Pchelnikov, Recollections; published in *MV*, 27 and 28 October/8 and 9 November 1900, and *RMG* (1900), no. 45, reprinted in *PVC4*, pp. 143–4.

# HERMAN LAROCHE

He never succeeded in becoming a master conductor, but remained on the level of a talented beginner – though, as often happens in our art (and perhaps in others), his talent here proved, through training and experience, to be incomparably more substantial [than it had first seemed]. A performance under his baton constantly left one wishing for this or that detail, but was in general lively and interesting; his choice of tempo (I am speaking of those comparatively rare occasions when he conducted pieces by others) was correctly made but with, nevertheless, a noticeable inclination to *fast* tempi . . . This corresponded completely with his disposition and habits – quick walking, quick letter writing . . . quick reading (I remember how, at evening tea or on a train, he would get through three or four newspapers in succession at a speed I found incomprehensible).

Herman Laroche, *VOC*; reprinted in *LIS2*, pp. 168–9, and *PVC4*, pp. 38–9.

Tchaikovsky initiated his professional career as a conductor by directing the first performances of *Cherevichki*, which took place in Moscow in January 1887. Within a year he had set out on a tour of Western Europe, conducting in Leipzig, Hamburg, Berlin, Prague, Paris and London.

# DAVID CHERNOMORDIKOV
## (1869–1947)

David Chernomordikov was a composer and pianist who was present at Tchaikovsky's public concerts in Paris early in 1888.

The hall was full. In the left-hand box (the directors') sat Edvard Grieg exchanging greetings with his musical acquaintances. When the orchestra and the audience were in their places, Edouard Colonne came out from the wings; behind him came Tchaikovsky. The composer gave the impression of an old man, though he was then still not 50 years old. I recall his stately figure, the gentle and pleasant features of his face. As he appeared on the stage he was very pale; it was as though he was being dragged out by force. Advancing to the footlights, Colonne presented the composer to the public with a broad gesture of his hand, and left the stage. The audience greeted the composer with loud, friendly applause. When the hall had fallen silent Tchaikovsky mounted the rostrum, took the baton and, after a pause, began waving it.

You sensed that Pyotr Ilich was very agitated. This showed itself both in the uncertainty with which he took hold of the baton and in a certain sluggishness in his hand movements. When the orchestra began playing the Serenade for Strings the composer's baton, as it were, swam through the air. One got the impression that, if the conductor had stopped conducting, the orchestra would have gone on playing just the same. After each item the audience applauded the composer cordially, and from the directors' box Edvard Grieg clapped his hands with great enthusiasm . . .

Tchaikovsky's second appearance was as successful as his first. This time it appeared that Pyotr Ilich felt more assured; there were not the nervous quiverings in his beat as during the first concert. But his baton, as before, 'swam' through the air.

David Chernomordikov, Recollections; published in *SM* (1940), nos. 5 and 6, reprinted in *PVC4*, pp. 244–5.

# FRANTIŠEK ŠUBERT

Šubert recalled a conversation he had with Tchaikovsky in Prague in 1888 at a banquet in Tchaikovsky's honour (attended by Dvořák) about a possible opera production in Prague. Šubert was, of course, mistaken in believing Tchaikovsky had never conducted opera before.

I expressed the hope that before long we might see the maestro again in Prague, and that as conductor of one of his operas.

'Don't wish for such a thing,' said Tchaikovsky with a smile. 'That would serve you ill. I don't know how to conduct operas.'

There were objections, but the maestro stood his ground.

'In concerts I feel confidence in myself, but the conducting of my operas I am glad to leave to other conductors.'

I no longer remember whether he added that up until then he had never conducted even one of them.

'And which of my operas would you wish to give? I don't know whether they will please anyone outside Russia.'

We assured him that he would mortally wound the entire Czech public if he doubted their interest in Russian and Slavonic subjects in general.

'I don't know, I don't know,' the maestro insisted sincerely, 'whether any of my works will be to your Slavonic taste. *The Oprichnik, The Enchantress. [Vakula] the Smith (Cherevichki*) and others: all these are perhaps only for us Russians; elsewhere they would find it difficult to gain a permanent foothold.'

'Which of your works is your favourite?' I asked.

'My favourite?' repeated Pyotr Ilich. He leaned against the back of his chair and his eyes fastened on me firmly – unusually so. Excitement greater than I could have expected was noticeable on his oblong face, which recalled the image of St Peter. Expectation flitted across it and, at the same time, fear of disappointment.

He leaned forward in his chair, bent his head towards the table, as it were strumming something with his right hand, and in a rather muffled, almost constrained voice, said:

'There's one of my operatic works which is my favourite, but outside Russia it is completely impracticable.'

'Which one?' I persisted.

'It is not a dramatic piece, but only scenes.'

Then, looking sideways, he repeated: 'It would be altogether impracticable.'

A human word can be completely understood only when we hear it and, at the same time, see the speaker. The word is a mask, a veil, is a balsam averting the ache [which would follow], should another utter it; it is the opposite of the wish. The truth lies in the tone of the speaker, in his look, the expression on his face.

'Here in Prague, as far as the arts are concerned, things are possible which probably in another place would not be understood,' I replied. 'We [Czechs and Russians] are closer to each other than to foreign nations. And so perhaps you will tell me what your favourite work is called.'

'*Eugene Onegin*,' Tchaikovsky burst out, adding equally quickly, 'But it is not an opera at all, not a drama; it is only lyrical scenes . . .'

To my good fortune and to Tchaikovsky's joy, I could not say other than that which I now uttered. His eyes sparkled with happiness. He got up. Across the table he grasped my hand – I was sitting opposite him – squeezed it, and said only: 'I'll come, I'll come.'

It was only then that those present at the reception . . . learned what we had been talking about. In an instant tankards and glasses were clinking to the première of the opera *Eugene Onegin* in Prague, and to a further visit by the composer . . .

Thus was *Eugene Onegin* accepted for the National Theatre amid glass clinking; everything else [at the banquet?] followed the usual course – and in November of the same year we were already welcoming Tchaikovsky in Prague for the première.

At the première of *Onegin* a rather unusual role fell to the chief conductor of the National Theatre: the role of prompter. Pyotr Ilich, in saying that he did not feel at home in conducting operas, had been merely speaking the truth. Not very accustomed to it, he directed his attention chiefly to the orchestra without concerning himself much with the stage. To forestall any unwelcome shipwreck at the première the first conductor sat in the prompt box and co-operated in the performance exactly as Italian operatic prompters do, who not only prompt but also give the singers the beat and all other necessary directions. He differed from them only in being invisible to the audience.

At rehearsals, and especially at the performances, the composer was very excited, and as a keen smoker went out after every scene to smoke a cigarette. In our theatre, especially after the fateful 'epidemic' of theatre fires which had occurred in the 1880s of the last century, smoking was out of fashion. Indeed, according to the theatre's internal regulations, it was strictly forbidden. But because Tchaikovsky as a smoker was uncontrollable, everyone turned a blind eye when he took refuge in the conductor's room near the orchestra. There, by an open window (in December), along with Knot, a member of the orchestra, he rolled his cigarettes and lit up, drinking mineral water with cognac.

František Šubert, *Moje vzpomínky* (Prague, 1902), pp. 108–13.

## 'B-moll'

In December 1889 Tchaikovsky conducted in St Petersburg, on consecutive days, two concerts of music by his former teacher Anton Rubinstein as part of the celebrations of the golden jubilee of Rubinstein's first appearance as a performer. One concert ended with Rubinstein's sacred opera, *The Tower of Babel*, in which massed choirs participated. This seems to have posed insoluble difficulties: as Alina Bryullova, who was singing in one of the choirs, described it, the performance 'truly was a babel'. The identity of 'B-moll' is unknown.

I was in one of the numerous choirs which took part in the concert. At first the choirs rehearsed separately, then several general rehearsals were arranged. The first rehearsal of the massed choirs, with piano and without soloists, took place in the palace of the Grand Duchess Ekaterina Mikhailovna. It was there that for the first time I saw Pyotr Ilich at close quarters.

It was evening. Towards eight o'clock the choirs aspiring to participate in *The Tower of Babel* began to assemble. Almost all the Russian and German choirs that existed in St Petersburg were there and, as is well known, there are a lot of them; German was heard almost as much as Russian.

I cannot remember who pointed out to me the sympathetic and already completely grey head of Pyotr Ilich, who met with us in one of the palace's rooms. Our choirs filled the entire hall assigned for the rehearsal. There were six hundred of us. It was not without difficulty that we were deployed, during which each conductor stood alongside his choir to show his charges, the majority of whom were amateurs, the way. But finally everything was in its proper place. The men stood, the women sat. Our choir was at the front, right below the rostrum and the piano, so that Pyotr Ilich was in our sight all the time. Mounting the rostrum, he began talking to us, immediately revealing the most agreeable simplicity and naturalness. He indicated the speed at which we should sing the first movement of *The Tower of Babel*, quoting the words of the composer himself. The tempo proved to be very fast, and the first movement of *The Tower of Babel* is nothing other than the most intricate of fugues, written daringly and effectively. We all subsided into the most reverential silence, looking expectantly towards the conductor. The first chords of the accompaniment and the introductory phrase rang out. Then Pyotr Ilich waved his baton on our side and directed at us the authoritative gaze of the conductor. The machine trembled, and all the massed choirs filled the hall with the sounds of this unwieldy, effective, many-voiced fugue depicting the crowds of people who are building the Tower of Babel.

Alas! We had not managed to sing ten bars before it fell to pieces in the most shameful fashion. The Arkhangelsky Choir on one side, the Lieder-tafel on the other: here the tenors, there the basses – in a word, a veritable Babylonian babel! Pyotr Ilich began tapping with his stick; half the choirs fell silent as though from the waving of a magic wand, but the half at the rear, neither seeing nor hearing the conductor through such a mass of voices and people, gave the impression of some avalanche uncontrollably rolling down from above. At this Pyotr Ilich summoned all his resources; in desperation he waved his arms, calling to order the raging choral elements, and when they at last fell into confused silence, asked us to start again, exhorting us to be more careful. The same story was repeated several times. After half an hour Pyotr Ilich was already in utter despair. It was evident he had from the start pulled out all his stops; there was now no hint of calm and method. Quite the contrary! At the very beginning of the rehearsal he was already completely rubicund, and sweat was shower-ing from his brow. His whole, small frame became yet more convulsed. It seemed he wanted, through the totality of his own energy, to inspire this huge sluggish mass of voices which he had to conduct . . . One has to admit that the separate choirs had been well rehearsed and sang well – but just ask them to sing this fugue of innumerable voices, and manage all the pauses, and especially at such a diabolical tempo! . . .

'Ah, gentlemen, you must look at me, please, not at your music,' cried

Pyotr Ilich. 'How can you begin if you aren't looking at the conductor!' He appealed to us in both Russian and German, and finally got us to sing at least half the fugue without stumbling. But whether it was that we were frightened of fudging something, or whether it was simply that many had become hoarse from the influenza that was going through the city, we sang only timidly and even quietly.

'But why are you so quiet, gentlemen! Here you must be *fortissimo*. Let's have your full force! You must deafen me, and I can barely hear you!' said Pyotr Ilich. He was particularly distressed by the altos, who made up a separate choir of spirits from hell in the last movement of *The Tower of Babel*. The demons here were thin on the ground, and they got lost in the general mass of voices.

Tormented by the refractory elements in the choirs, Pyotr Ilich finally lost his self-control. He screamed at us and struck out so mercilessly with his baton that it finally broke and one end flew off into one of the choirs; but all these thunderings were permeated with such exceptional good nature, such immeasurable Russian mildness that you could not get angry with the conductor, the more so since his situation was in reality very difficult . . .

The rehearsals with the orchestra and soloists were located in the Dvoryanskoye Assembly Hall. We were arranged on the stage like warriors before battle . . . Hardly had Pyotr Ilich mounted the rostrum than he called out quietly: 'Vasily!' An attendant appeared and began raising Pyotr Ilich above the crowd by turning on one side some sort of lifting screw. When Pyotr Ilich was high enough, he gave a sign to the orchestra – and the fun began. The choirs now showed themselves to be adequately drilled, and it was much easier to sing with the orchestra. But the orchestra, being used to playing without a choir, became confused, and we were slow in entering after the soloists. Now the basses weren't there, now the tenors were missing, now the drum spoiled everything.

'*Kann man so dummköpfig sein!*' cried Pyotr Ilich, turning to the Germans after losing all patience. 'That's where the tenors enter; we'll try repeating that phrase,' he said, turning to Mr Mikhailov. Mr Mikhailov sang a second time; again the chorus got it wrong.

'Now listen, gentlemen, I'll sing it to you,' said Pyotr Ilich, and began singing in a completely true but totally unmusical voice. He sang the whole recitative diligently, drawing out all the notes in hope of success. And so what? Once again the choir did not enter.

'What's the matter with you, gentlemen!' Pyotr Ilich exclaimed, disenchanted. 'I deliberately sang it all to you in my frightful voice, and again
you're late!'

And so on. Thus it was that Pyotr Ilich exhorted us when we blundered
– but afterwards he was quick to praise us when things went well.

'Please, gentlemen, can't you be a little quieter?' He turned to the
orchestra. 'As it is, we can't hear his beautiful voice.' This compliment
concerned the tenor Mikhailov.

In the end all went well. At the final rehearsal we sang well, at the
concert better still. But it was Pyotr Ilich who had taken such pains with
us. His gentle simplicity, his good-natured scolding, and the whole tone in
which he delivered both his reproofs and his encouragements won him the
heart of every huge choir in *The Tower of Babel*.

Anonymous; published in *NV* (1893), no. 6355, reprinted in *PVC4*, pp. 227–9.

# ISAAK MATKOVSKY
## (1862–1940)

Isaak Matkovsky had been a piano student at the Moscow Conservatoire. He had participated in the concert Tchaikovsky conducted in Tiflis on his final visit to that city in 1890.

Visiting the orchestral rehearsals before the concert, I was satisfied that
Tchaikovsky could be not only gentle and tactful, not only sweet and
affable, but also exacting and insistent. He did not rest content until he had
obtained from the orchestra the required nuances.

At the concert I could not recognize our opera orchestra. The opinion,
which at one time was quite widespread, that Tchaikovsky was a weak
conductor is profoundly mistaken. The concert passed off with unpre-
cedented success.

Isaak Matkovsky, 'Nezabïvayemoye' ['An unforgettable event']; published in *Ogonyok [Light]* (1940), no. 12, reprinted in *PVC4*, p. 403.

# MIKHAIL IPPOLITOV-IVANOV

Referring to the same concert as Matkovsky.

Pyotr Ilich had begun getting worked up a couple of days before the concert and [was agitated], especially on the day of the concert. We tried to divert him in every way; we took him off to the Botanical Gardens where he loved to walk, then showed him the giant in one of the booths, and in conclusion even went on one of the roundabouts, which greatly amused him, and then took him home before the concert and put him to bed. In the evening he was bright and cheerful, only complaining that he had totally forgotten his [First] Suite and could not remember how the introduction to the fugue began. But it was all his imagination; he conducted the fugue outstandingly from memory, not once glancing at his score.

Mikhail Ippolitov-Ivanov, *IRM*; reprinted in *PVC4*, p. 235.

# FREDERIC LAMOND

## (1868–1948)

Frederic Lamond was a Scottish pianist who studied with von Bülow and Liszt.

A notable experience was mine in connection with the Valse in the slow movement of the B flat minor Pianoforte Concerto. Tschaikowsky took it very quickly, but only as quickly as would allow the soloist to bring out the keyboard figuration distinctly and *pianissimo*: he made the strings play with half bows, the wood-wind extremely soft, but all without the slightest alteration of tempo – the effect was magical. Many a famous, even very famous conductor, takes this middle section at such a breathless tempo, that he has practically finished before he has begun: and some pianists make out of this tender, delicate fabric a German waltz, horrible to listen to! Both conceptions are absolutely wrong! I have listened to this work twice under the composer's direction, so I can bear witness.

Frederic Lamond, *The Memoirs of Frederic Lamond* (Glasgow, 1949), p. 94.

# WALTER DAMROSCH
## (1862–1950)

In 1891 Tchaikovsky travelled to the USA to conduct in concerts inaugurating the new Carnegie Hall.

He was not a conductor by profession and in consequence the technic of it, the rehearsals and concerts, fatigued him excessively; but he knew what he wanted and the atmosphere which emanated from him was so sympathetic and love-compelling that all executants strove with double eagerness to divine his intentions and to carry them out. The performance which he conducted of his Third Suite, for instance, was admirable, although it is in parts very difficult; and as he was virtually the first of great living composers to visit America, the public received him with jubilance . . .

Walter Damrosch, *My Musical Life* (New York, 1923), pp. 143–4.

# IPPOLIT PRYANISHNIKOV
## (1847–1921)

Ippolit Pryanishnikov created the part of Lionel in Tchaikovsky's *The Maid of Orleans* in 1880, and the name part in the St Petersburg production of *Mazepa* in 1884. In 1889 in Kiev he organized an opera company which was run as a co-operative. Tchaikovsky was greatly impressed both by this initiative and by its results, and when the company attempted a short season in Moscow in May 1892, he offered to appear as a conductor for them, directing Rubinstein's *The Demon* and Gounod's *Faust*, as well as his own *Eugene Onegin*.

In such well-known and already established operas as *The Demon* and *Faust* he managed to discover new and, in the highest degree, artistic shades. To comments on the novelty of these nuances he always replied: 'Perhaps it is accepted that they should be performed differently, but that's how I feel that phrase.'

Here it is pertinent to note a peculiarity – namely, that Pyotr Ilich directed all rehearsals and performances standing up, so that the conductor's platform had to be lowered for him, and he even asked that the stool should be removed completely. He explained this through the habit of directing concerts [standing up] – that when sitting on an orchestral chair he felt himself so attached to it that he positively lost every ability to be carried away and to give himself fully to his task.

I recall something which happened at one of our performances, and though it does not touch upon Pyotr Ilich's musical activities, it is interesting as demonstrating his calm and coolness in a moment of danger.

By way of explanation I must say that in the Shelaputina Theatre [in Moscow] the one and only tiny exit from the pit (and that under the stage) was built so inconveniently that, in the event of fire, by far the greatest danger threatened the orchestral players and the conductor, so that hardly any of them would be able to escape. As luck would have it, during one of the performances in which Tchaikovsky was participating, namely, in the third act of *Faust*, from somewhere in the totally packed auditorium there spread a slight smell of burning. At first the audience, though it was glancing round, sat quietly, but unfortunately two gentlemen in the front row quietly got up and headed for the exit, then others followed their example, and after this all the stalls became restless. Suddenly someone cried: 'Fire!' – and the whole audience jumped up and in panic made for the doors. While from the stage I was managing to calm everyone down, reporting that there was no fire, that it was not known whence was coming this quite chance smell of burning, and while the audience and the orchestra were settling themselves back into their seats, a good deal of time passed. And during all this panic Pyotr Ilich did not leave his place but, turning to face the audience with his arms crossed, calmly waited until all this commotion had finished and I had given him a signal that he could continue the performance.

Ippolit Pryanishnikov, Recollections; published in *RMG* (1918), no. 9, reprinted in *PVC4*, pp. 256–7.

# LEONID NIKOLAYEV

## (1878–1942)

Leonid Nikolayev was a pianist and composer who became a professor at the St Petersburg Conservatoire in 1909. He recalled

Tchaikovsky conducting in Kiev in January 1892 (Nikolayev was only 13).

When conducting Pyotr Ilich normally became agitated and confused. While conducting in Kiev, because of his agitation he sometimes stamped mechanically with his foot out of time with the beat, which somewhat confused the cellists sitting at his feet.

Leonid Nikolayev, Recollections; published in *PVC4*, pp. 263–4.

# ISAAK BUKINIK

## (1867–1942)

Isaak Bukinik was a violinist who founded a music school in Kharkov. In the concert Tchaikovsky conducted in Kharkov in March 1893 Bukinik was the deputy leader of the orchestra. Tchaikovsky was greeted at the railway station by a crowd of admirers.

I never saw such a brilliant reception. There were members of the Musical Society with the director, Ilya Slatin, at its head, there were also teachers and pupils from the music school, and among those who met him were music-loving students and other admirers of the great composer's talent. When the train drew up Slatin and the teacher, Konstantin Gorsky, entered the carriage and quickly returned to the platform with Pyotr Ilich. Those who had gathered greeted our exalted guest with loud applause. He was loaded with fresh flowers. Everyone tried to push forward to see him better, to shake his hand. But he was, it seems, embarrassed and agitated, shook the hand of the person standing in front of him, and slowly moved towards the exit, encircled by people.

Phaetons were waiting at the station. Pyotr Ilich, accompanied by Slatin and Gorsky, sat in a phaeton. The crowd surrounded the phaeton, again applauding, and for a long time would not let it move. Slatin had told me that they were going straight to the Hotel Europe and would come with Pyotr Ilich to the rehearsal in two hours, and he had asked me to tell the orchestra all to be in their places. The complement of the orchestra which would play in the forthcoming concert was unusual. Never before in

Kharkov had there been an orchestra of more than forty to forty-five persons. This time the orchestra was augmented to seventy. It was made up of players from the opera, teachers from the music school, of music-school graduates who had even been invited from other towns, and of the best pupils of the music school . . . Besides the orchestra there was also in the hall a choir of pupils from the music school.

At about one o'clock someone ran into the hall and cried:

'They're coming, they're coming – they've come!'

In an instant we had all sat down, each had taken his instrument, and the whole orchestra froze in expectation . . .

Pyotr Ilich and Slatin appeared in the doorway. Tchaikovsky was of medium height, completely grey, very elegant, dressed in a brown suit of French cut. While still in the doorway he bowed, and quickly moved towards the orchestra. Everyone stood up. The orchestra and choir met our precious guest with a musical greeting. They performed the 'Slava' from his opera *Mazepa*.

When the greeting was finished, Pyotr Ilich mounted the rostrum and turned to the orchestra:

'Allow me to introduce myself – Pyotr Ilich Tchaikovsky.'

The orchestra and choir again applauded loudly.

When it was quiet Pyotr Ilich gave me his hand and asked how many first violins there were. I replied sixteen. How many second violins? Twelve. How many violas? Eight. How many cellos? Eight. How many double basses? Six.

Having acquainted himself with the complement of the orchestra, it seemed Pyotr Ilich was well satisfied. He took hold of his baton, and said:

'So, let's rehearse.'

All the orchestra's attention was directed at the conductor. I recall how everyone was terribly struck by Pyotr Ilich's manner of conducting. He did not hold the baton as most conductors do; he held his baton not in his fingers but firmly in his fist. He raised it above his head, on the first beat brought it down sharply, on the second raised it to his left shoulder, on the third to his right shoulder, and on the fourth again raised it. The players were not accustomed to such a way of conducting. Everyone glanced around, but the sense that the composer himself was conducting the piece we were going to play made us quickly forget this initial awkwardness, and we tried to play our best – and by the end of the rehearsal we were already accustomed to Pyotr Ilich's idiosyncratic way of conducting.

We were rehearsing Tchaikovsky's Second Symphony. The players became so carried away that they did not notice how Pyotr Ilich was all the time listening attentively and observing each performer, and that all the time his face never lost its smile of satisfaction. I recall that while the first horn was playing the main theme Pyotr Ilich directed special attention to the player. He played his part with such inspiration that Pyotr Ilich positively beamed and nodded his head to him in thanks. During the first break Pyotr Ilich went up to the first horn, held out his hand to him, and expressed delight at his playing. They began a friendly conversation . . .

After the break we rehearsed the orchestral fantasia *The Tempest* (after Shakespeare). The rehearsal lasted more than three hours. When the rehearsal was over Pyotr Ilich thanked the orchestra, and all were enchanted by the great composer's charming manner . . .

The long-awaited concert took place on 26 March 1893 at two o'clock in the Hall of the Nobility. It was a true festival. The hall and the platform were adorned with fresh flowers and tropical vegetation. There was nowhere to pass on the platform; it was with great difficulty that they accommodated an orchestra twice the usual size and the choir from the opera house. We were so excited by the forthcoming concert that it was a long time before we could get settled, get ready, compose ourselves appropriately. I awaited the beginning of the concert with inner trembling. It began in an unusual way, with unusual ceremony. In tails and white tie Pyotr Ilich came onto the platform unnoticed, modestly, and began stealing towards his place. The audience spotted him before the orchestra. They applauded, cried, 'Hurrah! Bravo! Greetings to the great composer! Greetings to our guest!' and everyone applauded and applauded. The orchestra (standing) and the choir performed the 'Slava' from the first [in fact, last] act of *Mazepa*.

The audience's greeting did not stop after the 'Slava', and the whole hall and the platform turned towards Pyotr Ilich, who stood near the rostrum, a little pale, leaning on a chair, and looking straight in front of him. He bowed several times, and this drew an even greater greeting. Finally he mounted his rostrum, the hall fell silent, we prepared to begin playing. But it appeared that the beginning of the concert was still a long way off. Suddenly there mounted the platform Velichenko, a member of the Musical Society, and delivered an address to Pyotr Ilich in the name of the directorate of the Musical Society. The audience, orchestra and choir stood up to listen to this address . . .

When Pyotr Ilich had received the address, the audience again applauded frenziedly. And when Velichenko left the platform, his place was taken by another member of the Musical Society, who presented Pyotr Ilich with a wreath from the members of the Musical Society. Then he was given a silver wreath from admirers, a silver wreath from the opera company, a wreath from the newspaper, *Yuzhnïy Kray [The Southern Region]*, a wreath from the teaching staff at the musical school; from the pupils of the music school there were marvellous flowers. All the while the audience applauded noisily; it seemed there would be no end to this stream of greetings and ovations.

These greetings and ovations continued right through the concert, and reached their strongest at the end of the overture, *1812*. This overture had been well performed at the final rehearsal, and was still better performed at the concert itself. The performers were totally at one with the conductor.

I remember that this universal enthusiasm actually resulted in an extraordinary occurrence. The concert was already long over; Pyotr Ilich had already left the rostrum, was taking his bows, but somewhere in the distance bells were still being struck. The audience was already streaming towards the stage. All were in a happy, excited state. But the bells continued to ring out with all their strength. Pyotr Ilich several times winced and said:

'Why doesn't that sound of bells stop? Are they getting ready to bury me?'

And because I was sitting at the nearest desk, Pyotr Ilich turned to me: 'Can't someone tell whoever is responsible to stop that noise? It distresses me.'

I ran to the place where the bells had been set up. It seems that, to play the bells, Slatin had assigned one of the pupils from the singing class in the music school, a very tall, healthy fellow, and a great lover of music. He was several rooms distant from the orchestra. Because of the noise from the ovation he had not heard that the orchestra had stopped playing and that the concert was already over, and he was continuing to strike even when I arrived. When the sound of the bells was stopped and the ovations continued, Pyotr Ilich became himself again, was caught by the general mood, bowed in all directions, signalled to the orchestra that they also should stand to acknowledge the applause . . . But some of the young people in the audience and pupils from the music school ran to the platform, sat Pyotr Ilich in an armchair, and carried him right across the hall, accompanied by greetings and applause. The members of the Musical Society, with Slatin at their head, installed Pyotr Ilich in his phaeton, and bore him off in his tie and tails to be photographed.

Isaak Bukinik, Recollections; published in *PVC4*, pp. 291–3, 296–8.

# VIII

## Three composers

On 31 December 1887 Tchaikovsky arrived in Leipzig for his first ever appearance as a conductor outside Russia. On New Year's Day following, quite unexpectedly, there occurred an historic meeting.

# Mrs A. BRODSKY

## (?-?)

Mrs Brodsky was the wife of the violinist Adolf Brodsky (1851–1929), who in 1881 had given the first performance of Tchaikovsky's Violin Concerto. From 1880 Brodsky was senior professor of violin at the Leipzig Conservatoire. In 1895 he settled in Manchester where he became senior violin professor at the Royal Manchester College of Music.

In the winter of 1887 the Gewandhaus Committee [in Leipzig] invited Tschaikovsky to conduct some of his own compositions, and as he had received similar invitations from other towns in Germany, he decided to accept them and so, for the first time, came abroad to conduct his own works. He arrived in Leipzig on Christmas Eve:* it was a cold frosty evening, and the snow lay thick on the ground. My husband went to the station to meet Tschaikovsky, and my sister Olga and her little son who were our guests at that time helped me prepare our Christmas tree. We wished it to be quite ready before Tschaikovsky arrived, and to look as bright as possible as a welcome to him. As we were lighting the candles we heard the sound of a sledge, and soon afterwards Tschaikovsky entered the room followed by Ziloti and my husband.

I had never seen him before. Either the sight of the Christmas tree or our Russian welcome pleased him greatly, for his face was illuminated by a delightful smile, and he greeted us as if he had known us for years. There was nothing striking or artistic in his appearance, but everything about him – the expression in his blue eyes, his voice, especially his smile – spoke of great kindliness of nature. I never knew a man who brought with him such a warm atmosphere as Tschaikovsky. He had not been an hour in our house before we quite forgot that he was a great composer. We spoke to him of very intimate matters without any reserve, and felt that he enjoyed our confidence.

The supper passed in animated conversation, and, notwithstanding the

*Mrs Brodsky is writing of the Russian Orthodox Christmas Eve (i.e. 5 January 1888). In fact Tchaikovsky had arrived in Leipzig earlier, on the last day of 1887, and his first meeting with the Brodskys had taken place that evening.

fatigues of his journey, Tschaikovsky remained very late before returning to his hotel. He promised to come to us whenever he felt inclined, and kept his word.

Among his many visits one remains especially memorable. It was on New Year's Day. We invited Tschaikovsky to dinner, but, knowing his shyness with strangers, did not tell him there would be other guests. Brahms was having a rehearsal of his [C minor] trio in our house that morning with Klengel and A[dolf] B[rodsky] – a concert being fixed for the next day. Brahms was staying after the rehearsal for early dinner. In the midst of the rehearsal I heard a ring at the bell, and expecting it would be Tschaikovsky, rushed to open the door. He was quite perplexed by the sound of music, asked who was there, and what they were playing. I took him into the room adjoining and tried to break, gently, the news of Brahms' presence. As we spoke there was a pause in the music; I begged him to enter, but he felt too nervous, so I opened the door and softly called my husband. He took Tschaikovsky with him and I followed.

Tschaikovsky and Brahms had never met before. It would be difficult to find two men more unlike. Tschaikovsky . . . had something elegant and refined in his whole bearing and the greatest courtesy of manner. Brahms with his short, rather square figure and powerful head, was an image of strength and energy; he was an avowed foe to all so-called 'good manners'. His expression was often slightly sarcastic. When A.B. introduced them, Tschaikovsky said, in his soft melodious voice: 'Do I not disturb you?'

'Not in the least,' was Brahms' reply, with his peculiar hoarseness. 'But why are you going to hear this? It is not at all interesting.'

Tschaikovsky sat down and listened attentively. The personality of Brahms, as he later told us, impressed him very favourably, but he was not pleased with the music. When the trio was over I noticed that Tschaikovsky seemed uneasy. It would have been natural that he should say something, but he was not at all the man to pay unmeaning compliments. The situation might have become difficult, but at that moment the door was flung open, and in came our dear friends – Grieg and his wife, bringing, as they always did, a kind of sunshine with them. They knew Brahms, but had never met Tschaikovsky before. The latter loved Grieg's music, and was instantly attracted by these two charming people, full as they were of liveliness, enthusiasm and unconventionality, and yet with a simplicity about them that made everyone feel at home. Tschaikovsky with his sensitive nervous nature understood them at once. After the introductions and greetings were over we passed to the dining room. Nina Grieg was seated between Brahms and Tschaikovsky, but we had only been a few moments at the table when she started from her seat exclaiming: 'I cannot sit between these two. It makes me feel so nervous.'

Grieg sprang up, saying, 'But I have the courage,' and exchanged places with her. So the three composers sat together, all in good spirits. I can see Brahms now taking hold of a dish of strawberry jam, and saying he would have it all for himself and no one else should get any. It was more like a children's party than a gathering of great composers. My husband had this feeling so strongly that, when dinner was over and our guests still remained around the table smoking cigars and drinking coffee, he brought a conjuror's chest – a Christmas present to my little nephew – and began to perform tricks. All our guests were amused, and Brahms especially, who demanded from A.B. the explanation of each trick as soon as it was performed . . .

We were sorry when our guests had to go. Tschaikovsky remained till the last. As we accompanied him part of the way home A.B. asked how he liked Brahms' trio.

'Don't be angry with me, my dear friend,' was Tschaikovsky's reply, 'but I did not like it.'

A.B. was disappointed, for he had cherished a hope that a performance of the trio in which Brahms himself took part might have had a very different effect and have opened Tschaikovsky's eyes to the excellence of Brahms' music as a whole. Tschaikovsky had had very few opportunities of hearing it, and that was perhaps one reason why it affected him so little.

During Tschaikovsky's frequent visits to Leipzig we saw him in every possible mood, in all his ups and downs, and always loved him more as we knew him better.

Being of an exceedingly nervous temperament, he passed from one mood to another very rapidly. One night I remember well. It was the evening before his debut in Leipzig. A.B. was absent, playing at Cologne. My sister Olga and I had finished our supper some time before when Tschaikovsky suddenly called on us, apologizing for being so late. We were struck by the sadness of his expression and thought he must have heard some bad news. We gave him a warm welcome without asking any questions, and did our utmost to cheer him. We soon succeeded, and he told us it was the thought of tomorrow's concert which had depressed him so greatly, and that, if he could, he would have been glad to give up all his engagements and return to Russia immediately.

Such excitements were often more than he could bear; they brought on moods of terrible depression in which he seemed to see death in the form of an old woman standing behind his chair and waiting for him. Tschaikovsky often spoke of death and still more often thought of it.

He was greatly attached to life and loved many things passionately: people he knew, natural beauty, and works of art. He had no firm belief in a future life and could never be reconciled to the thought of parting with all that was beautiful and dear to him . . .

Sometimes Tschaikovsky would send us a telegram from Berlin, or any other town where he happened to be, to this effect: 'I am coming to see you. Please keep it secret.' We knew well what this meant: that he was tired and homesick and in need of friends. Once after such a telegram Tschaikovsky just arrived in time for dinner; at first we had him quite to ourselves, but after dinner, as he was sitting in the music room with his head leaning on his hand as was his custom, the members of the Brodsky Quartet quietly entered the room bringing their instruments with them as had been previously arranged. They sat down in silence and played Tschaikovsky's own String Quartet no. 3, which they had just carefully prepared for a concert. Great was Tschaikovsky's delight! I saw the tears roll down his cheek as he listened, and then, passing from one performer to the other, he expressed again and again his gratitude for the happy hour they had given him. Then turning to Brodsky he said in his naïve way: 'I did not know I had composed such a fine quartet. I never liked the finale, but now I see it is really good.'

This time he did not reproach us for having disobeyed his wish about the incognito.

He was very fond of meeting the Griegs at our house and, knowing this, we arranged it as often as possible. The dinners were usually followed by music. Madame Grieg would sing her husband's beautiful songs and he himself would accompany her at the piano. She always put great enthusiasm in her singing and stirred us deeply. It was a treat to hear her, and Tschaikovsky never failed to express his delight.

The composers soon became intimate friends and, as a token of his great esteem, Tschaikovsky dedicated to Grieg his [fantasy-] overture to *Hamlet*, a tribute which the latter highly esteemed.

Mrs A. Brodsky, *Recollections of a Russian Home* (Manchester and London, 1904), pp. 153–67.

# IX

## Tchaikovsky – and others: both general and personal

Few composers have built up a warmer relationship with society at large than did Tchaikovsky. The affection in which he was held was as great among professional musicians as among the general public. And though it was clearly the appealing qualities within his music that prepared the way, it was only after 1887, when he began his conducting career by directing the first performances of his opera *Cherevichki*, that the open adulation began. After this it became increasingly impossible for him to appear at performances of his music in Russia without the audience responding ecstatically to his presence. Though his wish to expand the opportunities for more people to hear orchestral music excited hostility in some established musical circles, it also won him deep affection from those who benefited from his initiatives. And with professional musicians, too, it was his personal concern and kindness as much as his musical endowment that won their hearts.

# VIKTOR CHECHOTT

## (1846–1917)

Viktor Chechott was a Russian critic, composer and pianist. On 16 September 1889, in Kiev, Tchaikovsky slipped into a performance of his own opera *Eugene Onegin* which Chechott was attending.

The eminent composer managed to remain incognito only until the end of the opera's fourth scene. Little by little the news had spread through the audience that the composer was sitting in one of the right-hand lower boxes. The portion of the audience who were in a position to see him turned towards where he was, and this gave the signal for an ovation which quickly rose to enormous proportions. For a long while Mr Tchaikovsky bowed from his box; in consequence of the growing cries of 'Come on to the stage!' he set off thither. The applause continued during all the time he was making his way round the theatre. At last the curtain rose and the composer appeared at the footlights surrounded by the soloists and acknowledging the applause which rang out with redoubled strength. The orchestra played a fanfare. More than once attempts to lower the curtain led only to fresh bursts of applause and cries of 'Composer!' so that the stage remained open for a long while. And when at last they managed to lower the curtain, they had to raise it again immediately at the demand of an audience who wanted yet again to see the artist to whom they were indebted for so many unclouded moments of aesthetic pleasure. The sincere and hearty ovation of the evening I have described will doubtless long remain in the memory of all who participated in it. It came straight from the heart of admirers of our famed compatriot's great talent; in it there was no shadow of an official or formal character.

Viktor Chechott, 'Chaykovsky v Kiyeve' ['Tchaikovsky in Kiev'], in *Kiyevlyanin [The Kievian]*, 6/18 September 1889; reprinted in *PVC4*, p. 412.

# EMILIYA PAVLOVSKAYA

## (1853–1935)

Emiliya Pavlovskaya was the soprano who created the parts of Mariya and Kuma in Tchaikovsky's operas *Mazepa* and *The Enchantress* respectively. She was impressed by the efforts of Tchaikovsky and the Moscow RMS to broaden their audience by repeating a formal concert the following morning at prices within the reach of all. This had happened with an all-Tchaikovsky programme conducted by the composer himself in November 1887. It seems probable that this reminiscence was written down during the Soviet period.

The hall was filled to overflowing, the audience (for the most part ordinary office-workers, factory-hands and working-men) greeted Pyotr Ilich excitedly, and despite the malicious croaking [of the critics] that (so they said) such a crowd had not achieved an understanding of serious music, that one ought not thus to mock the 'real' audience which (so they say) will not be able to attend together with 'the crowd', that the concert was foredoomed to failure by this and similar ridiculous predictions, the concert went off so successfully that it [the experiment] was actually very soon repeated, despite the whole stream of aspersions and insinuations which rained down in abundance on the heads of Tchaikovsky and the main promoter of the concert, Taneyev. Pyotr Ilich himself told me that the success of these concerts especially gladdened him not only for himself personally, but for its discrediting of the malicious critics, who were totally ignorant of the mood and taste of the people and did not understand that art would always find its true route to the people's heart and spirit.

Emiliya Pavlovskaya, Recollections; published in *PVC4*, p. 149.

# PYOTR RYAZANTSEV

## (1881–?)

Pyotr Ryazantsev was a trumpet player who later worked within the Moscow Conservatoire. As a 12-year-old he played in the concert Tchaikovsky conducted in Kharkov in March 1893.

Pyotr Ilich knew how to identify himself with the world of the players with the utmost speed; he not only got to know us, but interested himself in our life, our way of existence. Could I possibly pass over the following incident, so extremely characteristic of Pyotr Ilich? The clarinettist Feofan Panchenko, whom Tchaikovsky had known earlier, could not take part in the concert because he was seriously ill in hospital. Pyotr Ilich noticed that Feofan Panchenko was not in the orchestra. Having discovered that Panchenko was ill and in the Alexandrovskaya Hospital, Pyotr Ilich found time to pay a personal visit to the sick man; moreover, he personally helped in a material way this needy musician.

Pyotr Ryazantsev, Recollections (1944); published in *PVC4*, p. 416.

# FREDERIC LAMOND

To this great personality and perfect gentleman, Tschaikowsky, I owe my first engagements in Russia. I wrote to him, in my youthful enthusiasm, after a meeting in Frankfurt, that his three piano forte concertos: *viz* the B flat minor, the G major (in the old unabbreviated edition) and the *Fantaisie de Concert*, had become a part of myself, for I knew these works to the smallest dot and loved them ever more and more. I thought no further of this letter. About six weeks later, the postman came to my lodgings. 'Here is a letter from Moscow.' I tore the cover with trembling hand – 'Herr Gott, a letter from Tschaikowsky!' It was written in French. 'Dear Fellow Artist, I understand with joy from your letter that you play my pianoforte concertos. Perhaps an opportunity may be found to play here in Moscow, and I have spoken warmly about it to Monsieur Safonov [principal conductor of the Moscow Branch of the RMS]: tout à vous, Tschaikowsky.'

Months passed, and I learned to my infinite sorrow of his death in St Petersburg. One Sunday there came a telegram from the head of the Wolff Bureau in Berlin – 'Can you play in Moscow on October 10th, Tschaikowsky's B flat minor Concerto stipulated. If in the affirmative, arrange passport immediately.' In those happy, oh so happy days, no passport was necessary in Europe, except in Russia. An engagement was arranged at the last moment in Warsaw – with excellent results. I journeyed on to Moscow, as in a dream, seeing the gloomy, endless Steppes: all enveloped in snow. Under the auspices of the Imperial Russian [Musical] Society and with Safonov conducting, I had a sensational success, and at the supper which followed the concert, Professor Gaymaly [presumably the violinist, Jan Hřímalý] said: 'Do you know whom to thank for this wonderful result? No one else than Tschaikowsky. At one of the last meetings of the Imperial Symphony Society that he attended, he insisted that we should engage you. All concerts were arranged while he was still living . . .'

Yet another example of the unusual goodness of Tschaikowsky. It was in those days the custom to present a 'cachet' of 300 roubles to artists who appeared for the first time at the Symphony Concerts. Tschaikowsky, who was by no means rich himself, would say to the treasurer – 'Monsieur or Madame X has had travelling expenses': would take one hundred roubles out of his wallet (in those days approximately twelve pounds in English currency), add them to the 300, fasten the envelope, and the treasurer would hand it to the soloist. It is to be noted that those were artists whom Tschaikowsky did not know, and in whom he had not the slightest interest.

Tschaikowsky had the exquisite manners of the aristocrat of former times. But he was more than an aristocrat. He was, to wit, a nobleman of the spirit: one of God's chosen, and his memory will for me remain unforgettable.

Frederic Lamond, *The Memoirs of Frederic Lamond* (Glasgow, 1949), pp. 95–8.


# IVAN LIPAYEV

## (1865–1942)

Ivan Liypayev was a horn player who founded a mutual aid society for orchestral players. From 1912 he taught at the Saratov Conservatoire. Initially he is recalling Colonne's morning rehearsal of Tchaikovsky's symphonic fantasia *The Tempest* in Moscow in February 1891.


Alongside me I heard furtive footsteps – and a man, dressed extremely simply but tastefully, was leaning against a marble column. It was Tchaikovsky, *The Tempest*'s creator himself. Probably by habit he ran his right hand through his silver hair and, with a passing glance in my direction, headed purposefully towards the orchestra. This proved inopportune. One by one the players stopped, began whispering, and did not listen to the conductor, who was impatiently tapping his desk with his baton. But suddenly everything became animated, and a deafening fanfare of wind and strings rang through the hall. It seemed that those massive, solid columns would not survive the wild, tempestuous outburst of sound, that the ceiling was trembling and all would perish as concertedly as the players played their welcome to Pyotr Ilich Tchaikovsky. In embarrassment he began bowing from a distance, but on hearing this insistent, fervent welcome, he shyly directed himself towards the stage. From the hearty way he pressed the players' hands, the way he smiled affectionately at them, and by the way in which their faces lit up at the sight of Tchaikovsky, you could say with certainty that the relationship of this artist-creator with his performers was most warm and sincere.

Until that day I had not been closely acquainted with the great musician. True, on meeting we had bowed, shaken hands, exchanged some general and brief phrases; however, all this had had the character of no more than a casual, nodding acquaintance. But then in the spring of 1892 there arrived in Moscow Pryanishnikov's Opera Association [from Kiev]. Tchaikovsky strongly sympathized with this Association which had come with the intention of mounting Russian operas. He demonstrated this by agreeing readily and without remuneration to conduct three operas: his own *Eugene Onegin*, Rubinstein's *The Demon* and Gounod's *Faust*. At that time I was in the Association's orchestra. It was from this that, strictly, my acquaintance with Tchaikovsky began. Once, during a performance of Borodin's *Prince Igor*, Mr Pribique, the permanent conductor of the Association, came up to me, took my arm, and led me to the theatre office. Tchaikovsky stood in the middle of the room and, while talking with Valentina Serova [widow of the composer, Alexander Serov], was drawing hard on a cigarette. On our appearance Serova went off to the next room. Tchaikovsky looked at me with surprise, then at Mr Pribique, and, laughing, said:

'Iosif Vyacheslavovich! But I've been a long time acquainted with him, a long time . . .'

After this Mr Pribique left and I remained face to face with Tchaikovsky. He hastily finished his cigarette, took out another, and offered one to me.

'I have business with you, and very important,' he said. 'There's no time now, and this isn't a suitable place to talk. Be so good as to drop in on me – only, in the morning at eight or earlier; I shall already be up.'

Several days passed and I did not manage to get to Pyotr Ilich because

*Eugene Onegin* was in rehearsal, and its composer was pretty tired. At one rehearsal Tchaikovsky came up to me in a very agitated state. It turned out that the cause of this was the breaks for the most ordinary of reasons which had extended the rehearsal to a late hour.

'Is it really always like this?' he asked me anxiously.

'They know your opera well,' I replied, 'and the company's discipline is exemplary — and it could be worse.'

'Yes, but how can an orchestra sit all the time and learn their parts with the singers?!' he observed.

It is pertinent to say that Tchaikovsky, because of his nervousness, did not like to remain sitting in one place. He stood not only during rehearsal but also during the performance when he was conducting, and in his apartment either paced from corner to corner, or else tried as often as he could to alter the position of his body on his chair.

While conducting an opera — and not only his own but one by another composer — he became extremely worked up. The slightest slip on stage or in the orchestra affected him painfully. On such occasions Tchaikovsky's face now turned white, now became covered with red blotches; the stick trembled in his hand, his eyes shot in all directions, and he often resorted to a glass of water.

At the end of *Eugene Onegin* Pyotr Ilich put his baton down on his conducting desk and, paying no attention to the calls and applause, quite distinctly declared:

'What agony!'

We met at the orchestra's exit door into the stage, and I simply did not recognize him. He seemed terribly exhausted, white, weary. His handkerchief, soaked with perspiration, trembled in his hand, and his whole body seemed literally feverish.

'When will you come?' he asked, turning to me.

I went the very next day. At that time Pyotr Ilich was occupying two rooms in the Moscow Grand Hotel, opposite the Duma building. It was still only half-past seven. A sleepy servant was only just wandering along the corridors. Nevertheless Tchaikovsky, wrapped in a dressing gown, was already sitting drinking tea. The room was smoke-filled. The morning papers lay on the divan, and on the table were the latest issues of fat journals.

Pyotr Ilich met me with uncommon attentiveness and courtesy. He poured me a glass of tea, and was beginning to talk about something when a lackey entered the room and gave him a telegram from which he learned that he had been elected an honorary member of the Odessa Society of Musical Workers.

That morning we did not manage to talk about the matter for which Tchaikovsky had summoned me. While he was speaking about the Odessa Society someone knocked at the door and a general [of the civil service] entered the room. Behind him came the director of one of the provincial opera houses, then the designer and the conductor. Pyotr Ilich talked with each for a very long time, and his conversation revealed great erudition. There was no branch of art with which he was not acquainted at least partially, if not entirely. He only avoided responding to questions about music and about its agents, even though some [of his visitors] both provoked and pressed him to do so.

More than a month passed before we succeeded in talking about our business. At this time I was witness of several characteristic features of the composer. He commanded an outstanding memory and did not forget the numerous requests made of him. On returning from his artistic travels Pyotr Ilich would immediately fly off to the Conservatoire or to people who had some connection with it. In the most touching, most heartfelt manner he described the lot of 'a young, talented person' who was wasting away in the provinces and who had been recommended to him.

'What a pity that we have only two conservatoires,' he said, 'while there are so many wanting to learn that have to be refused. It is possible that out of them might come good musicians.' . . .

In general Tchaikovsky was very attentive, sympathetically concerning himself with young artistic people. He inspired them with his attentions, invigorated them, and directed them along their art's thorny path. On two occasions while I was present he received through the post manuscripts from composers asking him to look through, or to pronounce upon, a piece. He did not begrudge the time – time which was often very dear to him – given to correcting a manuscript, if only so as not to delay returning it. On one occasion I found him looking over pages of music. He was marking them with his blue pencil, humming the melody quietly and evaluating it aloud.

Tchaikovsky also paid extreme attention to orchestral players. He frequently asserted:

'They work so hard and receive very little reward. It's not fair. Look at singers: they gain big money which is not always deserved. Is it really impossible to do something about this?'

Tchaikovsky willingly became a member of musicians' benevolent societies, and persuaded others to join these institutions, explaining the sound principle of solidarity. In a word, he tried, at least in something, to show his sympathy with orchestral players.

I was witness to such a scene. For some reason one morning the leading violin of a private orchestra came to Pyotr Ilich. He asked Pyotr Ilich to write a testimonial of his performing accomplishments. The latter readily sat down at the table, and said several times:

'Very happy to do so!'

Tchaikovsky had not managed to finish his testimonial when a second player came in with the very same request. Again Tchaikovsky wrote. After him came a third, then a fourth.

'Are you the last?' Tchaikovsky suddenly asked.

'N-no . . . There are still . . .'

The door was slightly open, and in the corridor, indeed, some eight or nine men were waiting their turn. Pyotr Ilich could not contain himself, and good-naturedly burst out laughing.

'All right, gentlemen,' he said. 'I'll have them ready tomorrow.'

At this he noted down each name, surname, and the speciality of the players who had performed under his direction, asking all of them to come for their 'certification' the following day.

But then, at last, after several months had already passed, we managed to talk about our business.

'You published an article on the life of musicians,' he said, for a long while reflecting, and stroking his brow. 'I confess I read it avidly. I have long been interested in the life of these industrious people. The progress of music depends upon their well-being. An orchestra is an instrument of a particular kind. For a good instrument we begrudge neither means, nor care, nor attention; we do the same for the dead wood and metal from which it is made. How then can we not treat sympathetically the living instrument – the orchestra? Do you agree?'

'Of course.'

'Perhaps my comparison is not all that good, but that's not the point. In your article you lament that there are few benevolent societies for musicians. That's true. A society is the guarantee of the best life for each man, and for the artist in particular. Have you not tried to pass beyond theory and put your ideas into practice?'

I replied that I had not. There followed a long silence. Pyotr Ilich again reflected, and then asked:

'You would like to devote yourself to this cause?'

I replied affirmatively, but also pointed out the many factors obstructing the fulfilment of such a dream.

'Ah, what are the factors!' he retorted impatiently. 'You need money, connections. I am ready for anything.'

And again he fell silent. In these moments I simply did not recognize Tchaikovsky. [Before] more or less calm, now he seemed to me extremely agitated.

'We'll take it it's absolutely essential some time to do this,' he continued. 'I myself haven't the time, already I have too many preoccupations.'

These were his last words and, in essence, our conversation concluded with this. I began assembling materials for drawing up the regulations of a Mutual Aid Society for Orchestral Players, drawing these [materials] from whatever source I could. Reading them over to Tchaikovsky, I hoped through this to fix his attention on a public institution of some sort. But this did not satisfy him.

In the spring of 1892 he went abroad. As guidance he promised to send me some regulations of German societies [*Vereins*]. I waited a long time: however, no package arrived. Meanwhile I had to be in St Petersburg where I was playing in the symphony orchestra at the 'Aquarium'. At that time the orchestra was conducted by Kajanus and Engel. At an evening devoted entirely to works by Russian composers, Mr Engel included the suite from Tchaikovsky's ballet *The Nutcracker*. In St Petersburg at least it was being performed for the first [in fact, second] time. And what was my surprise when in the hall I saw Tchaikovsky, who had come specially to hear his piece. In the interval I rushed into the hall, but encountered the composer at the door.

'Bah!' he exclaimed. 'How glad I am . . .'

We went out into the garden and withdrew unnoticed into one of its remote alleys.

'Please don't blame me. I tried to find regulations, but nothing came of this. I think it will have to be postponed until the autumn.'

I tried to calm him as best I could, and said that I had gone on to devise regulations for myself without borrowing from others. While we were managing to exchange a few words on this, the bell rang. I hurried back to the orchestra, and we parted.

Tchaikovsky forced his way through a thick wall of bystanders and stood in a corner – but Rimsky-Korsakov came up to him and carried him off to the stalls. *The Nutcracker* so delighted the audience that the orchestra had to repeat nearly every number of the suite. When it was over Tchaikovsky quickly rose and headed for the exit. But his way was barred and he was not allowed to reach the door. Someone called out: 'Composer!'

'Composer! Composer! Come on to the stage!' cried hundreds of voices.

Four people grabbed Tchaikovsky by the arms and literally dragged him onto the stage. Dumbfounded, confused, he began bowing, and an unimaginable din and clamour rose in the hall, especially when the orchestra played a fanfare. The ladies tore flowers from their buttonholes and threw them at Tchaikovsky. When the ovation had subsided a little, Pyotr Ilich, all dripping with perspiration and breathing heavily, came to our artists' room. He thanked the players for their good performance and, going round each in turn, exchanged kisses with everyone.

After this we again went into the garden. Even here the audience began applauding him. Completely overcome by this, Tchaikovsky rushed headlong for the doors of the main exit, jumped into a cab, and disappeared.

Two days later I was walking along the Nevsky Prospect. Someone called my surname. I turned and saw Pyotr Ilich. He was preparing to go abroad again, and promised without fail to bring back some regulations. After this I learned of Tchaikovsky only from the newspapers, and by the autumn of that year all news of him ceased.

It was only in the autumn of 1893 that I again met Tchaikovsky in Moscow. The first words with which he greeted me were:

'Ah, those regulations . . . Just imagine . . .'

'But they would now be superfluous. I have brought a prepared copy of the regulations for the intended institution.'

At this Pyotr Ilich was indescribably happy.

'Pour out some tea, and I . . .'

At this he grabbed the package from me and with a beaming face immersed himself in reading. At first he read quietly and calmly, but then began fidgeting, leaped up from his chair, went to the writing table, and began rapidly writing with a pencil. Now he was inserting question marks, now exclamation marks. I stood behind him and followed his annotations.

'Why can't fifty-year-olds join the institution?' he asked. 'That's not just. Why advantages, privileges? All must be equal.'

And fitfully Tchaikovsky underlined what seemed to him to be wrong. My God! After about an hour the whole list of regulations was besmirched with pencil marks. That the kindness and humanity of this being knew no bounds was evident from all his annotations.

'Pyotr Ilich,' I said. 'What will you leave of these regulations!'

'All right! . . . A lawyer must be consulted. There are many questions here for his specialist knowledge.'

Then he took his glass of tea, and reflected.

'What a complex matter this is,' he muttered. Pyotr Ilich thought about who should be invited to become founder members, and put forward several names. When I was about to go, he took his visiting card, quickly wrote on it several lines, and added:

'Give this card to my friend, the attorney [L. V.] Sh[adursky]. He will look over the regulations.'

It was now well into the autumn. The rain was freezing, the wind roared, there was slush about. Unusually, I had come to Tchaikovsky at six in the evening, but I found him at home. He was very pleased to see me, and most of all because, it appeared, I had brought into his solitariness a certain measure of variety. Something had dispirited him. Our conversation never got going. As he saw me out Pyotr Ilich said with a certain forced liveliness:

'Perhaps we shan't see each other . . . I am going to St Petersburg for a while. However, I shall return in a month. When you've finished with the regulations, send them to me. I'll give time to them. Write care of the head of the directorate of the state theatres, or of Mr Jurgenson.'

We said goodbye. At the first symphony concert Mr Safonov received a telegram. Pyotr Ilich was ill! This news spread with amazing speed not only among the musicians but even among the audience at the concert. From time to time Safonov enquired about Tchaikovsky's condition. Two days later I was at the Conservatoire. There I learned that Tchaikovsky had cholera! The frightful news was soon confirmed by telegrams from St Petersburg. Among the orchestral players depression was evident, which quickly turned to despair. Tchaikovsky had gone . . . The first theatre I went to with the sad news was the Shelaputina. I was forewarned: they were already celebrating a requiem there. I saw the first tears on the faces of the orchestral players . . .

Ivan Lipayev, Recollections; published in *RS*, September 1896, and *RMG*, (1896), no. 11, reprinted in *PVC4*, pp. 270–7.

# X
## Tastes, traits and idiosyncrasies

## NIKOLAY KASHKIN

Because Pyotr Ilich devoted himself to serious musical studies comparatively late, he was far from having totally clear opinions about music, as is
the case with people who have lived in a musical environment from their
childhood and who, in life itself, have been in close contact with certain
tendencies and sympathies as regards art. He had to acquire these tendencies and sympathies through conscious labour and, mainly of course,
through the study of the literature of music. As far as I can remember, at
that time (i.e. around 1870) he did not read orchestral scores with special
facility, and preferred to acquaint himself with symphonic literature
through piano duet transcriptions . . . At that time he knew little chamber
music, in particular string quartets, and he came to terms with that kind of
music with difficulty – even the very sound of the string quartet he found
at times tedious, and he could hardly bear the last quartets of Beethoven.
Apropos of which, he once confessed to me that he almost fell off his chair
from the drowsiness that overcame him from the great A minor Quartet of
Beethoven. As far as the combination of piano with stringed instruments
was concerned, he said that while admiring many compositions of this sort,
especially by Beethoven, he could not imagine himself ever wishing to
compose something for such a combination of instruments – though, as is
known, he himself later composed, in memory of Nikolay Rubinstein, a
piano trio that is colossal both in content and execution.

Nikolay Kashkin, *KVC*, p. 75.

## ALINA BRYULLOVA

> The period of which Bryullova is writing cannot be earlier than
> the late 1870s.

He [Tchaikovsky] liked very much to play piano duets. For instance, one
summer when he was staying with us at our dacha I played through with
him all Beethoven's quartets . . . In St Petersburg we had two grand
pianos, and when he came to dine alone, not to a formal dinner party, he

would immediately propose we should play piano, eight hands – he with his brother [Modest], and I with my husband. And always he began with [Beethoven's] overture *Leonora* no. 3 which, as regards drama, he placed the highest of all. 'My flesh creeps every time the sound of the trumpet rings out in the distance,' he said. 'I think such a stupendous effect is to be found nowhere else.' But while he bowed before the genius of Beethoven, he directed all his love towards Mozart.

Alina Bryullova, Recollections (1929); published in *PVC4*, pp. 115–16.

## PAVEL PCHELNIKOV

Tchaikovsky is known to have had an early enthusiasm for Italian opera, but it is clear that Pchelnikov is writing here of a later period in the composer's life. However, other evidence suggests that, as with Beethoven's quartets (and, indeed, that composer's music in general), Tchaikovsky's attitude was deeply ambivalent.

Pyotr Ilich's weakness for light Italian music seems odd. Very often he came to the theatre for [Verdi's] *Traviata*, [Rossini's] *The Barber of Seville*, and in particular for [Donizetti's] *Lucia*, of which he liked very much the sextet; after hearing this he often left the theatre. If all the stalls were sold, then he did not hesitate to take a seat in the gods. After these performances he always spoke of wanting to compose a comic opera on a Russian subject; he thought of seeking a libretto from the time of Peter the Great.

Pavel Pchelnikov, Recollections; published in *MV*, 27 and 28 October/8 and 9 November 1900, and *RMG* (1900), no. 45, reprinted in *PVC4*, p. 144.

## ALEXANDER GLAZUNOV

During the 1880s – and later also – Balakirev, Borodin, Cui and Rimsky-Korsakov, composers of Balakirev's circle, which had already little by little begun to disintegrate, regarded Tchaikovsky . . . with a certain reserve that was purely party-political, though the zealots of the circle looked upon him with some hostility and impatience. There were exceptions. Rimsky-Korsakov, who subsequently came to like and value *The Queen of Spades*,

once expressed to me his regret that he had not managed, while Tchaikovsky was alive, to tell him this, adding: 'He would certainly have liked to
hear my opinion of the best of his operas.'

On his part Pyotr Ilich regarded the music of composers of the new
Russian school rather neutrally, as he did the work of Liszt and Wagner,
since he was by nature not attracted to their trends and principles. It
seemed to me that his temperament was more drawn to the work of Anton
Rubinstein, though Pyotr Ilich not infrequently censured the shortcomings
of its style and the carelessness with which it was written. All the same,
Tchaikovsky praised the Parrot Song in [Musorgsky's] *Boris Godunov*,
rated highly the first movement of Borodin's Second Symphony and the
chorus of peasants in *Igor*, and admired Rimsky-Korsakov's craftsmanship.
Tchaikovsky regarded the works of César Antonovich Cui more nega-
tively, and was not over-fond of him either as a composer or as a music
critic who caused him not a little distress . . .

Tchaikovsky was interested in my work, noted and saluted its successes,
but expected more of me in the future.

Alexander Glazunov, *Pisma, stati, vospominaniya. Izbrannoye [Letters, Articles,*
*Recollections. Selected]* (Moscow, 1958); reprinted in *PVC4*, pp. 210–11.


## Traits and idiosyncrasies

As might be expected, Tchaikovsky abounded in highly personal
traits and idiosyncrasies, and it is often difficult to discern the line
that divided them. The following materials inevitably make a
very heterogeneous miscellany.


## MIKHAIL IPPOLITOV-IVANOV

His hospitality knew no bounds. Thus, for instance, when he was greeted
while abroad with a serenade, he issued an invitation to all those who had
taken part, and entertained them royally without thinking of the expense.
Such sudden outgoings always caused extreme alarm to his servant Alexey
Sofronov because of their unexpectedness. Playing host to his friends was
always a great pleasure to Pyotr Ilich, and he would spare no expense.
When Nikolay Figner [the leading tenor in the premières of Tchaikov-

sky's last two operas] asked him where his capital was, he replied with his characteristic humour:

'At the present moment in the "Moscow Bolshoy" [i.e. in hoped-for performance royalties], and sometimes in other similar institutions.'

Mikhail Ippolitov-Ivanov, *IRM*; reprinted in *PVC4*, p. 236.


## NIKOLAY KASHKIN

This is probably another version of the incident with Nikolay
Figner related by Ippolitov-Ivanov.

I remember an incident which characterizes Tchaikovsky's attitude towards money. Once in 1891 we went as guests to the estate of a well-known artist who came for us at the railway station, after which we set out together. We had to travel in the carriage an hour or more, and we talked about various things, in the course of which our Amphitryon asked:

'Pyotr Ilich, where do you invest your capital?'

In reply to this Pyotr Ilich at first opened his eyes wide in complete amazement, then collapsed in helpless laughter; never in his life had the thought occurred to him of the possibility of investing his capital other than in the form of expenses or presents. I, of course, immediately understood what the point was, but our companion remained puzzled as to the causes of this unexpected gaiety on the part of his guest. At last the latter, having almost completely suffocated from laughter, said with a catch in his voice that he had most recently invested his capital in the Hotel Moscow where he had stayed, and that he did not know where he would invest it next time. For a person at all practical such an attitude towards money was simply incomprehensible, but with Tchaikovsky that is exactly how it was.

Nikolay Kashkin, *KVC*, p. 141.


## VLADIMIR NÁPRAVNÍK

At Shrovetide Pyotr Ilich decided to divert himself and go to Moscow, but currently he did not have enough money. He obtained some from me, then told me to distribute the money in various books in his library. After this Alexey, who looked after the composer's finances, was summoned, and

Pyotr Ilich asked for money from him for the trip. After receiving a negative response Pyotr Ilich said with the most innocent expression:

'But see, Alexey, isn't there something in such-and-such a book, and in such-and-such?'

And he delighted in his servant's surprise like a child.

I will add another little detail. When I was about to leave Klin, Pyotr Ilich presented me with his bill and said:

'And now we must decide what tip you should give Alexey, and how much to the cook. There's so much for you to give Alexey, and so much for the cook.'

And despite all my energetic protests, he still pressed the money upon me.

Vladimir Nápravník, Recollections; published in *SM* (1949), no. 7, reprinted in *PVC4*, p. 221.


## ALINA BRYULLOVA

When Rimsky-Korsakov's *Spanish Capriccio* was first performed Tchaikovsky was so enraptured by it that straightway he ran out to buy a laurel wreath and presented it to the composer. But then he was tormented by doubt:

'Perhaps I shouldn't have done it, perhaps I acted tactlessly, perhaps they'll think that I'm after something. What do you think?' he asked in embarrassment, rubbing his forehead with his customary gesture . . .

On another occasion I was imprudent enough to say that there was a movement in the First Suite I did not like. The next time it was performed I hear with surprise that it has been left out.

'Why?' I asked.

'But you don't like it, and you're right; the suite's too long and it's all in $\frac{3}{4}$ [in fact, $\frac{4}{4}$].'

You can imagine my embarrassment.

Alina Bryullova, Recollections (1929); published in *PVC4*, pp. 116, 110.

## MIKHAIL IPPOLITOV-IVANOV

During our walk I began humming as was my habit, constantly repeating the theme from Liszt's First Piano Concerto, at which he [Tchaikovsky] observed rather irritably:

'Please don't remind me of that play-actor. I can't bear his insincerity and affectation!' I began trying to defend him, but the result was disastrous. Pyotr Ilich unburdened himself still more energetically, and I fell silent, not wishing to spoil his mood . . .

Tchaikovsky, who bowed before Lev Tolstoy as a great writer, set little value on his discussions of art in general and of music in particular, finding his judgements dilettantish and superficial. Tolstoy's opinion that Beethoven was ungifted made Pyotr Ilich profoundly indignant, but because of Tolstoy's persistent stubbornness he considered it useless to dispute with him and demonstrate the opposite. And so he always avoided talking with him on this matter, and moreover more than once, at the prospect of meeting Tolstoy in the street, availed himself of adjoining courtyards – as he himself confessed – to avoid encounters and discussions . . .

Mikhail Ippolitov-Ivanov, *IRM*; reprinted in *PVC4*, pp. 238–40.


## VLADIMIR POGOZHEV

Pogozhev speaks of Tchaikovsky's ready tolerance of oral and privately communicated criticism of his music, then ends:

As testimony to his good nature I give the following example. In 1885, I think (I cannot remember exactly), there was mounted on the stage of the Mikhailovsky Theatre the little German fairy-tale *Der gestiefelte Kater* (*Puss-in-Boots*). For some reason this merry piece concluded with an apotheosis including a comic procession of operatic composers and the heroes of their works. Thus, for example, there was a caricature of Faust along with Marguerite, of the composer Wagner with Lohengeld (instead of Lohengrin); the procession was accompanied by parodies of their corresponding melodies. The chief producer of the German troupe, Philipp Bock, expressed regret to me that in a concluding procession of make-believe beings on the St Petersburg stage there would be no parody of a

Russian opera. I suggested that to parody an opera that had had no success would have no point, and would be a mean act on the part of the management; I suggested the possibility of parodying an opera with an established reputation, for instance *Eugene Onegin*, and apropos of this pointed out a certain similarity between the theme of the well-known song 'The Little Arrow' and Onegin's melody in his scene with Tatyana in the garden at the words 'I love you with the love of a brother, the love of a brother.' This made it possible to put into the musical procession a caricature of Onegin who would cross the stage singing [the corresponding words of the popular song]: 'I want to tell you, to tell you.' Bock liked the idea very much, and on meeting Pyotr Ilich I risked asking his permission to the intended parody – being ready, of course, at the slightest sign of hesitation or mark of displeasure on Tchaikovsky's part to drop the idea. My fears were groundless; Tchaikovsky burst out laughing and straightway agreed to my project. However, as far as I remember, prudence caused this project to remain unrealized.

Vladimir Pogozhev, Recollections; published in *MV*, 27 and 28 October 8 and 9 November 1900, and *RMG* (1900), no. 45, reprinted in *PVC4*, p. 191.

## Mrs A. BRODSKY

On another occasion his extreme sensitiveness revealed itself in a different way. A telephone wire had just been laid between Berlin and Leipzig. Tschaikovsky and Brodsky arranged to speak through the telephone, the former from Berlin and the latter from Leipzig. At the appointed time Brodsky went to the telephone office hoping to have a chat with his friend, but he had only uttered a few words when he heard Tschaikovsky say in a trembling voice, 'Dear friend! Please let me go. I feel so nervous.'

'I have not got you by the buttonhole,' said A.B. 'You can go when you please.'

Later on Tschaikovsky explained to us that as soon as he heard his friend's voice and realized the distance between them his heart began to beat so violently that he could not endure it.

Mrs A. Brodsky, *Recollections of a Russian Home* (Manchester and London, 1904), pp. 164–5.

# YULIAN POPLAVSKY

## (1871–1958)

Yulian Poplavsky was a cellist who had studied at the Moscow Conservatoire. Here he has been talking about Tchaikovsky's good memory when it came to certain musical matters.

However, despite all this, Pyotr Ilich lamented his musical memory. For instance, he often would ask:

'Whose nice romance is that?' – and was very confused on receiving the reply:

'Tchaikovsky's!'

Yulian Poplavsky, Recollections; published in *Artist* (1894), no. 42, bk. 10, reprinted in *PVC4*, p. 325.

# MIKHAIL IPPOLITOV-IVANOV

At this period [the later 1880s] Pyotr Ilich spent more than a month in Tiflis; we were constantly in his company, and became friendly with him. He often came to us for breakfast or lunch, and loved playing for hours with my little daughter Tanya, whom he called his 'Little Lump'. Once he came to us when Varvara Mikhailovna [Ippolitova-Ivanova] was singing his romance 'The Canary', one of his very early compositions. He listened for a long while, and finally asked:

'What's that you're singing?'

She looked at him in amazement, but he went on:

'What is it? It's very nice.'

She, laughing, replied:

'It's more than nice!'

Pyotr Ilich was surprised, and said:

'Why are you laughing? I'm quite serious; I like it very much.'

Subsequently he laughed a lot himself when he learned it was one of his own works . . .

Once when I was playing cards with him I mechanically hummed a phrase from his opera, *The Enchantress*. For a long while he heard me without saying anything, and finally asked:

'Tell me, please: I've been listening to what you've been humming for more than an hour, and I simply cannot remember where it comes from. I know it's something familiar, but what I can't remember.'

Mikhail Ippolitov-Ivanov, *IRM*; reprinted in *PVC4*, p. 235.


# ALEXANDER GOLDENWEISER
## (1875–1961)

Alexander Goldenweiser was a pianist and composer who later became director of the Moscow Conservatoire.

The director of the Synod School, Stepan Vasilyevich Smolensky, told how, when Tchaikovsky came to Moscow, they usually arranged for the performance of some choral music for him at the School. Once, when sitting alongside Smolensky during one such performance, Tchaikovsky knit his brow while one of the pieces of church music was in progress. It was evident he did not like it. Finally he turned to Smolensky and asked:

'Tell me, what is that rubbish?'

In fact they were performing one of Tchaikovsky's own compositions, written a long time before, and apparently completely forgotten by him. Stepan Vasilyevich said to me that it was extremely awkward telling Tchaikovsky that it was his own work.

Alexander Goldenweiser, Recollections; published in *PVC4*, p. 314.


# A. KAUFMAN
## (? – ?)

A. Kaufman worked in Odessa. He is recalling Tchaikovsky's 1893 visit to the city.

I remember at one rehearsal of Pyotr Ilich's opera [*The Queen of Spades*] the conductor Emmanuel observed:

'But you know, Pyotr Ilich, in *Mazepa* are to be found echoes from *Eugene Onegin*, *The Oprichnik* and others [of your] operas.'

'But you know, maestro,' replied Tchaikovsky in the same tone, '*Mazepa* is also my opera, as is *Eugene Onegin* and *The Oprichnik*.'

A. Kaufman, 'Vstrechi s Chaykovskim' ['Meetings with Tchaikovsky'], in *Solntse Rossy [Sun of Russia]* (1913), no. 44, reprinted in *PVC4*, p. 419.

## TATYANA SHCHEPKINA-KUPERNIK

This incident took place on a trip down the River Volga in 1887.

All artists observed in particular the modesty and delicacy of Tchaikovsky, who was as cordial with the most insignificant members of the chorus as with prime ministers. Apropos of which, much later his brother [Modest] told me an amusing incident which happened to Pyotr Ilich during some trip on a steamer. Tchaikovsky disliked very much being recognized and fêted. He had not been recognized on the steamer, and he was indescribably glad at this. He quietly mixed with the other travellers, participated in their amusements, and even undertook to accompany some woman [on the piano]. When she performed one of his romances, he tried to show her what needed to be done in some place, but she observed in displeasure:

'Allow me to know how this should be sung; I went through this romance with my teacher, and Tchaikovsky himself had shown her how it should be performed.'

Tchaikovsky bowed respectfully . . .

Tatyana Shchepkina-Kupernik, Recollections; published in *KP*, 6 May 1940, reprinted in *PVC4*, p. 266.

# XI

Two contemporary evaluations

# ARTHUR POUGIN

## (1834–1921)

Arthur Pougin was a French writer on music who edited the
supplement to Fétis' *Biographie universelle*. The earlier portion of
the following entry in that supplement had given a highly selec-
tive and factually insecure account of Tchaikovsky's career up to
the time of his opera *Vakula the Smith* (1874).

M. Tchaikovsky is one of the most gifted and most interesting musicians
of the young Russian school. With a mind a little unsure perhaps, a little
too much permeated with the tiresome ideas which for a quarter of a
century have possessed so many heads, his rather hazy eclecticism has
doubtless prevented him up to now from showing the full measure of his
worth. It is because of this that his originality has not yet blazed forth
upon us strongly, and that his works, very inconsistent in character and
inspiration, draw attention to themselves sometimes for their truly exquisite qualities (as in his fine [first] piano concerto and his pretty vocal
melodies, so luscious and original), sometimes for [exhibiting] a kind of
wilful unintelligibility, a style stretched beyond its limits, a contrived,
tiresome extravagance which makes comprehension difficult and which
totally wearies the ears (as in his symphonic fantasia on Shakespeare's *The
Tempest* and in his overture *Romeo and Juliet*). One can find a little of every
style in M. Tchaikovsky's music – that of Schumann as much as that of M.
Richard Wagner, and that of Berlioz as much as that of Mendelssohn.
From this stems the lack of stability in [his use of] his resources, [the
lack] of consistency in his talent and of precision in what results; from this
also stems the critic's difficulty in classifying the artist and in allotting him
the position he is entitled to occupy.

Yet, when all is taken into account, one has to say that M. Tchaikovsky
is a quite remarkable artist, a learned musician, often inspired, a master of
all the secrets of his art, aware of and employing miraculously all the
resources of the orchestra, and whom one could not reproach for sometimes sacrificing the ideal side of music in his search for the effect that is
sensual and brutal.

Article: 'Tschaikowsky', *Biographie universelle des musiciens et bibliographie générale de la musique. Par F.-J. Fétis: Supplément et complément. Publiés sous la direction de M. Arthur Pougin,* i (Paris, 1881).

# EDWARD DANNREUTHER

## (1844–1905)

Edward Dannreuther was an English pianist of German origin, and a writer on music. As a pianist he introduced Tchaikovsky's First Piano Concerto to England, and suggested revisions of the solo part which the composer accepted. He contributed the entry on Tchaikovsky to the first edition of Grove's *A Dictionary of Music and Musicians*.

TSCHAIKOWSKY, Peter Iltitsch, one of the most remarkable Russian composers of the day, was born April 25 [old style], 1840, at Wotkinsk in the government of Wiatka (Ural District), where his father was engineer to the Imperial mines. In 1850 the father was appointed Director of the Technological Institute at St. Petersburgh, and there the boy entered the School of Jurisprudence, into which only the sons of high-class government officials are admitted. Having completed the prescribed course in 1859, he was appointed to a post in the ministry of Justice. In 1862, however, when the Conservatoire of Music was founded at St. Petersburgh, he left the service of the state, and entered the new school as a student of music. He remained there till 1865, studying harmony and counterpoint under Prof. Zaremba, and composition under Anton Rubinstein. In 1865 he took his diploma as a musician, together with a prize medal for the composition of a cantata on Schiller's ode, 'An die Freude'. In 1866 Nicholas Rubinstein invited him to take the post of Professor of Harmony, Composition, and the History of Music at the new Conservatoire of Moscow; he held this post, doing good service as a teacher, for twelve years. Since 1878 he has devoted himself entirely to composition, and has been living in St. Petersburgh, Italy, Switzerland, and Kiew. M. Tschaikowsky makes frequent use of the rhythm and tunes of Russian People's-songs and dances, occasionally also of certain quaint harmonic sequences peculiar to Russian church music. His compositions, more or less, bear the impress of the Slavonic temperament – fiery exaltation on a basis of languid melancholy. He is fond of huge and fantastic outlines, of bold modulations and strongly marked rhythms, of subtle melodic turns and exuberant figuration, and he delights in gorgeous effects of orchestration. His music everywhere makes the impression of genuine spontaneous originality

Edward Dannreuther, article: 'Tschaikowsky', in Sir George Grove, ed., *A Dictionary of Music and Musicians*, iv (London, 1890).

# XII

First impressions – and more
## II
1888–93

## ALEXANDRA AMFITEATROVA-LEVITSKAYA

On meeting with Tchaikovsky in Tiflis in 1890, ten years after her previous meeting:

When I saw Tchaikovsky for the first time at the Ippolitov-Ivanovs' I was struck by the change in his appearance; the sternly gloomy image of the Conservatoire professor, which had stamped itself on my memory, had completely gone. Before me was a Tchaikovsky unknown to me, with a nice welcoming smile and a good-natured expression on his face. Pyotr Ilich had gone very grey but did not seem like an old man.

Alexandra Amfiteatrova-Levitskaya, Recollections; published in *CIT*, reprinted in *PVC4*, p. 241.

## LEONID NIKOLAYEV

The last photographs of Tchaikovsky represent his appearance accurately. Of medium height, refined, with regular and handsome facial features, he was not remarkable for his youthful appearance but, rather, appeared older than his years. His eyes had already lost their glitter. Shortly before his arrival in Kiev he had lost one of his front teeth and he sometimes lisped as a result of this. He had none of the grandeur and imperiousness of Anton Rubinstein, who had been to Kiev two years earlier. He was simple and welcoming.

Leonid Nikolayev, Recollections; published in *PVC4*, pp. 262–3.

## MIKHAIL GAIDAI

### (1878–1965)

As a boy Mikhail Gaidai was a member of the choir of St Sofiya, Kiev. Later he became a choral conductor and teacher. Tchaikovsky's visit took place in 1890.

All the singers were in a state of excitement on hearing a rumour that Tchaikovsky – the Tchaikovsky whose compositions we frequently rehearsed and sang in the cathedral – was coming to hear our choir. And so it happened. A bell was heard, and there entered the hall a very sympathetic elderly man, with a large, prominent forehead and (what sharply stamped itself on my memory) with greying hair unusually – and rather untidily – sticking up on end.

Mikhail Gaidai, letter to *Muzïka i Peniye [Music and Singing]* (1903), no. 9; reprinted in *PVC4*, p. 410.

# YURY YURYEV

## (1872–1948)

Yury Yuryev studied acting in Moscow, and from September 1893 was an actor at the Alexandrinsky Theatre in St Petersburg.

I saw Pyotr Ilich for the first time in the Bolshoy Theatre in Moscow in November 1891 at the dress rehearsal of *The Queen of Spades*. What immediately lodged in my memory was his characteristic appearance which was imbued with a captivating inner grace and nobility; his voice was a pleasant low bass . . . For some reason I recall a curious detail: the abnormally large boxes of sweets which had been prepared as a gift for the children, the pupils of the theatre school, who had to appear in the opera.

Yury Yuryev, *Zapiski [Notes]* (Leningrad and Moscow, 1948); reprinted in *PVC4*, p. 278.

# IGOR STRAVINSKY

## (1882–1971)

Igor Stravinsky's father, Fyodor, was a bass who had a distinguished career in the Imperial Opera in St Petersburg. Tchaikovsky had a great respect for Fyodor, who created several minor roles in his operas. Igor Stravinsky claimed that he saw Tchaikovsky at the fiftieth anniversary of the première of Glinka's *Ruslan and Lyudmila*, which must have occurred in 1892, making Strav-

insky 10 years old at the time; if so, he was wrong in placing it a
fortnight before Tchaikovsky's death.

In the first interval we stepped from our loge into the small foyer behind.
A few people were already walking there. Suddenly my mother said to me:
'Igor, look, there is Tchaikovsky.' I looked and saw a big man with white
hair, large shoulders, a corpulent back, and this image has remained in the
retina of my memory all my life.

Igor Stravinsky and Robert Craft, *Expositions and Developments* (London, 1962),
p. 86.

# KONSTANTIN STANISLAVSKY

## (1863–1938)

Konstantin Stanislavsky was an actor and director who encountered and came to admire Tchaikovsky in the 1880s. In 1898 he
founded the Moscow Arts Theatre which in its early years was
especially associated with the plays of Chekhov (who had also
known Tchaikovsky personally and received encouragement from
him in the 1880s). In 1899 Chekhov's *Uncle Vanya* was being
prepared for performance, and a lively debate had arisen about
what sort of person Vanya was, Stanislavsky and the rest having
assumed that he was a conventional member of the landed gentry.
What finally issued was an interesting analogy.

The costume and general appearance of a landed gentleman are known to
all, high boots, a cap, sometimes a horsewhip, for it is taken for granted he
rides horseback a great deal. It was so that we painted him to ourselves.
But Chekhov was terribly indignant.

'Listen,' he said in great excitement, 'everything is said there. You
didn't read the play.'

We looked into the original, but we found no hint there unless we were
to reckon several words about a silk tie which Uncle Vanya wore.

'Here it is, here it is written down,' Chekhov tried to persuade us.

'What is written down?' We were in amazement. 'A silk tie?'

'Of course. Listen, he has a wonderful tie; he is an elegant, cultured man. It is not true that our landed gentry walk about in boots smeared with tar. They are wonderful people. They dress well. They order their clothes in Paris. It is all written down.'

This little remark uncovered the drama of contemporary Russian life: the giftless, unnecessary professor [Serebriyakov] enjoys life. He has a beautiful wife, he enjoys scholarly fame which he has not deserved . . . But in the end it is seen that Serebriyakov is a blown-up soap bubble who occupies a post in life that he has not earned, while the talented Uncle Vanya and his friend Astrov are forced to rot in the darkest corners of the provinces. One wants to call the real doers and workers to the source of power and to throw the giftless and famous Serebriyakovs from their high posts. From this time on, Uncle Vanya became for us a cultured, soft, elegant, fine type of man, almost like the unforgettable and enchanting Pyotr Ilich Tchaikovsky.

Konstantin Stanislavsky, *My Life in Art* (London, 1924), pp. 361–2.

## Foreign Impressions

### *Hungarian*

## LEOPOLD AUER
## (1845–1930)

Leopold Auer was the Hungarian violinist for whom Tchaikovsky had intended his Violin Concerto. From 1868 to 1917 Auer was professor of violin at the St Petersburg Conservatoire and also the court violinist.

In my mind's eye I see once more the great figures of those days. There is Tchaikovsky, with the personality and the manners of a French marquis of the eighteenth century; but very modest, with a modesty which could not be mistaken for a pose. He was too intelligent ever to attempt playing a part among his artist comrades, to whom, incidentally, he was always most cordial . . .

Tchaikovsky was excessively sensitive; modest and unassertive in his dealings with all, he was deeply appreciative of any interest shown in him or in his works.

Leopold Auer, *My Long Life in Music* (London, 1924), pp. 139–40, 202.

## *American*

# WALTER DAMROSCH

In the spring of 1891 Carnegie Hall, which had been built by Andrew Carnegie as a home for the higher musical activities of New York, was inaugurated with a music festival in which the New York Symphony and Oratorio Societies took part. In order to give this festival a special significance, I invited Peter Iljitsch Tschaikowsky, the great Russian composer, to come to America and to conduct some of his own works. In all my many years of experience I have never met a great composer so gentle, so modest – almost diffident – as he. We all loved him from the first moment – my wife and I, the chorus, the orchestra, the employees of the hotel where he lived, and of course the public . . .

He came often to our house, and, I think, liked to come. He was always gentle in his intercourse with others, but a feeling of sadness seemed never to leave him, although his reception in America was more than enthusiastic and the visit so successful in every way that he made plans to come back the following year. Yet he was often swept by uncontrollable waves of melancholia and despondency.

Walter Damrosch, *My Musical Life* (New York, 1923), pp. 143–4.

During his three and a half weeks in the USA Tchaikovsky also conducted concerts in Philadelphia and Baltimore. His every appearance in public, both on and off the concert platform, was scrutinized closely by the local press.

## ANONYMOUS

He is a fine-looking, stalwart, and dignified man, quiet and polished in his manners, and making himself understood either in broken English or one of the many European languages with which he, with the usual linguistical bent of the Russian, is thoroughly familiar. He has scant white hair and a white beard, and is younger than he looks, being 51 years old.

Newspaper: *The Sun*, Baltimore, 16 May 1891.

Tchaikovsky is a distinguished-looking man, apparently about 50 years of age, and looking more like a prosperous merchant or a United States Senator than a musician. His manner [as a conductor] is singularly unobtrusive and quite free from any kind of mannerism or affectation. He seems to think of nothing but that he is there for the purpose of directing the orchestra, and that duty, without any preliminary posturings or preludings, he at once proceeds to discharge. In conducting his methods are simple, clear, forcible, and masterly.

Newspaper: *North American*, Philadelphia, 19 May 1891.

*German*

## GUSTAV MAHLER
## (1860–1911)

Mahler first met Tchaikovsky in Leipzig in 1888. In 1892 in Hamburg he took over the performance of *Eugene Onegin* which the composer himself was to have conducted. Tchaikovsky had unstinted admiration for Mahler as a conductor. After this occasion Mahler described Tchaikovsky as:

An elderly gentleman, very likeable, with elegant manners, who seems quite rich and reminds me somehow of Mihalovich [a Hungarian composer and educationist].

Gustav Mahler, Letter to Justine Mahler, quoted in Henry-Louis de La Grange, *Gustav Mahler*, i (New York, 1973), p. 248.

## *English*

Tchaikovsky visited England on three occasions (1888, 1889 and 1893) as a conductor of his own works. The main purpose of his last visit was to receive the honorary degree of D.Mus. from Cambridge University, but he arrived in England a fortnight before the graduation ceremony to conduct a concert of the Royal Philharmonic Society in London, and he was much sought after by English musicians during the intervening time.

## SIR FREDERIC COWEN

## (1852–1935)

Sir Frederic Cowen became permanent conductor of the Royal Philharmonic Society in London in 1888; the following refers to Tchaikovsky's 1888 visit.

At the next concert Tschaikowsky made his début as composer-conductor before an English audience. His name was then little known here except among musicians, although he had already given to the world many of his finest compositions . . . His visits to London (he returned the following year) were so brief that I had little opportunity of being in his company except at the rehearsals and concerts. This I much regretted, for he seemed a man of a pleasant and friendly disposition and enthusiastic temperament, to whom one would be attracted more and more as one got to know him better. He did not speak English, and I had to stand at his side all the time and translate his wishes to the members of the orchestra.

Sir Frederic Cowen, *My Art and my Friends* (London, 1913), pp. 148–9.

# JOHN FRANCIS BARNETT

## (1837–1916)

John Francis Barnett was an English composer and conductor who met Tchaikovsky several times when the latter was in London.

Tschaikowsky had a striking personality. He was a finely-built man, and held himself so well he looked quite military in appearance.

John Francis Barnett, *Musical Reminiscences and Impressions* (London, 1906), p. 270.

# FRANCESCO BERGER

## (1834–1933)

Francesco Berger was an English pianist and composer, and secretary of the Royal Philharmonic Society.

This distinguished Composer and delightful man came to England in March 1888 to conduct some of his music at 'the Philharmonic'; he came again in 1889 and 1893. During this last visit to England he invited himself to dine with me at my house, stipulating that there should be 'no party' and 'no evening-dress'. Accordingly we were only four: Madame Berger, myself, the Composer, and one young lady (a talented Pupil of mine, Phoebe Hart, who has since distinguished herself by writing some very clever 'Monologues', published in various magazines).

Like most foreigners, Tschaikowsky was fond of English food, cooked English fashion, so our dinner consisted mainly of such. He told us that before he came as a Composer of Music he had once paid a flying visit to this country in another capacity. His conversation, carried on in French and German (for I do not speak Russian), was easy without being brilliant, and in all he said there was apparent the modest, gentle spirit which was so characteristic of the man. I noticed on this and other occasions that he never spoke of 'politics', and if in the course of conversation that topic cropped up, he would remark that 'Music and Art generally were fit matters for Musicians to discuss – not politics.'

Francesco Berger, *Reminiscences, Impressions, Anecdotes* (London, n.d.), p. 87.

# MATHILDE VERNE
## (1865–1936)

Mathilde Verne was an English pianist of German descent, a
pupil of Clara Schumann.

Tschaikowsky's appearance was utterly opposed to the mental picture I had
formed of the creator of such passionate and stirring music.

I saw at once that he was painfully shy and retiring, but I imagined that
if he took part in any actual musical performance he would lose all self-
consciousness and disclose some fire and sparkle, so when he accompanied
the great singer, Augusta Redeker (Lady Semon), in his own lovely song,
'Nur wer die Sehnsucht kennt', I was more than ever astonished at his
listless attitude. I can only say that his playing struck me as diffident and
unsympathetic.

Mathilde Verne, *Chords of Remembrance* (London, 1936), pp. 86–7.

# SIR GEORGE HENSCHEL
## (1850–1934)

Sir George Henschel was a British baritone of German extraction.
He had already met Tchaikovsky in Moscow over fifteen years
before, in 1875 or 1876.

Tschaikovsky, whom I had the pleasure of seeing nearly every day during
his short stay in London, seemed to me, though then on the uppermost
rung of the ladder of fame, even more inclined to intervals of melancholy
than when I had last met him; indeed, one afternoon, during a talk about
the olden days in Petrograd and Moscow, and the many friends there who
were no more, he suddenly got very depressed and, wondering what this
world with all its life and strife was made for, expressed his own readiness
at any moment to quit it. To my gratification I succeeded in dispelling the
clouds that had gathered over his mental vision, and during the rest of the

afternoon as well as the dinner in the evening he appeared in the best of spirits.

Sir George Henschel, *Musings & Memories of a Musician* (London, 1918), p. 365.

# SIR CHARLES VILLIERS STANFORD

## (1852–1924)

Sir Charles Villiers Stanford was an English composer, and pro-fessor of music at Cambridge University from 1887.

[While in Cambridge] Tschaikowsky stayed with the late F. W. Maitland, who spoke to me with enthusiasm of his culture and grasp of extra-musical subjects. He reminded me, in more ways than one, of his countryman Tourgéniew, whom I once met at Madame Viardot's. He had none of the Northern roughness, was as polished as a Frenchman in his manner, and had something of the Italian in his temperament . . . For all the belief which he had in himself, he was to all appearances the acme of modesty.

Sir Charles Villiers Stanford, *Pages from an Unwritten Diary* (London, 1914), p. 280.

# HERMAN KLEIN

## (1856–1934)

Herman Klein was an English singing teacher and critic.

In the June of 1893, Tschaikowsky came to England to receive the honor-ary degree of 'Mus.Doc.' at Cambridge University . . . By a happy chance I travelled down to Cambridge in the same carriage with Tschai-kowsky. I was quite alone in the compartment until the train was actually starting, when the door opened and an elderly gentleman was unceremoni-ously lifted in, his luggage being bundled in after him by the porters. A glance told me who it was. I offered my assistance, and, after he had recovered his breath, the master told me he recollected that I had been presented to him one night at the Philharmonic. Then followed an hour's delightful conversation.

Tschaikowsky chatted freely about music in Russia. He thought the development of the past twenty-five years had been phenomenal. He attributed it, first, to the intense musical feeling of the people which was now coming to the surface; secondly, to the extraordinary wealth and characteristic beauty of the national melodies or folk-songs; and, thirdly, to the splendid work done by the great teaching institutions at St Petersburg and Moscow. He spoke particularly of his own Conservatory at Moscow, and begged that if I ever went to that city I would not fail to pay him a visit. He then put some questions about England and inquired especially as to the systems of management and teaching pursued at the Royal Academy and the Royal College. I duly explained, and also gave him some information concerning the Guildhall School of Music and its three thousand students. It surprised him to hear that London possessed such a gigantic musical institution.

'I don't know,' he added, 'whether to consider England an "unmusical" nation or not. Sometimes I think one thing, sometimes another. But it is certain that you have audiences for music of every class, and it appears to me probable that before long the larger section of your public will support the best class only.' Then the recollection of the failure of his *Eugény Onégin* occurred to him, and he asked me to what I attributed that – the music, the libretto, the performance, or what? I replied, without flattery, that it was certainly not the music. It might have been due in some measure to the lack of dramatic fibre in the story, and in a large degree to the inefficiency of the interpretation and the unsuitability of the locale. 'Remember,' I went on, 'that Pushkin's poem is not known in this country, and that in opera we like a definite dénouement, not an ending where the hero goes out at one door and the heroine at another.' . . .

Tschaikowsky was to be the guest of the Master of Merton [in fact, Downing], and I undertook to see him safely bestowed at the college before proceeding to my hotel. Telling the flyman to take a slightly circuitous route, I pointed out various places of interest as we passed them, and Tschaikowsky seemed thoroughly to enjoy the drive. When we parted at the college, he shook me warmly by the hand and expressed a hope that when he next visited England he might see more of me. Unhappily, that kindly wish was never to be fulfilled.

Herman Klein, *Thirty Years of Musical Life in London, 1870–1900* (London, 1903), pp. 343–8.

# ETHEL SMYTH

## (1858–1944)

Ethel Smyth was an English composer who studied in Leipzig and met Tchaikovsky there in 1888. Tchaikovsky's reaction to Marco, as recorded by Ethel Smyth, is surprising; normally he liked dogs.

Of all the composers I have known the most delightful as personality was Tchaikovsky, between whom and myself a relation now sprang up that surely would have ripened into close friendship had circumstances favoured us; so large minded was he, that I think he would have put up unresentingly with all I had to give his work – a very relative admiration. Accustomed to the uncouth, almost brutal manners affected by many German musicians as part of the make up and one of the symptoms of genius, it was a relief to find in this Russian, whom even the rough diamonds allowed was a master on his own lines, a polished, cultivated gentleman and man of the world. Even his detestation of Brahms's music failed to check my sympathy – and that I think is strong testimony to his charm! He would argue with me about Brahms by the hour, strum passages on the piano and ask if they were not hideous, declaring I must be under hypnotic influence, since to admire this awkward pedant did not square with what he was kind enough to call the soundness of my instinct on other points. Another thing that puzzled him was my devotion to Marco [her dog], of whom he was secretly terrified, but this trait he considered to be a form of English spleen and it puzzled him less than the other madness. For years I have meant to inquire whether dogs play no part in the Russian scheme of life or whether Tchaikovsky's views were peculiar to himself; anyhow it amused me, reading his Memoirs, to find Marco and Brahms bracketed together as eccentricities of his young English friend.

On one point we were quite of one mind, the neglect in my school . . . of colour. 'Not one of them can instrumentate,' he said, and he earnestly begged me to turn my attention at once to the orchestra and not be prudish about using the medium for all it is worth. 'What happens,' he asked, 'in ordinary conversation? If you have to do with really alive people, listen to the inflections in the voices . . . there's instrumentation for you!' And I followed his advice on the spot, went to concerts with the sole object of studying orchestral effects, filled notebook upon notebook with impressions, and ever since have been at least as much interested in sounds as in sense, considering the two things indivisible.

Ethel Smyth, *Impressions that Remained* (London, 1919), pp. 167–8.

# XIII

## The last years

# NIKOLAY KASHKIN

Outwardly Tchaikovsky did not appear to be particularly strong, but in reality he was healthy and hardy. Accustomed to walking in the country in all weathers, he was almost immune to colds; only windy weather did he fear greatly, not so much as being harmful as unpleasant. His single ailment was a kind of gastric fever which appeared in him from time to time accompanied sometimes with a quite high temperature: but all this quickly passed of its own accord, yielding to domestic remedies (Pyotr Ilich did not like resorting to doctors). However that might be, with the approach of his 50th birthday the marks of old age and weariness began to appear, though right up to his death there were never any of the diseases and indispositions of old age. Outwardly Pyotr Ilich aged drastically in his last years; his thin hair turned completely white, his face became covered with wrinkles, he began to lose his teeth, which he found especially unpleasant since it sometimes hindered him from talking with complete clarity. Still more perceptible was the gradual weakening of his eyesight which made reading in the evenings by the fire difficult, and this deprived him of his chief diversion within the creative life he pursued in the country, so that sometimes solitude became distressing for him, especially in the long winter evenings.

Weariness began to reveal itself in that a newly projected composition no longer engrossed him as totally as had happened earlier; there began to appear more often moments when thought required rest and diversion in some trivial occupation requiring no mental effort. Pyotr Ilich sometimes said that the possibility of having a party for vint (three rubbers: he could hardly play more with pleasure) in the evening would provide significant satisfaction, but that it was impossible to arrange this in the country without bringing over company from Klin, which he did not want to do at all because he wished to preserve his absolute freedom. As far as I can see, there were all the same few evenings of melancholy solitariness for Tchaikovsky; more frequently than before he could live in the composition that was occupying him at the given moment. On the other hand, besides his own compositions, those of others occupied him; if he liked some new piece, then for hours, and with pleasure, he would study it. Thus, for instance, he was for a very long while inseparable from the score of Rimsky-Korsakov's *Spanish Capriccio*, in which the novelty and brilliance of the orchestral effects captivated him; I remember that when he arrived in Moscow for several days he brought this score along with him, although he probably knew it all by heart. But he found it pleasant, without troubling his memory, to open the score and read through yet again what he already knew well . . . In the evenings it was easier to read scores than books because musical print is easier for the eye to grasp – and so such reading could sometimes fill his free time for him. I should also add playing patience, with which my late friend sometimes occupied himself, though not for more than a few minutes at a time – enough for the two kinds of patience he knew (he had not learned any other). But his patience cards were an essential accessory in his writing desk; he even nearly took them with him on his travels.

Nikolay Kashkin, *KVC*, pp. 151–3.

> There was a steady increase in Tchaikovsky's self-assurance as what he felt to be the scandal of his marriage slipped further into history; above all, his overwhelming success as a composer and the personal esteem he enjoyed, as evidenced in the rapturous reception given him wherever he went, made him much more ready to mix with people socially. He could even gossip and joke obliquely about his marriage, retailing his own half-comic version of what happened, in which all responsibility for the affair is shifted to the woman.

# NIKOLAY RIMSKY-KORSAKOV

In the years following [on 1890] Tchaikovsky's flying visits [to St Petersburg] became quite frequent. The time we spent together usually ended with sitting in a restaurant until three or four in the morning with Lyadov, Glazunov and others. Tchaikovsky could drink a lot of wine, while retaining total control of his faculties, both bodily and mental; few could keep up with him in this regard.

Nikolay Rimsky-Korsakov, *RKL*, 9th edn (Moscow, 1982), p. 223.

# ISAAK BUKINIK

Bukinik recounts something that happened at the banquet following Tchaikovsky's concert in Kharkov in 1893. What is surprising is not what Tchaikovsky relates (though if he is referring to
his relationship with Antonina Milyukova it is not by any means
congruent with the known facts, and the end is false), but that he
should have related it at all.

Pyotr Ilich recounted a strange romance he had had with one of the
students at the Moscow Conservatoire. It turned out he did not know of
her love for him, and he was terribly disconcerted when she appeared at his
apartment, fell on her knees, and declared that she could not live without
him, that she had come to die at his feet. And, indeed, she pulled out a
revolver, and was going to shoot herself. Pyotr Ilich related how he was
terribly afraid, promised to marry her, and how it cost him a great effort
to escape from this madwoman.

Isaak Bukinik, Recollections; published in *PVC4*, p. 299.


# WALTER DAMROSCH

Damrosch was a guest in Cambridge in June 1893.

The following year in May I went to England with my wife, and received
an invitation from Charles Villiers Stanford, then professor of music at
Cambridge, to visit the old university during the interesting commence-
ment exercises at which honorary degrees of Doctor of Music were to be
given to five composers of five different countries – Saint-Saëns of France,
Boito of Italy, Grieg of Norway, Bruch of Germany, and Tschaikowsky of
Russia . . .

In the evening a great banquet was given in the refectory of the college
[King's], and by good luck I was placed next to Tschaikowsky. He told
me during the dinner that he had just finished a new symphony which was
different in form from any he had ever written. I asked him in what the
difference consisted and he answered: 'The last movement is an adagio and
the whole work has a programme.'

'Do tell me the programme,' I demanded eagerly.

'No,' he said, 'that I shall never tell. But I shall send you the first orchestral score and parts as soon as Jurgenson, my publisher, has them ready.'

We parted with the expectation of meeting again in America during the following winter, but, alas, in October came the cable announcing his death from cholera, and a few days later arrived a package from Moscow containing the score and parts of his Symphony No. 6, the 'Pathétique'. It was like a message from the dead.

Walter Damrosch, *My Musical Life* (New York, 1923), pp. 144–5.

# MIKHAIL IPPOLITOV-IVANOV

Ippolitov-Ivanov recalls one of his last meetings with Tchaikov-sky, this time at Taneyev's in Moscow, where the company was to hear the piano duet version of the new Sixth Symphony.

It was played by Lev Konyus and Sergey Ivanovich [Taneyev]. Whether it was the frequent stops to make corrections of details, or the nagging interruptions from Pyotr Ilich, who was somehow especially edgy that evening – but the symphony did not make an impression on us, and Pyotr Ilich was blacker than a cloud.

That evening I met for the first time Sergey Rakhmaninov, who had finished at the Conservatoire a year before my arrival in Moscow . . . At the end of the evening Rakhmaninov acquainted us with his only just completed symphonic poem *The Crag* (after the poem by Lermontov, and without question [composed] under the influence of Rimsky-Korsakov). Everyone liked this [symphonic] poem very much, and especially Pyotr Ilich, who delighted in its colourfulness. The performance of *The Crag* and the discussion of it diverted Pyotr Ilich somewhat, and his former benevolent mood returned. He cheered up completely when Sergey Ivano-vich, seeing that Pyotr Ilich was about to smoke, reminded him that smoking was only permitted in the passage by the chimney, whither he advised him to direct himself; moreover, near the chimney there hung an extract from an article by Lev Tolstoy about the harmfulness of tobacco, to which Sergey Ivanovich considered it his duty to draw the attention of all smokers. After the prolonged musical performance everyone hastened to occupy the place closest the flue, near which there always gathered a large company and where there proceeded a discussion of current matters. Although Tchaikovsky protested against such autocratic behaviour towards his visitors on the part of their host, he still assented and went off with everyone to smoke into the chimney.

Mikhail Ippolitov-Ivanov, *IRM*; reprinted in *PVC4*, pp. 239–40.

## YULIAN POPLAVSKY

Poplavsky is recalling a visit to Klin made a little more than a fortnight before Tchaikovsky's death. Tchaikovsky is about to leave his home for the last time.

[At Klin railway station we were met] by a curly-haired, jaded-looking coachman who took us to the entrance of a two-storey wooden house with a glass-covered balcony, the last along the Moscow highway.

Pyotr Ilich occupied the upper storey. A large room with bookcases for music along the walls and a piano in the middle, a dining room, and a bedroom – that was all that was necessary for this solitary musician; all the remaining spacious rooms, except the two or three for guests, were given into the care of Alexey, his devoted servant. Except for the drawing room not one of the rooms suggested the dwelling of the most popular of Russian composers, the creator of the opera *Eugene Onegin* . . . In the bedroom, besides a bed, washing and toilet tables, there was by the window an unpainted pine table and a simple chair with arms. On the table stood a simple cut-glass inkwell, a surprisingly finely crafted china Pierrot head, and several small items of the crudest primitive workmanship. There also lay music paper, pens, and the manuscript of the last [E flat] piano concerto, which Pyotr Ilich was looking over when we arrived . . .

Strictly speaking, this bedroom was also Pyotr Ilich's work room. Its windows looked out onto a small garden shut in by a wall, with flowerbeds sown by Pyotr Ilich himself. If, sitting in the chair, you looked straight ahead, then there was nothing to distract your gaze except the clouds above, the uniform expanse of fields to the horizon, and the enigmatic smile of Pierrot. Pyotr Ilich worked at this pine table, getting up at seven every morning. Neither among the mountains of Switzerland, nor on the shore of the Adriatic, nor in America was Tchaikovsky so inclined to compose as at home here in Klin. In the drawing room not far from the fireplace was situated a large pedestal writing desk with a beautiful, expensive writing set and a mass of no less valuable, exquisitely fine things. This desk was assigned exclusively to correspondence . . .

Tchaikovsky's library of scores was unusually varied. First and foremost: a bookcase with the magnificent Leipzig edition of the complete works of Mozart. There were works by the most recent composers – almost all with warm inscriptions. Scores by Glinka occupied an honoured position. In the margins of several of the scores by younger composers was a mass of corrections, observations, and frequently advice in Pyotr Ilich's own hand. He was interested in all that was new, and had looked over each attentively.

One of the bookcases was devoted to masters of words and thoughts. Here, alongside Pushkin, Heine, Alexey Tolstoy and Hugo, there were grandly disposed, weighty volumes, their titles on their spines: Wundt, Schopenhauer, Mill, Spencer – and the names of philosophers whom artists generally were more in the habit of respecting than reading. Also there stood a small bookcase with sumptuous, for the most part English, editions of world poets – Dante, Shakespeare, Byron, Milton. In the corner a cabinet with precious gifts; of these there caught the eye a gold pen, cups and wine bowls, and a silver Statue of Liberty brought from America . . .

The portraits on the walls of Bach, Handel, Mozart, Beethoven, Glinka, Anton Rubinstein, and other musicians – many of them with autographs ('à mon ami', 'to a great artist', or 'to a fellow musician') – alternated with silver wreaths and family portraits. In a cosy corner with softly upholstered furnishings, on an oval table, lay artistically crafted document cases with addresses from Russian and foreign institutions, learned and musical societies. Here also stood beautiful morocco boxes filled with photographs, distributed according to shape and size in separate, differently shaped compartments; here also among artists, singers, poets, composers and virtuosi of the whole world it was, I confess, a not unpleasant surprise to see beneath some beardless face its own signature . . .

It was around ten in the evening. Klin was already asleep, the family of Alexey, who was serving us, had evidently retired. Suddenly, in the almost absolute silence, there sounded a chord pure as a tuning fork, there trembled and resounded through the whole house the strokes of silver bells. The thirds and minor sixths merrily widened into octaves, [though] sometimes delayed in the passing notes, and two bells with the purest and lowest tones angrily disputed in fourths and, like the bass main spring, vibrated long and resonantly through the air. It was a stone clock, which Tchaikovsky had obtained in Prague, at play. The clockmaker, recognizing the purchaser as the conductor of the previous evening's concert, had insisted on accepting only the cost of the materials and labour . . .

Pyotr Ilich proposed that we should jointly look through the Cello Concerto of Saint-Saëns which he did not know and which Anatoly Andreyevich [Brandukov] was proposing to play in St Petersburg under Pyotr Ilich's direction, and we got up from the table. It was not without emotion that I sat at the piano and opened the orchestral score, even though I had looked it through earlier. When I struck the first chord I involuntarily lifted my hands from the keys – I had never before encountered a piano so out of tune. I recalled the assurances of some 'shrewd' persons that Pyotr Ilich composed only at the piano. It would be difficult to find more obvious proof of these absurd conjectures. Having rooted out together the most unsuitable keys, we proceeded to the performance. Pyotr Ilich followed and put in the wind instrument parts with his left hand, while Anatoly Andreyevich sang the cello part. This improvised trio with Pyotr Ilich participating will always remain in my memory.

Until eleven o'clock, when Pyotr Ilich usually went to bed, the time passed unnoticed. Our genial host showed us to the rooms which had been prepared for us to satisfy himself that Alexey had furnished us with all that was necessary. He brought us with his own hands rugs and a coat as he feared the night might be cold, and only then wished us a quiet night.

In the morning at half-past eight I found Pyotr Ilich at tea. He was reading the papers, sitting alongside a little round table at the drawing-room window. Every morning he drank two glasses of hot tea, looked through the papers, and read through the enormous number of letters which were brought to him once a day from the station. Then he transferred to the writing desk and wrote a reply to almost every letter. He kept all his letters in the bottom drawers of the desk; at the end of a year the drawers were emptied and all his correspondence, packed into a file with the year written on it, was given to Alexey for safe keeping. Pyotr Ilich was always going to sort out this huge archive (twenty years' worth) and extract from it the more interesting letters.

Pyotr Ilich showed and translated (the correspondence was in five languages) several amusing letters for me and Anatoly Andreyevich . . . In one, for instance, he was invited to somewhere in the south of Germany to participate in a concert; moreover he was asked to 'drag along Anton Rubinstein and Glinka (?!)'. It further appeared that almost all the celebrities who were pursuing their occupations on our capitals' platforms had been invited on advice from Pyotr Ilich or through his mediation.

Pyotr Ilich, as always, bore off his now cold third cup of tea to his working table in his bedroom . . .

At one o'clock we set off into the wood, which was not more than two-thirds of a mile away. If what Pyotr Ilich wore indoors was more than simple, the coat in which he appeared on the streets of Klin might easily have competed in an exhibition of antique fashions. It had been bought in Vienna a very long time before. In all weathers, in winter and summer, Pyotr Ilich walked for two hours. Every tree was familiar to our guide. We proceeded to the ditch – the remains of the work on building a canal which, during the reign of Nikolay I, was planned to join the Volga with the River Sestra. Being very familiar with this place, Pyotr Ilich retailed to us the sad plight of the serfs who had worked on this project. During this he lamented that he had not managed during the summer to carry out the plan he had thought up, together with Nikolay Kashkin, of walking along this canal all the way to the Volga on foot – and he was hoping to accomplish this project during the next spring. Dear Pyotr Ilich, I too had hoped to accompany you!

Unnoticed we had arrived at a wonderful spot. A small clearing suddenly arose in the wood; on the right the Sestra meandered, on the left a level field as far as the eye could see – and if you stood with your back to the wood, before your eyes on both sides was the embankment of the Nikolayevsky Railway. In the distance Frolovskoye was visible . . .

After this it was decided to return home. Alexey, looking displeased, reported that our meal was not yet ready, and to occupy the time Pyotr Ilich suggested we should look over Laroche's overture to *Karmozina*.

As we ate Pyotr Ilich spoke of his last symphony. We, seeing his particularly good spirits, approached him with our perpetual request – that he should write a cello concerto.

'Why don't you play my [Rococo] Variations?' was always the one and the same reply.

I repeated the old line about how some of the variations were uncomfortable for the cellist, that in them there was little singing.

'They can't play them, and so they pester me,' Pyotr Ilich joked. 'I've always said that the best composition by Tchaikovsky is sung by Krutikova in *The Queen of Spades* – not one of us is in debt to that!'

And everyone laughed . . .*

After our meal we went to one of the best grocers' shops in Klin. The proprietor met us at the door – a tall, strong local merchant, with a peaked cap made greasy by the heat. On meeting him Pyotr Ilich extended his hand to him. Being far removed from music in general and the works of the composer standing before him in particular, this estimable trader showed his esteem for Pyotr Ilich only by calling him 'Your Excellency'. From all the products offered some apple *pastila* [a sweet made of fruit and berries] was selected. Before it got dark Pyotr Ilich showed us his uncomplicated economy: his warm-air heating, his stores of firewood for the winter, his stores of cabbage which had to be chopped up, in which operation Pyotr Ilich himself not infrequently shared.

At five o'clock we began getting ourselves ready for Moscow. The contents of the two suitcases well known to me, Pyotr Ilich's invariable companions, were looked over and packed by Alexey. Egorka, Alexey's 2-year-old son (and the master's godson), appeared. Bidding them farewell, Pyotr Ilich exchanged kisses with both father and son. Alexey, entrusting the master with sixty roubles, told him to buy some cloth for a coat in Moscow, and other necessities for his wardrobe. We sat in the carriages and in twenty minutes were already happily boarding a coach of the evening train.

Yulian Poplavsky, Recollections; published in *Artist* (1894), no. 42, bk. 10, reprinted in *PVC4*, pp. 318–24.

# MIKHAIL IPPOLITOV-IVANOV

Not long before he left for St Petersburg, Pyotr Ilich dined with us together with Sergey Taneyev, who demonstrated to us a machine someone had invented for 'perpetuum mobile' – perpetual motion, which was obtained by heating (with the warmth of your own hands) the little blades

---

*Tchaikovsky is referring to the aria 'Je crains de lui parler la nuit' from Grétry's opera *Richard, Coeur de Lion*, which he has the old Countess sing to herself in the bedroom scene in *The Queen of Spades*.

of a propeller which was placed in the sealed interior of a small glass gadget, and from this [heat] these blades were set in motion. Pyotr Ilich laughed good-naturedly at the attraction Sergey Ivanovich found in such inventions which had no practical use, but Sergey Ivanovich tried to vindicate the scientific value of such experiments with an insistence that would have been more worthily applied elsewhere. Their good-natured altercation created that atmosphere of friendly intercourse, the memories of which you retain all your life.

Mikhail Ippolitov-Ivanov, *IRM*; reprinted in *PVC4*, p. 240.

# KONSTANTIN SARADZHEV

## (1877–1954)

Konstantin Saradzhev was a Russian violinist and conductor. In 1934 he was to conduct the first performance of Tchaikovsky's early Concert Overture in C minor.

In 1893 Tchaikovsky was at the [Moscow] Conservatoire before his final departure for St Petersburg (I was a 15-year-old student), and from manuscript the Sixth Symphony was played through in the orchestral class, reinforced by teachers and professors (Hřímalý, von Glenn, Sokolovsky and the professors of wind instruments) . . . Safonov was conducting. Alexandra Ivanovna Hubert, the inspector, took pains to see that no one except those in the orchestra remained in the building. I, being both curious and mischievous, contrived to conceal myself so that neither the security men nor the supervisors saw me. The performance in the hall began at four, and I managed to creep up to the door and listen for two hours. There were many stops: it seems they were correcting mistakes in the parts and in the performance. Of course I understood nothing – but all the same I remember that I felt something out of the ordinary was taking place. When the class had finished, the students immediately left the hall. They went out very excited, all feeling that this was something unlike anything they had heard before. Then I saw Tchaikovsky, Safonov and Hřímalý leaving the hall together, and at some distance after them the other teachers. Tchaikovsky was carrying a very large score. His face was very especially red, very agitated. Safonov and Hřímalý walked a little after him, and all were silent. It was difficult to comprehend what all these people had just lived through, but it was clear to me that something out of the ordinary, exceptional, had taken place.

Konstantin Saradzhev, Recollections (1938); published in *Stati. Vospominaniya [Articles. Recollections]* (Moscow, 1962), reprinted in *PVC4*, pp. 316–17.

# XIV

## How did Tchaikovsky die?

### ANONYMOUS

The most contradictory rumours are afloat in the city with regard both to the causes of P. I. Tchaikovsky's illness, and to his death.

Newspaper: *NBG*, St Petersburg, 26 October/7 November 1893; quoted in *PTS*, p. 219.

This editorial comment, which appeared on 7 November, the day following Tchaikovsky's death, set squarely in the public domain a mystery which in recent years has become a subject of intense, sometimes acrimonious controversy. What is not in dispute is that Tchaikovsky arrived in St Petersburg on 22 October to prepare for the première of his Sixth Symphony, and much of his time and energies up to 28 October, when this took place, must have been absorbed by preparations and rehearsals for this. On 31 October he attended a performance of Anton Rubinstein's opera, *Die Makkabäer*, and on 1 November had lunch with a friend, in the evening going to the theatre to see Ostrovsky's play *The Passionate Heart* before dining with relatives and friends in Leiner's Restaurant, one of the most noted in St Petersburg. The following day, 2 November, his illness began. After this he never left Modest's apartment; his death was reported on 6 November.

Included below are the main statements relating to Tchaikovsky's death. First come the differing accounts of the circumstances which gave rise to his supposed illness, then the detailed records of its progress by Modest Tchaikovsky and Lev Bertenson, one of the doctors who attended the composer, as set out in the pages of the St Petersburg press; next come some other relevant materials, and finally the story of the court of honour.

# YURY DAVÏDOV

## (1876–1965)

Yury Davïdov was the youngest of Tchaikovsky's nephews, and at the time of the incident described below would have been 17 and still at school. During his final years he was curator of the Tchaikovsky Musuem at Klin. He was one of the party who attended the performance of Ostrovsky's play *The Passionate Heart*, on 1 November.

At the end of the play, which had been brilliantly performed, we all left the theatre together except for Uncle Modest, who stayed to talk with Mariya Gavrilovna Savina [an actress]. He promised to catch us up if we were walking . . . On the way Pyotr Ilich . . . suggested we went to Leiner's Restaurant, where we had often been with him, for it was one of the few restaurants which would admit us students through the back door (at a price, of course). That evening there were a lot of us who had no right of entry to the restaurant . . . and so we all went into the courtyard and waited until Pyotr Ilich had arranged the matter with the proprietor, and we were summoned. We did not have to wait long. We were conducted to a large private room, and found ourselves reunited . . . At the moment we entered Pyotr Ilich was engaged in ordering supper for everyone . . .

Having completed his order, Pyotr Ilich turned to the waiter and asked him to bring a glass of water. A few minutes later the waiter returned and reported that there was no boiled water. Then Pyotr Ilich, with some stress and irritation in his voice, said:

'Then give me some that's cold and unboiled.'

Everyone began dissuading him from drinking unboiled water, bearing in mind the cholera epidemic in the city. But Pyotr Ilich said that those were precautions in which he did not believe. The waiter went off to carry out his instruction. At that moment the door opened and Modest Ilich came into the private room, accompanied by the actor Yury Yuryev, and exclaimed:

'Ah-ha, what a good guesser I am! As I was passing I came in to ask whether you were here.'

'And where else would we be?' replied Pyotr Ilich.

Almost immediately on Modest Ilich's heels the waiter entered, carrying a glass of water on a tray. Having discovered what was happening and what the continuing dispute with Pyotr Ilich had been about, Modest Ilich became really angry with his brother, and exclaimed:

'I absolutely forbid you to drink unboiled water!'

Laughing, Pyotr Ilich leaped forward to meet the waiter, and Modest Ilich pursued him. But Pyotr Ilich outstripped him, pushed his brother aside with his elbow, and succeeded in gulping down the fateful glass at one go. Modest Ilich reproved him angrily – and then the merriment began.

Yury Davïdov, 'Posledniye dni P. I Chakykovskovo' ['Tchaikovsky's last days'] (1943); published in *PVC4*, pp. 332–3.


# MODEST TCHAIKOVSKY

The account which Modest was to publish in his three-volume biography of his brother (*TZC3*, pp. 648–54) was patently drawn from the following newspaper contribution, as the two accounts are almost word for word the same. Lev Bertenson's account (see below, pp. 213–15), to which Modest refers, had been published five days earlier. Initially Modest described what had happened before Bertenson had arrived.

As a supplement to the short but thoroughly accurate account by Lev Bertenson of the last days of my brother's life, I feel it necessary, in order to dispel all the conflicting rumours, to give you for publication as full an account as possible of everything I witnessed.

On Tuesday evening my brother was at a performance of *The Passionate Heart*. From the theatre he went . . . to Leiner's Restaurant. I had to arrive late and when I got there about an hour later . . . everyone had already finished eating . . .

On the Wednesday morning, 2 November, when I came out of my bedroom, my brother was not as usual taking tea in the drawing room, but was in his own room, and complained to me of having had a bad night because of a stomach disorder. This did not particularly disturb me, because he often had such disorders: they were always very short and sharp. At eleven a.m. he changed and set out for Nápravník's, but in half an hour he returned, not having got there. He decided to take certain measures in addition to the flannel which he had earlier put on. I suggested he should send for Vasily Bernardovich Bertenson, his favourite doctor, but he firmly refused to let me. I did not press the point, knowing that he was accustomed to illnesses of this sort, and that he always got over them by himself. Normally in such instances he found castor oil beneficial. Being convinced that he would resort to this on this occasion, and knowing that in no way could it do him any harm, I was quite unconcerned about his condition, went about my own business, and until one p.m. did not see any more of him. After lunch he had a business appointment with Fyodor Mühlbach [a friend of both Tchaikovsky brothers]. In any case, from eleven a.m. to one p.m. the deceased was well enough to be able to write two business letters; but he was not in the mood to write a third letter in full, and confined himself to a short note. During lunch he was not averse to food; he sat with us, but did not eat – but only, it seems, because he recognized it might be harmful. It was then that he told us that instead of castor oil he had taken Guniadi water. I think that this lunch had a fatal significance, for it was just while we were talking about taking medicine that he poured out a glass of water and took a sip from it. The water was unboiled. We were all alarmed; he alone viewed it with indifference, and reassured us. Of all illnesses cholera was the one he always feared least. Immediately after this he had to leave because he began to feel sick. He did not return to the drawing room, but lay down in his own room so that his stomach might get warm. All the same, neither he nor those of us around him were at all concerned. All this had happened frequently before. Although his indisposition got worse, we put this down to the action of the mineral water. I again suggested I should send for Vasily Bernardovich, but again my proposal was firmly rejected; moreover, a little later he improved, and asked to be allowed to go to sleep. He remained alone in his room and, as I assumed, went to sleep. Having satisfied myself that all was quiet in his bedroom, I went out on my own affairs, and was not back home until five p.m. When I returned the illness had worsened to such an extent that, despite his [Tchaikovsky's] protest, I sent for Vasily Bertenson. However, there were still no alarming signs of a mortal illness.

At about six p.m I again left my brother after putting a hot compress on his stomach. At eight p.m., when I returned, my domestics were tending him, and had managed to transfer him from his bedroom into the room where, later, his coffin stood, because during this time, i.e., from six p.m.

to eight p.m., the vomiting and diarrhoea had become at once so severe that my valet, not waiting for Vasily Bernardovich to arrive, had sent for the first doctor he could find. But all the same, nobody was thinking in terms of cholera.

Vasily Bertenson arrived at eight-fifteen p.m. The vomiting and diarrhoea were all the time becoming more frequent, but the patient was still strong enough to get up every time he needed to. Because none of his excretions had been preserved the doctor could not at first establish that it was cholera, but he was convinced at once of the extreme seriousness and severity of the illness. Having prescribed all that was necessary in such circumstances, the doctor soon judged it essential to call in his brother, Lev Bernardovich Bertenson.

Modest Tchaikovsky, 'Bolezn P. I. Chaikovskovo' ['Tchaikovsky's illness'], in *NV*, 1/13 November 1893.


# GALINA VON MECK
## (1891–1985)

Galina von Meck was a child of the marriage engineered by Tchaikovsky and his patroness Nadezhda von Meck between her son Karl and Tchaikovsky's niece Anna. Though she had no memories of her great-uncle, she knew intimately many of the other principals in the matter (including Modest), and she retails yet another version of the unboiled water story as handed down within the family.

[On 2 November] the composer came back home seemingly very upset by something – we shall never really know what – and not feeling very well. He asked his brother for a glass of water. When told that he would have to wait for the water to be boiled (Petersburg water not being fit to drink unboiled as the town stood on boggy ground) he ignored his brother's protests, went into the kitchen, filled a glass of water from the tap and drank it, saying something like: 'Who cares anyway!'

That same evening he felt quite ill; the doctor who was sent for the next morning diagnosed cholera, which was then ever-present in Petersburg. Three days later the composer died in great agony . . .

Galina von Meck, Epilogue in *Piotr Ilyich Tchaikovsky. Letters to his Family: An Autobiography*, trans. Galina von Meck (London, 1981), p. 555.

## LEV BERTENSON

### (1850–1929)

Lev Bertenson was a doctor, a music enthusiast, and a friend of Modest Tchaikovsky and the composer. What follows here is the newspaper contribution referred to by Modest Tchaikovsky (see p. 210) which had provoked yet more rumours and prompted Modest Tchaikovsky's response. It picks up from the conclusion of Modest Tchaikovsky's account given above. An editorial preamble to Bertenson's article ran: 'The conflicting accounts that have appeared in print concerning the illness of the late Pyotr Ilich Tchaikovsky have caused us to turn to Dr Lev Bertenson, who was in charge of the treatment of the late composer.'

I was called to see Pyotr Ilich on the evening of Thursday, 2 November, with my brother, Vasily Bertenson, who was a close friend of Tchaikovsky's family, and who was in continuous attendance upon all members of that family. When, at about ten p.m., I arrived at Modest Ilich Tchaikovsky's apartment, where Pyotr Ilich was, I found the deceased in the so-called algid phase of cholera. The symptoms were thoroughly characteristic, and I could not but recognize immediately a very serious case of cholera. We instituted all the various measures prescribed for such a situation. By two a.m. we had succeeded in almost stemming the spasms which, before my arrival, had been so violent that the patient had cried out aloud. The bouts of diarrhoea and vomiting became significantly less frequent and less severe. I departed before morning, leaving my brother with the patient. On the Friday morning, while I was absent, there was a further deterioration in Pyotr Ilich's condition: the spasms returned, and the action of the heart became so weak that my brother had to give Pyotr Ilich an injection of muksus and camphor. Early on Friday morning my brother was replaced by my assistant, Dr Mamonov, and I arrived at eleven a.m. The patient's condition was such that I was convinced that the attacks which had threatened his life during the night had passed.

'How do you feel?' I asked Pyotr Ilich.

'Vastly improved,' he replied. 'Thank you, you have snatched me from the jaws of death.'

The convulsive phase of cholera could be considered over. Unfortunately the second stage – the reaction – had not begun. The point is that in cases of cholera as serious as that which Pyotr Ilich had, the kidneys normally cease to function through rapid deterioration. Complete failure of the deceased's kidneys had been apparent from the beginning of the illness. This is a very dangerous manifestation, for it involves blood poisoning from the constituents of the urine [uraemia]. On the Friday, however, there were no very marked signs of this poisoning. All measures were taken to revive the action of the kidneys, but all these proved unavailing. Nevertheless I did not take one measure – a [hot] bath – until Saturday, and this is why: the mother of the late Pyotr Ilich had died of cholera – and had died at the very moment they had placed her in the bath. Pyotr Ilich knew this, and this had instilled in him and all his relatives a superstitious terror of the bath. On Saturday signs of uraemia became apparent, and there was simultaneously a new and very significant increase in the diarrhoea, which now indicated the paralytic condition of the intestines. The diarrhoea had a very depressing effect upon the deceased, and he turned to me, saying:

'Let me go! Do not torment yourself: it's all the same to me if I don't get better.'

I suggested to Pyotr Ilich that we should give him the bath. He readily agreed. When he had been placed in it, I asked:

'Do you find the bath unpleasant?'

'On the contrary, it's pleasant,' he replied, but after a while he began asking to be lifted out, complaining of weakness.

The immediate result of the bath was beneficial: a hot sweat occurred, and with this, a hope that the uraemia would diminish, and that the functioning of the kidneys would be restored. But by evening this hope had gone. Drowsiness set in, and there was a sudden weakening of the heart action, so severe that Dr Zander, who had been left with Pyotr Ilich, gave the patient a muksus injection, and sent for me. I found Pyotr Ilich comatose, and with a drastically weakened heart action; it was possible to revive him from this only for a very short time. Thus, for example, when he was offered a drink, he took it with full consciousness, saying, 'That's enough', 'Some more', and so on. At ten-thirty p.m. all hopes that there might possibly be a favourable turn in his illness completely disappeared.

His drowsiness became deeper still, his pulse became imperceptible despite frequently repeated injections of stimulants. At two a.m. the death throes began, and at three a.m. Pyotr Ilich was no more.

Lev Bertenson, 'Bolezn P. I. Chaikovskovo' ['Tchaikovsky's illness'], in *NV*, 27 October/8 November 1893.

## MODEST TCHAIKOVSKY

This is a continuation of Modest's narrative, and is his account of the events already described by Lev Bertenson.

The situation was getting more alarming. The motions were becoming more frequent and very copious. The weakening so increased that the patient could not move unaided. The vomiting was especially unbearable; while vomiting, and for several moments afterwards, he became thoroughly frenzied and cried out at the top of his voice, never once complaining about the ache in his abdominal cavity, but only about the unbearably awful state of his chest. On one occasion he turned to me and said: 'I think I'm dying. Farewell!' He subsequently repeated these words several times. After every motion he sank back on the bed completely exhausted. However, as yet there were no lividity or spasms.

Lev Bertenson and his brother arrived at eleven p.m. and, after examining the patient and his motions, declared it was cholera. Immediately they sent for a medical attendant. Including the doctors there were eight of us present with the patient: the two [in the original 'three'] Counts Litke, our nephew [Vladimir] Davïdov, my valet Nazar Litrov, the medical attendant, and myself. At midnight my brother began complaining of spasms and crying out aloud. We began directing our collective efforts to massaging him. The patient was fully conscious. The spasms appeared simultaneously in various parts of his body, and my brother asked us to massage now this part of his body, now that. His head and bodily extremities began to turn very blue and were completely cold. Shortly before the appearance of the first spasms, the deceased asked me:

'It's not cholera, is it?'

However, I concealed the truth from him. But when he heard the doctor give an instruction about precautionary measures against infection, he cried out:

'So it is cholera!'

It is difficult to recount the details of this phase of the illness. Right up to five a.m. it was one unbroken struggle with his numbness and his spasms which, the longer they were, the less they were amenable to our energetic rubbing and warming of his body. There were several moments when it seemed that death had come, but an injection of muksus and a tannin enema revived the patient.

By five a.m. the illness began to abate. My brother became relatively calm, complaining only of his depressed condition. Up to this point the most alarming thing had been those moments when my brother had complained of the pain around his heart, and of being suffocated. Now this ceased. Three-quarters of an hour of complete calm went by. The vomiting and motions lost their alarming appearance, but were quite frequently repeated. The spasms occurred whenever he tried to move. He developed a thirst, but said that drinking was incomparably more pleasing in his imagination than in reality; on being given a teaspoonful of something to drink, he turned away from it in distaste. Yet a few minutes later he was asking for the same thing again. In general what troubled him most was the anxiety that the outward signs of his illness occasioned to those around him.

During the most serious attacks he, as it were, apologized for the trouble he was causing. He feared that some things would elicit revulsion, and retained his awareness sufficiently to be able to joke sometimes. Thus he turned to our favourite nephew [Vladimir Davïdov], saying:

'I'm afraid you'll lose all respect for me after all these unpleasant things.'

All the time he was telling everyone to go to bed, and thanked us for the slightest service. Early in the morning, as soon as the patient no longer needed nursing, Vasily Bertenson sent me to give an oral notification to the police of what had happened.

On Friday, 3 November, at nine a.m., Vasily Bertenson, who had not left my brother for an instant, was replaced by Dr Mamonov. At that time a relative calm had lasted for about an hour. Vasily Bernardovich gave the case history to Dr Mamonov and left without waiting for my brother to wake up. At this time the lividity had gone, but there were black spots on his face. These quickly disappeared. There came the first remission. We all breathed more freely, but the attacks, though significantly less frequent, still recurred, accompanied by spasms. In any case his general state was sufficiently improved for him to feel he was out of danger. Thus when Lev Bernardovich arrived at about eleven a.m., he said:

'Thank you. You have snatched me from the jaws of death. I'm incomparably better than during the first night.'

He repeated these words more than once during that day and the following. The attacks accompanied by spasms finally ceased about midday. At three p.m. Dr Zander replaced Dr Mamonov. It seemed that the illness had yielded to the impeccably careful treatment, but already the doctor was in fear of the second phase of cholera – inflammation of the kidneys and *status typhosus*, though at that moment there were still no signs of either illness. His only discomfort was an unquenchable thirst. This condition continued until the evening, but by night it was so improved that Dr Mamonov, who came to replace Dr Zander, insisted that we all went to bed, since he saw no threatening symptoms that night.

On the morning of Saturday, 4 November, there was no improvement in the patient's morale. He seemed more depressed than the previous evening. His belief in recovery had vanished.

'Leave me!' he said to the doctors. 'Nothing you do can make any difference. I shan't get better.'

Some irritability began to show itself in his treatment of those around him. The previous evening he had even joked with the doctors, had argued with them about his drink – but on this day he merely obeyed their instructions submissively. The doctors began applying all their efforts to getting his kidneys to function, but all to no avail. We all pinned our hope above all on the hot bath which Lev Bertenson was preparing to give him that evening. I must tell you that our mother died of cholera in 1854, and death came as they placed her in the bath. My elder brother and I automatically had a superstitious fear of this necessary measure. Our fear increased when we heard that, when the doctor asked my brother whether he wished to take the bath, he replied:

'I'm very glad to have the bath, but I shall probably die like my mother when you put me into the bath.'

We were forced to abandon the bath that evening because his diarrhoea again worsened, became uncontrollable, and the patient weakened. Lev Bernadovich left after two a.m., worried by the state of things. Nevertheless the night passed relatively well. After two enemas the diarrhoea decreased significantly, but his kidneys still did not function.

By the morning of Sunday, 5 November, the position was still not hopeless, but the anxiety of the doctors about his kidney failure increased. My brother's general state was very bad. To all inquiries about his condition, he several times replied:

'Terrible!'

To Lev Bernardovich he said:

'How much kindness and patience you are wasting on me! I can't be cured!'

After he had slept his consciousness seemed duller than on the other days. Thus he did not immediately recognize his valet Sofronov, who had arrived that morning from Klin; but he was nevertheless glad to see him. Up to one p.m. the position seemed to those around him to remain unchanged. There was not a drop of urine, so we did not examine it even once. Lev Bernardovich arrived at one p.m. and at once deemed it necessary to resort to the extreme (so it seemed to us) measure for restoring the kidney function: the bath. The bath was ready at two p.m. My brother was in a semi-conscious state while it was being prepared in the same room. He had to be roused. It appears that he did not at first grasp what they wanted to do with him, but he subsequently agreed to the bath, and when he was put into it was fully conscious of what was happening. When the doctor asked him whether he found the hot water unpleasant, he replied:

'On the contrary, it's pleasant.'

But very quickly he began asking to be taken out, saying that he was weak. And, indeed, from the moment he was taken out of the bath his drowsiness and his sleep took on a certain peculiar character. The bath did not have the anticipated result, though it did produce a strong sweat; at the same time, according to the doctors, it reduced for a while the signs of uraemia. The perspiring continued, but at the same time the pulse, which up till then had been comparatively regular and strong, again weakened. Again it was necessary to resort to an injection of muksus to restore its strength. This was successful; despite the sweat, the pulse revived and the patient became calmer. Up to eight p.m. his condition seemed to us to improve. But at eight-fifteen p.m., soon after Dr Mamonov had left, his replacement, Dr Zander, again observed a sharp weakening of the pulse, and was sufficiently alarmed to consider it necessary to inform Lev Bernardovich immediately. As the doctors put it, the patient was at this time in a comatose condition, so that when I went to him in his room, the doctor advised me that I should no longer leave him even for an instant. His head was cold, his breathing laboured and accompanied by moans. However, the question: 'Do you want a drink?' could bring him momentarily to consciousness. He would reply 'Yes' or 'Of course'; afterwards he would say 'That's enough', 'I don't want any', 'I don't need it'. A little after ten p.m. Dr Zander diagnosed the beginning of emphysema, and Lev Bernardovich quickly arrived. At the request of those around, a priest of St Isaak's Cathedral was sent for. The condition of the dying man could be maintained only by increased injections of heart stimulant. All hope of an improvement vanished. The father who came with the Holy Sacraments was unable to administer them because of my brother's unconscious state, and simply read loudly and clearly the prayers for the dying, of which it seems not a single word was heard by my brother. Soon after this the fingers of the dying man moved in a peculiar way suggesting that he felt an itch in various parts of his body.

The doctors continued tirelessly to apply all possible measures to maintain the action of the heart as though they still expected a miracle of recovery. During this time the following persons were at the dying man's bedside: three doctors, the two Litke brothers, Buxhövden, Nikolay Figner, Bzul, our nephew [Vladimir] Davïdov, my brother's valet Sofronov, Litrov, the medical attendant, our brother Nikolay, and I. Lev Bernardovich decided there were too many people for the small room. They opened the window. Figner and Bzul left. Bertenson, considering all hope to be lost, departed in extreme exhaustion, leaving Dr Mamonov to witness the last moments. He [Tchaikovsky] breathed less frequently, though he could, it seems, be brought back to awareness by questions about a drink. He was no longer responding in words but only by positive or negative signs.

Suddenly his eyes, which up until then had been half-closed and glazed, opened wide. There appeared an indescribable expression of full consciousness. In turn his gaze rested upon the three people who were standing near him, then he looked up to the sky. For a few moments his eyes lit up, and then faded with his last breath. It was a little after three a.m.*

---

*The fullest discussions of the circumstances surrounding Tchaikovsky's death and of the relevant evidence are in Alexandra Orlova's book, *Tchaikovsky: A Self-Portrait*, trans. R. M. Davison (Oxford and New York, 1990), pp. 406–14, and in articles by Orlova (*OTL*) and Alexander Poznansky (*PTS*).

Modest Tchaikovsky, 'Bolezn P. I. Chaykovskovo' ['Tchaikovsky's illness'], in *NV*, 1/13 November 1893.

## DOCTORS' BULLETINS

The medical bulletins of 5 November 1893 posted on the door of Modest's apartment:

*2.30 p.m.* The dangerous symptoms are still present, and are not responding to treatment. There is complete retention of the urine, together with drowsiness and a marked general weakness.

*10.30 p.m.* Since three p.m. there has been increasing weakness . . . There are very strong signs of uraemia . . . Since ten p.m. the pulse has been almost undetectable, and there is emphysema.

*OTL*, p. 145.

## GALINA VON MECK

There were, besides his brother Modest and the doctor, several other people present [at the composer's deathbed] and the interpretation of some of the things said by the dying man in his agony, according to what I know from the composer's nephew [in fact, first cousin once removed], young Count Alexander Litke (Sania Litke) who was present, was completely different from the way his brother Modest related them.

Galina von Meck, from Epilogue to *Piotr Ilyich Tchaikovsky. Letters to his Family: An Autobiography*, trans. Galina von Meck (London, 1981), p. 555.

## OFFICIAL REGULATIONS

In the case of death through cholera [the body] is to be removed from the home as quickly as possible in a tightly sealed coffin; in addition, funerals and funeral banquets attended by many people should be avoided.

Government bulletin: *Directions concerning measures of personal protection against cholera*, 2/14 July 1892; quoted in *OTL*, p. 129.

Isolation of cholera patients should be effected either in the homes where they have fallen ill or by removal of the patient from his home to a medical institution . . . The bodies of those who have died from cholera should be wrapped in a shroud moistened with a sublimate solution and, insofar as possible, placed quickly in the coffin . . . Homes in which there have been cases of illness or death from cholera should be visited immediately and without fail by those persons specially designated to carry out measures concerning disinfection of excretions, clothing, linen, bed and rooms of the sick or dead.

Government bulletin: 9/21 June 1892 and 25 March/6 April 1893; quoted in *PTS*, p. 219.

## VASILY BERTENSON

### (1853–1933)

Vasily Bertenson, the brother of Lev, openly admitted that he had never encountered a case of cholera before Tchaikovsky's.

Despite the fact that all thinking Russia (and not only Russia but all Europe also), grieving at such a loss, has read with the keenest interest every detail of Pyotr Ilich's last days written down by his brother, Modest Ilich, and printed in *Novoye vremya [New Time]* and *Novosti [News]*, despite the presence at the sick man's bedside of four doctors, yet there were then, and there are now, people who said, and say, with confidence that Pyotr Ilich did not die of cholera at all, but committed suicide with poison!

Vasily Bertenson, 'Za tridtsat let – Pyotr i Modest Chaykovsky (listki iz vospominany)' ['Thirty years – Pyotr and Modest Tchaikovsky (pages from recollections)']; published in *IV*, xxviii (June, 1912), reprinted in *PVC4*, p. 343.

## ALEXANDRA ORLOVA

Alexandra Orlova is a former Soviet musical scholar who emigrated to the USA in 1979, bringing with her the court-of-
honour story (see below, pp. 224–5).

By the 1920s Vasily Bertenson no longer concealed the truth about the
cause of Tchaikovsky's death. And so he told the musicologist, Georgy
Orlov, a friend of the now aged doctor's son, the pianist Nikolay Bertenson, that Tchaikovsky committed suicide. At about the same time the
doctor Alexander Zander told the same story to his son Yury (Yury Zander
was also a friend of Georgy Orlov and told him what his father had said to
him). All this became known to me too, since in the 1930s Georgy Orlov
married me and we talked a lot about Tchaikovsky's death. Professor
Alexander Ossovsky, the Director of the Research Institute for Music and
Drama, where I worked after the war, also talked of Tchaikovsky's suicide. In other words the fact of the composer's suicide had long ceased to be
a secret.

Alexandra Orlova, *Tchaikovsky: A Self-Portrait*, trans. R. M. Davison (Oxford
and New York, 1990), p. 411.

## PRESS BULLETIN

The deceased lies on a couch, as if he were alive, and looks as if he is
asleep. A photograph of the deceased was taken by the photographer of the
Imperial Theatres.

Report in *NV*, 26 October/7 November 1893; printed in op. cit., p. 410.

## NIKOLAY RIMSKY-KORSAKOV

Rimsky-Korsakov visited Modest Tchaikovsky's apartment to pay
his respects to the composer's body.

Several days [after the première of the Sixth Symphony] news was flying
about of his serious illness. Several times a day everyone went to his
apartment [in fact, Modest's] to inquire about his health. His unexpected

end struck everyone, and then followed the requiems and the funeral. How strange that, though death came from cholera, there was free access to the requiems [before the open coffin]. I remember that Verzhbilovich, quite drunk after some carousal, kissed the deceased on the head and face . . . The composer's sudden end, which raised all sorts of gossip . . .

Nikolay Rimsky-Korsakov, *RKL*, p. 246.

## ALOYS MOOSER (1876–1969)/
## MARY WOODSIDE

Aloys Mooser was a Swiss musicologist and critic who worked in St Petersburg from 1896 to 1909. The following incident is narrated in his unpublished memoirs compiled during the last three years of his life, but based upon notes made while he was still in the Russian capital. Mary Woodside, an assistant professor in the Music Department of the University of Guelph, has edited these memoirs for publication. Unfortunately Dr Woodside has been unable, for copyright reasons, to provide a direct transcription of Mooser's text, and the following is her published summary of his account.

It was during his [Mooser's] first winter in the capital that he heard the rumors of Tchaikovsky's homosexuality and some unspecified time later the related story of the composer's suicide, just three years before Mooser's arrival. His informant was Riccardo Drigo, composer and conductor of the Imperial ballet troupe, who had worked with Tchaikovsky on that composer's three ballets. Somewhat incredulous, Mooser verified the story with the composer Alexander Glazunov, whose upright moral character, veneration of the composer, and friendship with Tchaikovsky are stressed in his introduction as a 'witness'.*

Mary Woodside, Communication to 'Comment and Chronicle', in *19th Century Music*, xiii, no. 3 (Spring 1990), pp. 273–4.

*In a private communication, André Lischke, the French scholar, informed the present writer that his father had been a pupil of Glazunov in Petrograd in 1920, and that Glazunov had told him that Tchaikovsky had committed suicide.

# ALEXANDER VOITOV

## (*d* 1966)

Alexander Voitov became curator of coins at the Russian Museum in Leningrad. A pupil at the School of Jurisprudence during its last years before the First World War, he had already developed a passion for the history of the school, and had amassed a great deal of information about former pupils. The following was taken down by Alexandra Orlova from Voitov's oral account in 1966.

Among the pupils who completed their studies at the School of Jurisprudence at the same time as Tchaikovsky there occurs the name of Jacobi. When I was at the school I spent all my holidays at Tsarskoye Selo with the family of Nikolay Borisovich Jacobi, who had been senior procurator to the Senate in the 1890s and who died in 1902. Jacobi's widow, Ekaterina Karlovna, was connected with my parents by ties of affinity and friendship. She was very fond of me and welcomed me warmly. In 1913, when I was in the last but one class at the school, the twentieth anniversary of Tchaikovsky's death was widely commemorated. It was then, apparently under the influence of surging recollections, that Mrs Jacobi, in great secrecy, told me the story which she confessed had long tormented her. She said that she had decided to reveal it to me because she was now old and felt she had not the right to take to her grave such an important and terrible secret. 'You,' she said, 'are interested in the history of the school and the fate of its pupils, and therefore you ought to know the whole truth, the more so since it is such a sad page in the school's history.' And this is what she told me.

The incident took place in the autumn of 1893. Tchaikovsky was threatened with a terrible misfortune. Duke Stenbok-Fermor, disturbed by the attention which the composer was paying his young nephew, wrote a letter of accusation to the Tsar and handed the letter to Jacobi to pass on to Alexander III. Through exposure Tchaikovsky was threatened with the loss of all his rights, with exile to Siberia, with inevitable disgrace. Exposure would also bring disgrace upon the School of Jurisprudence, and upon all old boys of the school, Tchaikovsky's fellow students. Yet the honour of the school uniform was sacred. To avoid publicity Jacobi decided upon the following: he invited all Tchaikovsky's former schoolfriends [he could trace in St Petersburg] and set up a court of honour which included himself. Altogether there were eight people present. Ekaterina Karlovna sat with her needlework in her usual place alongside her husband's study. From time to time from within she could hear voices, sometimes loud and agitated, sometimes dropping apparently to a whisper. This went on for a very long time, almost five hours. Then Tchaikovsky came headlong out of the study. He was almost running, he was unsteady, and he went out without saying a word. He was very white and agitated. All the others stayed a long time in the study talking quietly. When they had gone Jacobi told his wife, having made her swear absolute silence, what they had decided about the Stenbok-Fermor letter to the Tsar. Jacobi could not withhold it. And so the old boys [of the school] had come to a decision by which Tchaikovsky had promised to abide. They required him to kill himself . . . A day or two later news of the composer's mortal illness was circulating in St Petersburg.

Alexander Voitov, oral account noted down by Alexandra Orlova in 1966, printed in *OTL*, pp. 133–4.

## NATALIYA KUZNETSOVA-VLADIMOVA

Nataliya Kuznetsova-Vladimova is the granddaughter of Vera Kuznetsova (*née* Denisyeva), a younger sister of the wife of Tchaikovsky's eldest brother, Nikolay. This private letter to Alexandra Orlova was prompted by reading Orlova's retelling, in the Russian-language journal *Kontinent*, of Voitov's account of the court of honour.

From my childhood I had certain knowledge of Tchaikovsky's suicide through my paternal grandmother Vera Sergeyevna Kuznetsova (*née* Denisyeva). Her elder sister, Olga Sergeyevna, was married to Tchaikovsky's brother Nikolay Ilich. Vera Sergeyevna told the same version that you do. She lived in Leningrad . . . dying at the beginning of 1955 at a great age, but sound in mind and good in memory. [She had heard it] probably from Olga Sergeyevna, but in fact spoke of it most reluctantly, seeing in this court of honour a kind of besmirching of a gentleman's honour for Tchaikovsky. But more than once she referred to Jacobi very aggressively . . . While writing to you I could hear how she pronounced that name . . .

Vera Sergeyevna said that Alexander III knew of the letter *after* Tchaikovsky's death. I well remember that at our home in 1952 my grandmother
talked with Yury Iosifovich Slonimsky, the author of books on ballet, and
when he said that the cause of Tchaikovsky's suicide was that he had paid
improper attention to the heir [to the throne], she had corrected him. 'No,
it was to the nephew of Count Stenbok and not to the heir . . .'

Nataliya Kuznetsova-Vladimova, private letter written in 1987 to Alexandra
Orlova.

# XV
# Posthumous notes and obituaries

# A variety of personal reactions

## ANTON CHEKHOV
### (1860–1904)

Tchaikovsky first met Chekhov at the end of 1888, and between
1889 and 1891 they corresponded; there was even talk of an
operatic collaboration between them. Chekhov's admiration for
Tchaikovsky led him to dedicate a collection of stories to him.

The news staggered me. It is a terrible anguish. I loved and revered Pyotr
Ilich very much, and I am indebted to him for much. You have my
heartfelt sympathy.

Anton Chekhov, telegram to Modest Tchaikovsky, 8 November 1893; published
in Chekhov (A.P.), *Pisma v 12 tomakh [Letters in 12 volumes]* (Moscow, 1974–), v,
p. 240.

## ANTON RUBINSTEIN
### (1830–94)

Anton Rubinstein had been Tchaikovsky's principal teacher at the
St Petersburg Conservatoire in the 1860s. As a personality he
remained an object of veneration to Tchaikovsky for the rest of his
life, and it was a bitter disappointment to the latter that Rubinstein found very little he could like in Tchaikovsky's own
music. Yet this was far from the sum total of Rubinstein's view of
his former pupil's talents.

What do you say about Tchaikovsky's death? Is it possible this is the will of
God? What a loss for music in Russia! Yet you know, he was in the prime
of life, he was only 50 – and all this for a glass of water! What a nonsense
are all such tricks – and this life – and creation – and everything, and
everything.

Anton Rubinstein, letter to his sister Sofiya, 11 November 1893; published in

Rubinstein (A.), *Literaturnoye naslediye [Literary legacy]*, iii (Moscow, 1986), p. 140.

# IGOR STRAVINSKY

Tchaikovsky's death . . . affected me deeply. Incidentally, the fame of the composer was so great that after he was known to have cholera the government issued bulletins about the progress of his illness. Not everyone was aware of him, though. When I went to school and awesomely announced to my classmates that Tchaikovsky was dead, one of them wanted to know which grade he was in.

Igor Stravinsky and Robert Craft, *Expositions and Developments* (London, 1962), p. 87.

# MARIE SCHEIKEVITCH
## (?–?)

Marie Scheikevitch was a lady given to a certain literary embellishment – though there is no reason to doubt the essential truth of what she reports here. She recalls the meeting between her father and Tolstoy one winter's day.

Tolstoy says: 'Tchaikovsky is dead,' – and two huge tears (for everything is larger than life with him, she says), rolled down his great cheeks.

Marie Scheikevitch, as quoted in Paul Morand, *Journal d'un attaché d'ambassade, 1916–1917* (Paris, 1963), p. 65.

## Tributes and assessments

Except for the short excerpt from the reminiscences of Vasily Yastrebtsev, whose appreciation observes Tchaikovsky from a very different musical viewpoint within the Russian musical scene, the remaining materials in this final chapter are from two of his closest lifelong friends. Between them they draw together many of the threads spun in the preceding chapters.

# NIKOLAY KASHKIN

The first two-thirds of Kashkin's obituary of Tchaikovsky had traced his compositional career; this final portion reflects upon more general matters.

Tchaikovsky's significance for Russian music is huge. His symphonic compositions constitute the chief foundation of Russian musical literature, and rank with the best compositions of this kind in the most recent musical literature of all Europe, if they do not [actually] occupy the first place. Being by his fundamental nature a truly Russian man, by upbringing and education he belonged to the pan-European community, and the spirit of narrow nationalism was tótally alien to him; nevertheless, an attachment to his native land was one of the fundamental traits of his character. Revering nature and its beauty to the highest degree, he knew how to value it everywhere – in Germany, and in Switzerland, and in Italy, and in France – but from everywhere he was drawn back to his native woods and fields, which were in essence dearer to him than all the others. He was always particularly drawn to the surroundings of Moscow, which had for him (in his own words) a special charm. Being well versed in European literature, knowing how to assess writers of all countries, his truest sympathies were for Russian writers, among whom Pushkin, Gogol, Ostrovsky and Tolstoy occupied for him, I think, the first place: at least, he re-read them more often than the rest. These sympathies were also reflected in his attitude to music. Brought up in his childhood and youth on Italian music, he subsequently transferred his enthusiasm to the German classics and to Glinka, whom he considered one of the greatest of all composers. Along with these models of art music he felt a great attraction to native Russian song, but made a very sharp distinction between these and every counterfeit or urban modernization of a song. He felt total disdain towards the artificial style of what are called 'Ukrainian songs', finding that real Ukrainian folksongs were hardly at all distinguishable from Russian; he sometimes used such themes – for example, as the opening theme of his Second Symphony, as the theme of the finale, and in the finale of his First Piano Concerto. He could himself compose themes in a purely folk style – as, for instance, in the first peasant chorus in *Eugene Onegin*, where he took the words of a folksong, though because he did not like the tune he replaced it with a melody of his own. In his compositions the Russian element manifested itself not only in the folk melodies he took, but in the national shading, very obvious in very many of them, sometimes even in opposition to the main purpose of the work – as, for instance, in Ophelia's theme in the overture *Hamlet*. He also used harmonic devices that can be accounted for only by reference to the corpus of Russian folksong, which rarely permitted a sharpened leading note; but such harmonic peculiarities occurred in his work with complete naturalness, without any straining, and gave his harmony a particular colour.

Pyotr Ilich did not tolerate bombast in music, and so he did not rate Liszt very highly. He placed Wagner immeasurably higher, but the ultra-romantic lining of the subjects of his final operas, their contrived symbolism and the no less contrived solemnity in their actions were deeply antipathetic to him, so that he did not even go to see *Parsifal*, though he knew excerpts from it from concert performances and from the piano score. Most truly of all he loved the music of Mozart, being captivated both by its melodic beauty and by the spontaneous refinement of its work-manship. His love for Mozart had been transformed into a kind of rever-ential cult; he himself was sometimes surprised by the impression he made on him.

Pyotr Ilich visited the Moscow Conservatoire on 21 October, the last day of his stay in Moscow; they sang for him his own arrangement, for four voices with accompaniment (and on a text he had written himself), of a section of Mozart's C minor Fantasia for piano (Fantasie et sonate) [K475]. Pyotr Ilich sat beside me in the hall, and was so delighted that he was, so he said, ready to weep; the quartet was sung twice, and he himself proposed to perform it in one of the symphony concerts. Today his wish is being fulfilled, and the quartet 'Night' will be sung by the very same performers whom he heard for the last time at the Conservatoire. It was there at the Conservatoire that he told me, among other things, that the beauty of [Mozart's] melody was for him a mystery, and that he himself could not explain the inexpressible loveliness of that quartet's simple melody. Of course, it never entered the head of any of those who were at the Conservatoire on that occasion that this meeting would be a farewell, and that in little more than a fortnight this bright hope of Russian music would be no more, and that we should never again see this healthy, hale and hearty man, who bade farewell to everyone in expectation of a speedy reunion, since he intended without fail to be at the symphony concert on 4 November.

The loss of Tchaikovsky is a great and weighty one for all, but he must be especially mourned by all young Russian talents, for whom he was a trustworthy and powerful aid and protector. It is impossible to describe the exquisite kindness and delicacy with which he behaved towards all young people who brought or sent him their compositions. However much he valued his own time, he not only looked over carefully what had been sent to him, but very often wrote long letters with a detailed commentary, even if what had been sent merited this only a little – but, in any case, with a word of comfort or encouragement, even when the [compositional] instincts were not markedly good. If, however, he encountered something particularly talented, then he was always ready, even at personal expense and through efforts of all kinds, at the very least to advance a young talent. But the deceased behaved with the same heartfelt warmth towards everyone who turned to him for help; his heart, overflowing with love, could not bear the sufferings of others, and he was inclined rather to put himself in a difficult situation than deny help to someone in need.

Nikolay Kashkin, Obituary; published in *RV*, 6/18 November 1893, reprinted in *PVC4*, pp. 361–2.


# VASILY YASTREBTSEV

As a composer Tchaikovsky was without doubt one of the most gifted of his epoch. It seems to me it is in the contemporariness of his music that is concealed the fundamental reason, perhaps even the secret, of his huge popularity. Indeed, at the time when Musorgsky and Dargomïzhsky were forging an extreme naturalism and a genre that was not always artistic – when Borodin was submerging himself in a prehistoric epoch, with its alluring, powerful, heroic remoteness – when Rimsky-Korsakov, that indisputably greatest of contemporary musical artists, has been drawn into his own personal, clearly individual, pagan, fairy-tale (or, more precisely) 'illusory' world filled with the finest, almost unrivalled beauty and poetry – and when Cui with his amazingly talented [opera] *William Ratcliffe* flies off into a Scotland that is alien to us – Tchaikovsky has been filled totally with the spirit of the age, and with all the highly strung fervour of his deeply sensitive and impressionable nature has responded to its summons – and behold, while embodying in sounds images of the past, the epoch of our grandfathers and forebears, he has always remained true to himself and, perhaps without noticing it himself, has 'depicted us ourselves alone', with our unresolved doubts, our sorrows and our joys.

Vasily Yastrebtsev, Recollections; published in *RMG* (1899), no. 10, reprinted in *PVC4*, p. 215.

# HERMAN LAROCHE

The following extracts are taken from some of the posthumous tributes paid by Laroche to his departed friend. The first deals primarily with Tchaikovsky's non-musical characteristics and interests, the second with matters relating to music. The concluding obituary (which was, in fact, the earliest of these writings, appearing only four days after the composer's death) omits mention of Tchaikovsky's darker side, of his moods and depressive phases, and to a degree idealizes the man, but there is no doubt about the essential truthfulness of the rest.

Perhaps I am labouring under self-deception, but it seems to me the Tchaikovsky of the 1860s and the Tchaikovsky of the 1880s were two separate persons. The 22-year-old Tchaikovsky with whom I became acquainted at the St Petersburg Conservatoire was a young man of the world, completely clean-shaven (contrary to the already general fashion of that time), dressed rather carelessly in a suit that came from an expensive tailor but was not quite new, with manners that were enchantingly simple but, as it then seemed to me, cold. He had a host of acquaintances, and when we were going along the Nevsky Prospect together he was endlessly raising his hat. Mostly (though not exclusively) it was the smart set who exchanged bows with him. Of foreign languages he knew French and a little Italian; in particular he flaunted his ignorance of German, saying for instance '*Er ist an der Sehnsucht gestorben*' (meaning to say 'He died of consumption'), or '*Was dieser Mensch für ein Geheimniss hat*' (in Russian, 'What a memory that man has!'), or '*Ich habe grosse Gelegenheit zu schlafen*' (i.e. 'I'm longing to go to sleep'), from which the Germans in whose company he happened to be invariably went into stitches . . .

Of his other traits that I noticed [after he had entered the St Petersburg Conservatoire], his carelessness in his dress . . . increased so that in 1866 and 1867 his Moscow Conservatoire colleagues, who themselves had in no way made a speciality of being dandies, badgered and made fun of him for his slovenliness. He had unusually good health, but had an uncommon dread of death, even fearing everything that did no more than hint at death; you could not use in his presence the words coffin, grave, funeral, and so on. One thing that most distressed him in Moscow was that the entrance to his apartment (which through circumstances he could not change) was alongside an undertaker's. I will add that while in the 1880s Pyotr Ilich was an indefatigable walker, in this earlier period and for a long time afterwards he was no good at walking, and even for the very shortest distances would take a cab. And while I have just said that I walked along the Nevsky Prospect with him, then this was an exception which was characteristic of the St Petersburger: even those who in general did not walk walked along the Nevsky Prospect. This was particularly true of the 1860s, when people paraded aimlessly up and down its wide footway.

I think that many readers will view this characteristic with disbelief. The Tchaikovsky who is so well known to the present generation hardly at all recalls the earlier. With his hair as white as snow and thinning greatly, with his small, carefully trimmed beard, dressed not only irreproachably but invariably in a fresh, as it were, new suit, he resembled an old man only in the colour of his voice; in everything else he gave an impression of good spirits, liveliness and energy even greater than in the previous time. From being the obscure 'head of a desk' in a department of [the Ministry of] Justice, he had managed to become the world-wide celebrity. But his acquaintances had, it seems, become ten times fewer. In the 1890s I had occasion again, as thirty years before, to walk along the Nevsky Prospect with him, but it happened that we met not a single person he knew. Though he had become elegant and even fussy in his appearance, he had long since ceased to be a man of the world in the former sense of the word, was rarely in upper-class salons in the role of a 'star', but mostly knew and was friendly only with musicians, with whom he had hundreds of business connections – and, in many individual instances, also warm, heartfelt relations . . .

He began to play the piano less and less, but in all other branches of his art he did not stop going forward, and sometimes in his old age revealed totally new, unexpected abilities – as happened, for instance, with conducting. Italian he largely forgot, but began understanding German excellently, and spoke it quite animatedly, though inaccurately. He also tried to learn English, but soon gave it up. He looked upon death much more calmly, so that not only did he permit others to tell him that so-and-so had died or was about to, but would even bring up the subject himself – and, for instance, would recount in detail how one of his friends [Nikolay Kondratyev] had died in his arms in Aachen. Walking became for him not only a rule but also a panacea; he walked not only in the country, but also in large towns, where he was on flying visits, up to seven miles a day if that was possible, for the most part from two to four in the afternoon, asserting that this motion was the best remedy against headaches, nervous overstraining, lack of appetite, and a great number of other ailments. It may or may not be relevant to say that Pyotr Ilich, neither in his youth nor in his mature years, liked resorting to medical help, but treated himself, and only took medicine reluctantly and as infrequently as possible. Above all he relied on hygiene, of which he appeared, to my layman's view, to be a true master. He had managed to reduce to a precise art (I continue to speak as a layman) how to identify all that was good and all that was harmful to him, and on the basis of his observations subjected himself to a most strict regime little evident to the outsider because in the application of his rules he managed to show not the slightest finickiness. The sole exception was, if you like, the aforementioned afternoon walk; thanks to that, he often had to 'break up the party' and leave a more or less numerous company . . .

Laroche comments upon Tchaikovsky's liking for amateur theatricals, though Laroche never saw any of these performances for himself.

I would readily believe that he had a talent for dramatic and especially comic scenes because he was exceptionally observant and sometimes could imitate very successfully common acquaintances.

A passion for the theatre – that is, for going to the theatre – was one of the traits which, with almost equal force, was characteristic of both the young and the mature Tchaikovsky. In his youth he, completely in accordance with what were then his predominating social inclinations and habits, loved most of all the Italian opera and the Mikhailovsky Theatre, then the Alexandrinsky Theatre and the ballet; like a second Eugene Onegin, he spoke of the ballet in the tone of an expert, and regarded with the profoundest contempt the 'vulgarians' who went to the ballet only for the pleasure of staring at the long-legged dancers . . .

I cannot give myself up to my memories of Tchaikovsky without forth-

with talking about his literary abilities and occupations. In his life literature occupied a place much larger than in that of the average educated
person. After music, it was his main and most substantial preoccupation.
He was not at all interested in the arts of representation; like everyone he
went to exhibitions, but did not rush to go round museums and galleries
and, as though ridiculing his own ignorance, said that in all the Imperial
Hermitage he recognized only the hall of Russian painting. There is no
doubt that his love of literature contributed to this, and also his earlier
friendship with Apukhtin. But in my view the chief reason was that he
himself was to a significant degree a born literary person . . . When his
letters, or a portion of them, come to be printed (which will certainly
follow sooner or later), then it will be apparent how far a man, who lived
in a world of chords and rhythms, wrote more lucidly, more cleanly,
more logically and more gracefully than the majority of our contemporary
professional men of letters. In regard of the purity of the Russian language
and its logical application Pyotr Ilich was extremely strict, was affronted
by the illiteracy widespread in our daily press, and bought and read some
newspapers solely because of the comic pearls of style and thought with
which they abounded. There is no doubt that this conjunction in him of
musical and literary gifts would have made him a first-class writer on
music if he had had the slightest inclination for this. But to the degree that
he loved literature in general, to that same degree he ignored literature on
music, and he even felt oppressed by critical judgements about music. I
know of only one book which constituted an exception: Otto Jahn on
Mozart which, for several years on end, did not leave his table, and whose
margins are covered with various of his *boutades*, expressions of sympathy,
and so on. The reason for this was not so much the classical merits of the
work, to which there are very few equals among biographies, as to the
simple circumstance that it was the best book about Mozart, who was for
Tchaikovsky the ideal musician and artist in all aspects. The tiniest detail
concerning this individual of genius was filled with significance for him –
but this curiosity in no way extended to the history of music in general, and
I rarely saw an artist to whom the history of his art offered so little that was
attractive . . . Once he let me show him a passage from Giovanni Gabrieli
and it left him extremely unsatisfied. This dislike was not confined to the
period of the so-called strict style. Many years later, when we were already
in the 1880s, I showed him vocal scores of operas by Lully and Rameau –
more precisely, a single page (in many cases, two pages) of each. This time

I might have expected success, since Pyotr Ilich himself had at some time past acquainted me with Weckerlin's collection. *Echos du [temps] passé*, and one of the melodies Weckerlin had selected had so attracted him that later he even inserted it into his [opera] *The Maid of Orléans*. However, success did not ensue even here; he only asked in bewilderment: 'What's good in this?'

I have recalled his attitude to old music in order to observe a significant contradiction. That same Pyotr Ilich, who found nothing worthy of attention, nothing alive, in the history of music, loved political history passionately, though he loved it in his own way, after his own fashion. Besides poets and men of letters, on whom in general he did not fall avidly, having [instead] among them a little Parnassus of the chosen ones who satisfied him, he read exclusively history – moreover, almost exclusively Russian history. Works on Western history are to be found very rarely in his library; of ancient history only Herodotus in a French translation. He was interested least of all in the ancient history of Russia itself; the Russia of which he never tired of reading began with the accession of the Romanovs – and especially of Peter the Great. In his last years Pyotr Ilich's small library was constantly growing, and there began to appear in it books such as Petrushevsky on Suvorov, Bogdanovich on Alexander I, and so on. But such works did not epitomize his main inclinations. His true passion was memoirs – history of a sort where the fates of the state and of society vanish in favour of the description of individuality, of the detailed delineation of the psychological and the social. From the inception of popular historical journals filled with materials of precisely this kind, and until his last days, Pyotr Ilich was a constant reader of *Russky Arkhiv [Russian Archive]*, *Russkaya Starina [Old Russia]*, and *Istorichesky Vestnik [The Historical Herald]*. It goes without saying that in journals of a more general nature he would again settle down with the greatest curiosity to articles on Russian history.

Herman Laroche, *MTC*; reprinted in *LIS2*, pp. 178–83.

There are artists, at times highly talented, whose whole point of existence consists in bowing low to the crowd and flattering their instincts. In their hands art turns into the production of fancy merchandise. No inner content, no natural originality can hold out against their consuming craving for comfort and honours. Their life is sometimes brilliant but, by the nature of things, cannot be long-lasting; their compositions, quickly losing their *bouquet* and even their capacity for being remembered, remain for the historian as intriguing evidence to the taste (or lack of taste) of an epoch. There are other artists for whom the sympathy of the crowd has neither charm nor interest. Engrossed in themselves, they shun the noise of society, and dedicate themselves exclusively to the service of the chosen ideal. Their stern Muse, which arouses only bewilderment in the mass of people or which is even quite unnoticed, sometimes finds a close circle of ardent and staunchly true adherents. Neither material prosperity nor the delights of self-esteem are the lot of such artists; the strongest among them obtain a long and durable moral influence, become models for imitation, the founders of schools.

Pyotr Ilich belongs neither to the one nor to the other type. He was true to himself, and carried out every task he undertook with the greatest artistic conscientiousness. But this strictness with himself, this striving for an ideal, did not separate him from, but brought him closer to, the mass of the public. In the same way that his compositions satisfied him, they also satisfied others, and in order to please a broad circle of listeners he did not need to sacrifice the least part of his own cherished aims. His compositions traced, as it were, a middle path between Gounod and Schumann; they had outer brilliance and inner warmth, they pleased the uninitiated and the expert, could serve as a model for fashion, yet outlive its caprices . . .

Towards the end of his life his artistic fame was, of course, a great support, but I remember vividly that time when there was no fame – yet Pyotr Ilich just the same enchanted everyone who came into contact with him. One must also not forget that, while his artistic laurels drew many to him, they could also antagonize others towards him, provoking regrettable but almost inevitable manifestations of envy. In fairness it must be said that his profession[al life] was free from thorns of this kind to a rare degree. One does not have to be very well read in the biographies of great artists to observe that the majority of them endured incomparably more malice from their rivals than Pyotr Ilich. We would not be far from the truth if we said that in many instances his personal charm was the reason that they forgave him his artistic successes.

Herman Laroche, 'Pamyati P. I. Chaykovskovo' ['Memories of Tchaikovsky'], in *YIT*, *1892–3* (St Petersburg, 1894); reprinted in *LIS2*, pp. 188–9.

Several weeks before his death he discussed with me the subjects that, by turns, had attracted him for a new opera. During the current summer he had, among others things, read in a French translation *Scenes of Clerical Life* by George Eliot, for whose novels, beginning with *The Mill on the Floss*, he had an extremely strong affection during the last years of his life. Among the stories that made up this book was *Mr Gilfil's Love-story*, the action of which takes place in the eighteenth century, and whose pathos particularly captivated him. He found that 'you should be able to compose an excellent opera' on that subject. But a little earlier he had thought about (I dare not say whether he was in earnest or only mulling it over) *Karmozina* (after the well-known drama by Alfred de Musset), which had already in his early youth made a deep impression on him. Strange to say, he spoke with me least of all of [Pushkin's] *The Captain's Daughter*, about which there had been news in the papers on so many occasions; but on the other hand, more than once, and at various periods of his life, he mentioned *Romeo and Juliet*, and it appears to me that, of all these subjects, it was the Shakespearean one that drew him by far the most strongly.

Alongside the operas he was occupied with plans for various instrumental compositions: thus, two years ago he was going to compose a concerto for two pianos and orchestra for two of his friends, and when he had finished his string sextet [*Souvenir de Florence*], he declared that 'I should like to compose forthwith another sextet', probably because he felt that the sextet had turned out successfully, and because he was attracted to the unaccustomed complement of instruments. In this particular instance this was said half-jokingly, but in general musical thoughts and images, intentions and beginnings, occupied him persistently; he did not compose, as many (and even sometimes talented) Russian people do, 'from five to ten', but, in the literal sense of the word, *lived* in a world of sounds, floating in an infinite element, and though in the last ten to twelve years he had become much less productive, much more careful and severe with himself, this inner singing continued with its former strength – to me it even seemed as with a strength that was progressively increasing. People close to him, with whom he felt no constraint, know how often and abruptly he would fall silent during a conversation, or would not reply to questions, and they knew how not to exasperate him with a persistent 'why have you gone quiet?' or 'what's the matter with you?' knowing that in all probability, instead of the everyday subject which was being talked about, some chord of an augmented sixth for divided cellos had suddenly presented itself to him, some melody for cor anglais.

The hairs on his head had long since gone white, but this was the sole sign of old age in this robust, hale and hearty, and flourishing organism. To say that he 'had remained young at heart' would be not only trite, but also completely wrong. His youthful spirit challenged his weak and puny body. At home in Klin Pyotr Ilich would walk six or so miles a day, fearing neither rain nor snow, just as he had not feared last year [in fact, in 1891] the tossing on the stormy and dangerous crossing from Europe to America. Whenever he arrived in St Petersburg or Moscow for several days he, like a true denizen of the countryside whom the spectacles of the capital could not weary, spent his evenings at the theatre, knowing that in his backwoods he could not see a new French comedy, or the dramatic adaptation of [Gogol's] *Dead Souls*, or [Rubinstein's opera] *Die Makka-bäer*, or [Massenet's] *Esclarmonde*. He learned how to conduct only in the last years of his life, beginning in the mid–1880s; in the summer of 1884, living at his brother[-in-law]'s in the country, he took it into his head to devote *a quarter of an hour* each morning to learning English, and partly with the help of one of his friends, but more by teaching himself, in a short time he had made surprising progress. It was not only his creative imagination, but also his memory, his grasp, his ability for enjoying nature or art, his mental and physical energy that remained unimpaired in him until his final illness. As far as his creative imagination is concerned, I consider that it was constantly growing. True, he wrote with less facility, he neurotically destroyed entire compositions which he had completed, and which suddenly he did not like; but his music became richer in content, clearer, and more individual.

No, I cannot allow the thought that he had said everything, that he 'had completed everything of this world within the limits of this world!' On the contrary, I believe that he has carried with him to the grave a whole world of enchanting visions, that if he had lived only fifteen years longer, we would have recognized new and unexpected sides to his genius. He had within him that happy balance between 'the search for new paths' and an instinctive attachment to the classical tradition, which is precisely what gives the artist strength for the boldest novelties, for solid and artistic conquests. He loved Mozart passionately, loved him not in theory but in practice, and successfully advanced his cause – but in Tchaikovsky's own compositions there was no turning back, nothing archaic or in opposition

to the age, and it is significant that in the last years of his life, it is precisely
the most radical among our musicians, precisely our musical youth, which
one would expect must be under the influence of the [kind of] critique
which had once received his [Tchaikovsky's] first efforts with such hostility, that has grouped itself around him and become a circle of the most
enthusiastic admirers of his creations, the most devoted of his personal
friends.

When he was living at home he worked tirelessly and daily. Trips to the
capital, which of necessity broke this work, always oppressed him, and it
was with joy and eagerness that he returned to his country house, surrounded by its large garden, where he was accustomed to experiencing the
sweet torments of creation. From his youth it had become a law to him not
to let a day pass without work, and to compose at established hours. With
that light irony characteristic of him he said in an interview that 'he
worked just as though it were handicraft'. This intensive life in the world
of harmony was not free from a certain strain. Musical images pursued
him everywhere and, as he said more than once, they even appeared to him
in his sleep, fantastically interwoven with the images and events of the
everyday world. To the casual observer this absorption of the artist in his
business was little evident. Tchaikovsky was a true virtuoso in the use
of time, and he only in exceptional circumstances composed outside his
established morning and afternoon hours. In the remaining time he gave
the deceptive, though refreshing and reassuring impression of a man who
had finished with his daily tasks, who had no need to make up for something that had been lost, who was free and able to give himself up to his
favourite recreation, to playing piano duets with a friend who had come to
stay with him, or to playing vint for small stakes if several people had
arrived – or after an early, country supper, to listening to reading aloud
from his beloved Gogol, Lev Tolstoy, Turgenev, Ostrovsky and Flaubert.

Speaking of his musical genius, I somehow used the word 'balance'. I
cannot find another word that to a greater degree would characterize him
not only as a musician, but in general. In Burckhardt's book *Die Kultur der
Renaissance in Italien [The Civilization of the Renaissance in Italy]*, there is a
chapter, 'Die Entdeckung des Menschen' – 'The Discovery of Man'. It
has always seemed to me that this discovery has been made by those among
us who had the happiness to stand in some sort of close relationship with
Tchaikovsky. This was, if I may so put it, the consummate creation of this
great artist. Within him there reigned complete harmony; there was no

contradiction between his calling and what he did, between his drives and his tasks, between his mind and his character, between his way of life and his inner requirements. While loving in his symphonic poems to depict worldly sorrow, the sufferings of a restless soul, he himself, even in his younger years, seemed on the contrary to be a reconciled, lucid Faust of the second part [of Goethe's epic], contemplating life and people with love, but without agitation. They say such harmonized natures were more often encountered in ancient classical times than now. But they also say that in the ancient world the element of goodness, of warmth, was little in evidence. If such is the case, in no way could I bring myself to write that Pyotr Ilich had a classical nature.

In persons of genius we willingly forgive a certain egoism, a certain dryness of the heart. They have their preoccupation, and thanks to this [egoism] their preoccupation becomes a habit – perhaps even to an exaggerated and unfair degree – becomes a right, so that they [these persons of genius] pay no heed to their neighbour. There is nothing more widespread than that biographical fiction on the strength of which the great genius inevitably is also both a lovely person and the kindest of souls. The source of that fiction lies in our undemanding attitude. [But] the future biographer of Pyotr Ilich will have no need of this [undemanding attitude], will not ever need to search out facts for the sake of a predetermined and sugary idealization.

Pyotr Ilich was extremely kind. In him was that kindness which all behold, and which nobody suspects. He was kind in all ways and in all directions. Those who stood far from him could judge only by his financial generosity, which constituted only the most outward and least essential side of his kindness. Through the liveliness of his temperament, by no means incapable of outbursts of vexation or anger, he was somehow predisposed to kind actions of all sorts; he loved seeking out, and knew how to seek out, what was good both in a composer's works and in a man's soul. Without bustle and without efforts, through his presence alone he eased extremes [of tension], reconciled those who were quarrelling, brought warmth, light and happiness. For his art his loss is a severe blow – and perhaps to us, his contemporaries, this loss is insufficiently recognized; but even that loss pales by comparison with the loss which we have incurred in the person of this amazing embodiment of the bright sides of humanity.

Herman Laroche, 'Neskolko slov o Pyotre Iliche Chaykovskom' ['A few words about Pyotr Ilich Tchaikovsky'], in *TG* (1893), no. 21, 29 October/10 November; reprinted in *LIS2*, pp. 161–5, and *PVC4*, pp. 352–5.

# Index